August 93

ACTS FOR TODAY

D1149909

By the same author

ACTS FOR TODAY

First Century Christianity for Twentieth Century Christians

Michael Green

Hodder & Stoughton
LONDON SYDNEY AUCKLAND

Bible quotations are generally taken from the Revised Standard Version.

British Library Cataloguing in Publication Data
A catalogue record for this book is available from the British Library.

ISBN 0-340-55276 X

Copyright © 1993 Michael Green. First published in Great Britain 1993. All rights reserved. No part of this publication may be reproduced or transmitted in any form or by any means, electronic or mechanical, including photocopying, recording, or any information storage or retrieval system, without either prior permission in writing from the publisher or a licence permitting restricted copying. In the United Kingdom such licences are issued by the Copyright Licensing Agency, 90 Tottenham Court Road, London W1P 9HE. The right of Michael Green to be identified as the author of this work has been asserted by him in accordance with the Copyright, Designs and Patents Act 1988.

Published by Hodder and Stoughton,
a division of Hodder and Stoughton Ltd, Mill Road,
Dunton Green, Sevenoaks, Kent TN13 2YA.
Editorial Office: 47 Bedford Square, London WC1B 3DP.

Photoset by Phoenix Typesetting, Ilkley, West Yorkshire.

Printed in Great Britain by Clays Ltd, St. Ives plc.

Dedicated to
Zafar Ismail, Tim and Rachel Green,
partners in
cross-cultural mission

Contents

Preface

I am fascinated by the Acts of the Apostles. It is the only account we have of how the first Christians spread and multiplied during the thirty years following the death of Jesus. By that time they had become so numerous that the Fire of Rome in AD 64 could be attributed, albeit slanderously, to them. The book contains a tapestry of themes: the church, the ministry, the apostolic preaching, the Spirit, the charismata, church planting, Christian lifestyle, sacrifice, prayer, social concern and many more. The Acts has so much to say to our half-hearted and cold-blooded Christianity in the Western world. It rebukes our preoccupation with buildings and ministerial pedigree, our syncretism and pluralism, our lack of expectancy and vibrant faith. As such, it is a book supremely relevant for our time.

I have tried to learn principles of Christian life and ministry from this book for many years. They are so radical, so different from much that is taught and practised in the modern church. They are so difficult to carry out. Time and again I fall flat on my face. But better to try and to fail than not to try at all. It gives me a renewed zest to return to the book of Acts afresh, keen to discern more clearly the secret of the astonishing advance of the early church. So I have taken some major themes from the book and examined their relevance to today's church. And I am very grateful for churches I know in many parts of the world, mainly the Two Thirds World, which are seeking to live like the first disciples, and like them, are discovering the power of the Holy Spirit which seems only to be available to us when we make ourselves totally available to God.

I am deeply grateful to Jane Holloway who has not only worked with me for many years in mission and ministry, but has been generous enough to retype a messy manuscript.

Michael Green

I

Thirty Years That Changed
The World

Three crucial decades in world history. That is all it took. In the years between AD 33 and 64 a new movement was born. In those thirty years it got sufficient growth and credibility to become the largest religion the world has ever seen, and to change the lives of hundreds of millions of people. It has spread into every corner of the globe, and has more than sixteen hundred million current putative adherents. It has had an indelible impact on civilisation, on culture, on education, on medicine, on freedom, and of course on the lives of countless people worldwide. And the seedbed for all this, the time when it took decisive root, was in these three decades. It all began with a dozen men and a handful of women: and then the Spirit came.

We have some hints as to how this took place from scattered allusions in the letters of the New Testament, several of them written during these same thirty lyrical years; but there is only one connected account of this astonishing, volcanic eruption of the Christian faith, and that is contained in the Acts of the Apostles.

There are many ways of studying a book, and I do not propose to engage at any depth with the controversies which have racked New Testament scholarship over Acts. There are those who think it a highly imaginative account: there are those who think it sober history. My friend and colleague, Dr Ward Gasque, is one of the leading world experts on the technical aspects of this debate, and is currently writing a definitive commentary on the Acts. For the record, he regards it as a remarkably reliable account of the growth of the early church. Be that as it may, the fact remains that it is the only account that we have, and therefore we are driven to its pages if we want to know anything about those thirty critical years.

But just as I do not propose to take part in the controversies over the minutiae of historical and theological debate, neither do I propose to write a commentary on the book of Acts. There is no need to add to the hundreds already in existence. Instead, in this book I want to address a question which I think is commonly in the minds of Christian people when they read the Acts of the Apostles: what can we learn from these people who turned the world upside down in so short a space of time? Taking what they did at face value, how can it apply to our day? Who were these people who so changed the face of society? What did they preach? Why were they opposed? How did they live? What can we learn from the way they founded churches, from their pastoral care, from their social concern, their prayer, their priorities? What about their idea of discipleship, of leadership, and of church life? What about the Holy Spirit, who was so clearly a vibrant reality in their advance? What about the spiritual gifts that seemed so normal a part of the life of the early church?

I do not, of course, for one moment imagine that we can move from the pages of the Acts to contemporary church life as if there had not been 2000 years of Christian history in between. Even to attempt such a thing would be irresponsible; the undertaking itself would be impossible. I do not imagine that, for example, we can move directly from hints about church government in the Acts to the problems that exercise us in this area today, and solve them. That would be naïve. The circumstances are entirely different. What I do mean is that we cannot study themes like these in the Acts without great profit. We can learn much from the sacrifices, the lifestyle, the proclamation and the attitudes of our forebears in Christ. We can – and should – ask ourselves, 'If those people then acted in the way they did, what are the implications for disciples today, given all the differences brought about by culture, space and time?'

That is why I believe that to examine Acts for today is a valuable exercise: first-century Christianity has much to teach twentieth century Christians. The Christian faith has been around so long that it is easy to forget what it was like when it was new. It resembles a great ocean liner with its hull encrusted with barnacles. Studying the Acts in this way is like giving it the careening it needs. I think it is significant that it is the younger churches with no pretensions to Western 'sophistication' who look at the Acts, learn from it, and go out in the power of the same Lord expecting him to do equally mighty things through them. That is happening in Latin America, much of Asia, and a great deal of Africa. The Christians in these regions seem to have a facility we have lost for reading the story, learning from it, and applying it. I would dare to hope my re-examination of the leading themes in Acts will offer some helpful suggestions for our own church life and outreach in the West during the last decade of the twentieth century.

Many major denominations, such as the Roman Catholic, the Lutheran and the Anglican churches have set this decade aside as a time of determined endeavour to recapture the evangelistic outlook of the early church and to reach out with something like their zeal to the millions of our compatriots who know little or nothing of Jesus. Many of our churches are realising the weight of tradition under which they are labouring, and are looking for a fresh wind of the Holy Spirit to blow away dead leaves, strip them back to New Testament essentials, and to show them afresh the top priorities which Christians need to maintain. There is a hunger for renewal in the air. Where better to look than to this book which records the first white-hot eruption of Christians into society, and tells us so much about them that we cannot but be enriched if we will only listen?

A journal is published in the US called *Acts 29*. As its name suggests, it believes that much of what happened in those early days can happen today, given faith and courage and a fresh vision of Christ. My prayer for this present book is that it may encourage us to believe that Acts 29 is possible: that the fresh wind of God's Holy Spirit which launched the infant church is still available, still active, still ready to work in and through us if only we are willing.

I am reluctant to add to the number of treatises on the Acts, but I do want to awaken us to what these heroes did in so short a time, and to encourage us to go and do likewise. That, after all, is why the Acts was written. Luke wrote his Gospel to show what Jesus began to do and to teach when he was on earth. He wrote his Acts to show what Jesus continued to do and to teach after his resurrection, through the agency of the Holy Spirit in a handful of dedicated people whose message became irresistible. God is still engaged in this dynamic enterprise. He has not given up on us. That is why the study of the Acts remains so important. If those first Christians could accomplish so much in so short a space of time with such skimpy resources, what might the worldwide church today accomplish if only it was prepared for the vision, the faith and the dedication they exhibited?

2

Bridges and Ditches
in First Century Society

If we are going to understand something of the magnitude of the first Christians' achievement we must realise the forces working for and against them in the culture in which they found themselves. Both were substantial.

Bridges

There were three major bridges which the early Christians found it helpful to cross in their attempt to win the known world for Jesus Christ.

1. The first was *the Roman Peace*. This was a tremendous historical development, and reached deep into the consciousness of the people. The historian Polybius tells us that in the fifty years before 145 BC the Romans succeeded in subjugating nearly the whole world to their sole government, an achievement unparalleled in history. Rome became mistress of the world in those years, but Rome was not mistress of herself. During the next century she was torn apart by successive civil wars: names like Marius and Sulla, Crassus, Pompey and Caesar, Antony and Brutus succeeded one another in the attempt to gain overall power. Consequently the Roman world was war-torn and weary, thoroughly disenchanted with a hundred years of warring overlords seeking to feather their own nest.

At Actium in 31 BC, one of the decisive battles in human history, young Octavius Caesar emerged from the ruck, adopted the prestigious and numinous title 'Augustus', and modestly proclaimed himself on his coins to be 'the saviour of the world'. The man in the street

was so relieved at the end of this hundred years of carnage that he did
see Augustus in this light. Virgil's *Fourth Eclogue* talks of the Golden
Age returning, and that is how people felt. The Augustan Settlement
was one of the great constitutional settlements of all time. It was a
wonderful time to be alive. The sense of gratitude in ordinary common
folk comes through in one man's tombstone inscription, which speaks
of the forty-one years of happy life he has had and adds, 'now that the
world has been brought to peace again, the republic has been restored
and quiet and happy times have come back' (*ILS*, 8393).

This peace was substantial, and it had various side effects which
proved beneficial to the spread of the Christian cause. Peace led to
stability. Augustus brilliantly retained personal control of the frontier
provinces, and thus of the army to garrison them, while allowing
the senate to nominate governors for the lush, wealthy provinces in
the centre of the empire – where no troops were needed. In this
way he retained the loyalty of the armed forces and was their sole
supreme commander. This in itself was an enormous step towards
maintaining equilibrium. And thus, upon the great rivers, the Rhine,
the Danube and the Euphrates, which marked the boundaries of
the Empire, the Roman armies were deployed under the direct
control of the emperor himself.

Stability led to another invaluable side product of the Roman peace:
good communications. Romans were excellent at road building: in
Europe many of their roads still survive. They placed a high official
in charge of the road programme, because they knew how vital
these were for trade and for an efficient communications network
throughout the empire. This network fanned out from the Golden
Milestone in Rome. It must have been exhilarating, in some ways, to
live in those days. The New Testament records travel which would
have been impossible before the Augustan age. Indeed, there was
nothing comparable after the decline of Rome in the fourth century
until almost our own day. In the providence of God the gospel
came into the world at the time when there was unique ease of
communication. You needed no passport: customs dues were not high
and piracy had been put down. Travel was fast and safe. A tombstone
has survived from a merchant in the backwoods of Asia who records
having visited Rome on business no fewer than seventy-two times
in his working life (*CIG*, 3920). That would have been impossible
without the Roman peace, and the Roman communications system.
It is sometimes asked why the early Christians did not evangelise much
outside the empire. The short answer is that there were no roads!

2. If Roman peace was one major factor in the advance of the early church, *Greek culture* was another. There are three areas in particular which are important here: language, thought and religion.

It may surprise us to recall that although Latin was the official tongue of the empire, most people spoke Greek. They had it as a second or third language, to be sure, just as many people have English today, which comes near to being the *lingua franca* for the modern world, as Greek was in the ancient. But it was an invaluable way for the disparate nationalities of the empire to communicate. Greece had been captured by Roman armies in the second century BC, but soon took her captors captive through Greek language and culture. Greek professors were brought to Rome to educate the young, and Greek became very fashionable. It is interesting that St Paul addressed high-ranking Roman officials in Greek, not Latin, and to notice the centurion's surprise that Paul, an Oriental Jew, should speak Greek, the cultured language of the world, not Latin (Acts 21:37ff). The Roman poets of the first century complained that their women folk used Greek even in the bedroom! (Martial *Epigrams* 10:68).

This is of course why the New Testament was written in Greek: it enabled universal communication. And this was an enormous benefit: there are few other periods in world history when any one language would have been understood so widely. It had the added advantage of being devoid of any imperialistic overtones: it was the language of a subject people, and therefore caused little resentment – as Latin surely did.

Language leads naturally into thought forms. Greek is a flexible and cultured language, in a way Latin is not. And the Greeks used their language to make philosophic and literary distinctions that are not possible in the more rugged and earthy language of the Romans. This, too, was invaluable for the Christian cause as they began to wrestle with intricate problems like the relation of Jesus to God on the one hand and man on the other. They needed a flexible language, and in Greek they had a sophisticated tool. What is more, this flexible and beautiful tongue opened up the whole treasure chest of Greek literature. The poetry of Homer and the prose of Plato had reached all levels in society to some degree, and proved a preparation for the gospel. For Homer told of gods and men in fascinating terms, but the gods were just men and women writ large: they apparently engaged in the same jealousies and adulteries and murders as people on earth. How could they be worthy of mankind's worship?

And so it is not surprising to find a growing dissatisfaction in Greek thought with anthropomorphic polytheism, and a move towards belief in a single source of being from which the whole world derives. You find it in the later work of Plato and of Aristotle, and it made sense to a great many thoughtful people of the day. Moreover the Greeks were preoccupied, during the whole of their creative period, with the relation between the One and the many, and somehow they saw the many as coinhering in the One: the One is the source of the many, and holds it all together. As long ago as Xenophanes in the sixth century BC, we find a fragmentary statement like this, which might almost grace the pages of the New Testament: 'There is one God, the greatest of gods and men, unlike mortals in appearance and might and thought' (*Fragments,* 23). Only a fragment, but it shows the way the wind was blowing. That wind prepared the way for Christianity, which claimed, 'Of course we cannot believe in wars and adulteries among the gods. Your own best thinkers are moving to belief in one God. Let us tell you about him, and Jesus Christ whom he has sent to show us what he is like.'

It was a brilliant point of entry. And it was much appreciated, because official Roman and Greek religion did little to meet the hunger of the human heart. It was very much a matter of sprinkling incense before a statue of a god or perhaps the emperor; or else it was a matter of high philosophical debate in the various schools of the day, as their travelling teachers went round debating (and charging high fees). But it did nothing for the empty soul.

In the centuries before Christ, the emptiness had begun to get filled up with what were called mystery religions. Men and women observed the repeated cycle in nature and in human life of beginnings, growth, maturity, decay and death. Would it not be marvellous to be set free from this circle, this wheel of inevitability? And basically that is what the various mystery religions set out to offer. By identifying in the cult symbolically and dramatically with these primeval forces, the worshippers were offered a whiff of freedom, a hint of immortality. These religions were enormously successful in the first century. They catered to the personal hungers of the heart. They gave the thrill of being in a private club. They offered strict social equality – no mean gift in a heavily hierarchical society. They were full of colour and drama. And they reached out in hope towards immortality. Cynics have said, as they observed the similarities between Christianity and the mystery cults, that Christianity was simply the mystery religion that succeeded. I would stand that claim on its head. The mystery

cults were part of the divine preparation for what God was proposing
to do at the appropriate time in the incarnation, death and resurrection
of Jesus. None of the mystery cults was rooted in death and resurrection of an actual (and very recent) historical figure. They were the
shadows, pointing to the reality which was available not just to a
privileged élite of members, but to all people through the universal
redemption achieved by Jesus Christ.

The early Christians found the mystery cults a useful preparation
for the gospel. But they were also formidable competitors. Some of
the cults claimed to deal with guilt. They offered liberation from the
grip of demons and from the fatalism of bondage to the stars. And all of
those forces are perennial in human affairs. They are as relevant today
as they were in the first century. The mystery religions which constituted, at that time, the only spiritually powerful faith in the Graeco-
Roman world, opened up a direction and showed a way that the
earliest church was quick to follow. And many of these early Christians
from pagan backgrounds were profoundly grateful for the way Jesus
had broken the power of the occult in their lives, had given not sym-
bolic but real release from guilt, and had set them free from the terrible
fatalism of lives governed willy-nilly by the movements of the stars.

3) The third significant element in the amalgam which went to make
up the ancient world, was *Jewish faith*. Jews were everywhere. Their
eye for business took them to all the key points in the empire.
You have only to notice the list in Acts chapter 2 to see that they
were to be found all over the world.

The Romans never really understood the Jews, but they could
not help respecting them, and they allowed them special privileges.
Jews did not have to worship Rome and the emperor, so long as
they prayed for his well being. They did not have to be bothered
with any idolatrous paraphernalia from the Roman occupying forces.
They did not have to work on Saturdays, or enlist in the army. They
could have their own food regulations and courts of justice. Amazing
privileges!

At the same time the Jews were very unpopular. They were
foreign. They were usually rich. And their lifestyle was odd. Nevertheless they were very influential. Romans of high standing in society
were intrigued and attracted by Judaism. Some came over and became proselytes. Most did not, because they did not want what
seemed to them the mutilation of circumcision. Yet they were attracted, particularly by three things.

First, the monotheism of the Jews, to which, as we have seen, ancient paganism was increasingly being drawn. 'The Jews acknowledge one God only, of whom they have a purely spiritual conception,' wrote Tacitus. 'They think it impious to make images of gods in human shape out of perishable materials' (*Histories* 5:5). You can sense both his amazement and his attraction in those words. Jews disagreed with Plato who had said in the *Timaeus* (28c), 'To find the Maker and Founder of the universe is a hard task, and when you have found him it is impossible to make him known before all the people.' The Jews were clear that they *had* found him – or rather, he had found them, and the Scriptures *had* made him known. This confident monotheism was uniquely attractive. There must be some principle which holds together all the diversity in the universe, just as there is one emperor who holds together the differing strands within the empire. How intriguing to think he could be known!

The translation of the Old Testament into Greek in the second century BC was another powerful attraction. Here was a holy book which seemed to be both older and better than Plato. Here was what claimed to be the oracles of God. Could it, perhaps, be true? These writings (in the Septuagint, their Greek translation) were read by ordinary people, and they had an enormous impact.

Worship was the third facet in this attractive jewel of Judaism. There was nothing to be found anywhere in the ancient world which approximated to regular synagogue worship: synagogues were everywhere. It only took a dozen Jews to found one. Worship consisted of prayer, psalm singing, Scripture reading, and exhortation, or teaching. That was much more interesting and edifying than attending a temple to watch a priest pore over a chicken's entrails! And the element of exclusion even in the synagogue must have intrigued many a proud Roman. He could not pray, 'Lord God of our fathers'. He was not part of Israel. It must at best be, 'Lord God of your fathers'. That must have hurt a bit. Women, children and members of the Diaspora were all disadvantaged in Judaism, while of course no self-respecting male would submit to having his genitals attacked by a Jew with a knife! That is why there was never a major movement into Judaism despite the attraction it held for the Roman world.

There was a whole world out there which was open and intrigued but unlikely to be won over to Judaism. No circumcision, no idle Saturdays, no food laws, no membership of a despised Oriental nation for them, thank you! But when Christianity came along, requiring neither food laws nor circumcision nor Saturday idleness nor membership of

one particular nation – why that was a very different matter. It had all
the appeal of Judaism and none of the disadvantages. It proved to be
very attractive indeed. And the early Christians made the most of it.
They were, as the Acts shows us, conspicuously successful among the
people on the fringes of the synagogue, those who were examining
Judaism wistfully from the outside.

Those, it seems to me, were the main advantages which those early
Christians had. They derived from the Roman peace, Greek culture
and Jewish religion.

Ditches

But there were broad and deep ditches for those first Christians to
cross. They were very formidable. We would be ill-advised to think
'It was all very well for those first Christians to make an impact on
an unbelieving world. They had so much going for them.' For it
was a task of awesome difficulty.

To the Greeks, the message of these Christians was mad. To the
Romans it was weak, and to the Jews it was incredible. Everywhere
Christians were opposed as anti-social, atheistic and depraved. They
had a very bad press.

Stumbling blocks for the Jews
Look, first, at the major stumbling blocks that a Jew would find in
becoming a follower of Jesus. It is hard for a Jew to acknowledge
Jesus today, though a considerable number do, with great joy; and it
was hard then. Here are three reasons, among many.

1. As the Jew listened to the gospel for the first time, he would
have been struck by the fact that it was not rabbis speaking, but
unordained nobodies. That was not a good start. How could such
people instruct those who had the law of God, and stood in an
oral tradition of rabbinic teaching going back to Moses? That explains
the shock and outrage in Acts 4:13 that these followers of Jesus are
unlearned and ignorant men who have the nerve to operate in the
centre of normative Judaism. It was tremendously humbling for Jews
to accept talk about God from nobodies.

2. What is more, the message these men proclaimed of Jesus as
Messiah was *an affront to Judaism*. It was not easy for a Jew to see a
carpenter as the supreme climax of Israel's development. How could

that penniless unordained workman be greater than Abraham, than
Moses and than David? Not easy at all. And it made nonsense of
political hopes. Oppressed and insulted as the Jews were to have
God's holy land occupied by Gentile dogs, they were just waiting
for what the Messiah would do when he came. The seventeenth
Psalm of Solomon, written about forty years before Christ, spells out
some of their hopes: 'Behold, O Lord, and raise up the king, the
Son of David, and gird him with strength to shatter unrighteous
rulers, and purge Jerusalem from the Gentiles.' That was a widely
held hope. It lay shattered in pieces if Jesus were recognised as
Messiah. How could he be the Messiah if the leaders of the country
had not acknowledged him? How could he be the Messiah if he had
been killed in ignominy instead of liberating his people and driving
out the Romans? Manifestly, he was a failure. What is worse, he
rested under the curse of God, for he had ended up on a cross;
Deuteronomy had made it very plain that he who hangs upon a
cross is cursed by God (Deut. 21:23). This Jesus must, therefore, have
been not only a failure but accursed. How ludicrous, how offensive
to suggest he was the Messiah of Israel. How could the Son of the
Blessed land up in the place of cursing?

3. Then again, there was *the Christian ecclesiology*. It was a supreme
insult. They said, in effect, 'Scrap the temple and the sacrifices:
God has finished with those. Scrap the Jewish hierarchy. He has
no more use for that either. The congregation of Israel is no longer
where he is to be found: it is in the assemblies of the followers of
Jesus. Scrap circumcision, at least as a necessity for Gentiles joining
the church.' That was in straight contradiction of Genesis 17, and
must have seemed blasphemous and self-condemned to any Jew
considering this new movement. No wonder the mob went wild
and killed Stephen. These Christians were attacking the central and
prized bastions of Judaism: not only customs that had been hallowed
by long years of rabbinic teaching, but directions laid down by God
Almighty in the Old Testament. How could they be his people?
   The ecclesiology of the early church made it incredibly difficult for
Jews to share in it. Here were these followers of Jesus maintaining
that entry into God's people was free for all: while the *raison d'être* of
Judaism was the contention that it was not free for all in the slightest.
It was reserved for the seed of Abraham, the circumcised, those who
prized the temple and the sacrifices, those who obeyed the law of
God given to them directly in the Old Testament. No wonder the

Jew Trypho argues so powerfully with Justin, the Christian apologist, early in the second century. He says,

> This is what we are most at a loss about you, that you, professing to be pious, and supposing yourselves to be better than others, are not in any particular separated from them, and do not alter your mode of living from the nations, in that you observe no festivals, or sabbaths; you do not have the rite of circumcision; and further, resting your hopes on a man that was crucified, you expect to obtain some good thing from God while you do not obey his commandments. Have you not read that the soul shall be cut off from his people that is not circumcised on the eighth day? (*Dialogue*, 10).

It is hardly surprising that Justin could give no good answer to such charges. It is hardly surprising that the Jews found it well nigh impossible to join such a movement. And yet join it they did, in vast numbers. Nevertheless, the opposition and hatred which Christian tenets like these aroused among the Jews are eminently understandable. Wherever the Christians went there were riots, led by the outraged Jews. The peace of the ghetto was broken up by arguments about Christ, and reached the ears of the historians of the day. The Jews and the Messianic Jews were locked in conflict in Rome, and vast numbers of them were ejected by the emperor Claudius in AD 49, among them Aquila and Priscilla (Acts 18:2). It was bound to happen, wherever the two sides met.

On her side, the church retaliated by maintaining that the Old Testament did not belong to the Jews, and never had. It was the 'Christian' book from the beginning. The so-called *Epistle of Barnabas*, written about the end of the first century, shows this shameless process of the church stealing the Jewish Scriptures at its most blatant. Actually, the church was so successful at it that they took over the Septuagint, and the Jews felt compelled to produce an entirely fresh translation of the Old Testament into Greek to replace it.

By early in the second century we find Justin debating whether it was possible for a circumcised person, one of Jewish descent, to be a Christian! That is how far the relations between these two bodies of believers in the same God had deteriorated in a mere eighty years. It shows very plainly how hard it was to win Jews to Jesus. It is even harder today with centuries of bad relationships between Jews and Christians, and a shameful history of anti-Semitism. The remarkable

thing is that in some parts of the world there is among Jews a
substantial turning to Jesus as their Messiah; the joy when they find him
is indescribable. What is more, the depth of their faith seems to be so
much greater than that of comparable Gentiles. Perhaps this is because
faith in the one true God is so deeply rooted in their subconscious
assumptions and attitudes; now it has been fully realised.

Stumbling blocks for the Gentiles

If it was hard to win Jews to Jesus in the first century, it was no less hard
to win Gentiles, despite the advantages which, as we have seen, Christians enjoyed through Roman peace, Greek culture and language, and
Jewish faith. The attitude to Christians in the Graeco-Roman world
depended on the important distinction between *religio* and *superstitio*,
public religious observance, and private beliefs.

1. It was the Christians' *religious position* which most strongly evoked
opposition – and persecution. *Religio* was the official state cult, which
bound the state to the gods. The idea goes back to a supposed contract
between Numa, the first king of Rome, and Jupiter, the king of the
gods. In this, Numa undertook to keep Jupiter's altars well supplied
with the sacrifices which he loved, and Jupiter undertook to prosper
Rome's armies. It was a convenient and important arrangement,
which could not be jettisoned without danger to the state. Augustus
goes to great pains in his *résumé* of his achievements, known as the
Res Gestae, to stress that he had repaired numerous temples of the
gods which had fallen into disrepair during the preceding century
of chaos, and that he was disposed to regard his own spectacular
military success and the peace which ensued as a reward for his
piety. It is clear from the surviving literature that most sophisticated
people in Roman society did not actually believe in the ancient gods.
Nevertheless the cult must go on. The sacrifices must continue to
be offered. This was an important state event. Their mindset is
not difficult to compare with the continued church-going of many
leading Englishmen in the days of the British Empire, even when
they did not believe in God. Somehow the preservation of the
state and a token of respect towards the divine went hand in hand.
Atheism was distasteful, and dangerous.

Superstitio on the other hand, was any private faith you might
choose to hold. It might be the Mithras cult, the Osiris cult, the
worship of Dionysus or many others. The Romans were tolerant
of a wide range of personal faiths. There were only two things that

turned the colour of the litmus paper. One was when the *superstitio* led to actions which were harmful, such as magic: in that case the whole thing would be banished by act of the senate. The other was if adherence to the *superstitio* led to neglect or denunciation of the state religion. That, for example, was why the Druids had to go.

If you believed passionately and exclusively in one God, and refused to engage in the customary religious observance of the old gods, or offer a pinch of incense in the new temples to Rome and Augustus which were springing up in the big cities as a focus for the religious instincts of the Empire, then you were clearly a danger to the state.

Romans tolerated the Jews in this respect, but only just. They had been given permission to worship their one God in their own way back in the 60s BC, so long as they prayed for the good of the Empire. That was the one exception that the Romans allowed. Every other subject nation in the Empire had either to add the gods of Rome to the gods they already worshipped, or make some identification between the local and the Roman deities. The Christians were in an impossible situation. They were not Jews, most of them. And they were not a nation, so they had no national religion which might have precluded their worship of the gods of Rome. And of course they had received no edict of toleration from the authorities. They had no leg to stand on. Let them have their private *superstitio* if they must, but why should they imperil the good of the state by their unreasonable refusal to perform the ritual which was deemed to be the guarantee of its stability? If they refused to express their allegiance to Rome and Augustus in the normal way, that was an additional reason for regarding them as potential enemies of the state. On top of it all, they made a habit of denouncing the ancient gods as unworthy of worship, and thereby stirred up unrest. It is easy to see why they were regarded as traitors to the Empire.

As if all this was not bad enough, their private *superstitio* of faith in Jesus was getting a very bad press. They talked of eating his body, and that spelt cannibalism. They talked of love between brothers and sisters, and that spelt incest. Christians in the second century were often having to try to dispel rumours of their 'Thyestian banquets and Oedipean morals'. Their morals sounded terrible, even to the ears of dissolute Roman society.

2. Nor was that all. Christian *social life* looked unattractive to members of secular society. Why, they would not go to the theatre. They objected to the stories of the gods, their murders and their love

affairs, at school. They would not join the army, or become sculptors, painters or teachers, because they sensed the tang of idolatry in these professions. The man in the street thought them 'united in the hatred of the human race'. They were social misfits, a semi-secret society.

3. The tensions in *family life*, too, were great when one partner was a Christian and one was not. Listen to Tertullian on the subject:

> On all the memorial days of demons she will be agitated by the smell of incense, she will have to go out by a gate wreathed in laurel and hung with lanterns, as if from some whore house. She will have to sit with her husband in club meetings and taverns . . .
> If there is a meeting to be attended, her husband makes an appointment to meet his wife at daybreak at the baths. If there is a fast to be observed, the husband that same day arranges a supper party. If a charitable visit has to be made, never is family business more pressing (*Ad uxorem* 2:6).

It takes little imagination to see how unattractive it was for a pagan to have a Christian wife in the early church, and how very difficult for her to have a non-Christian husband. The differences in lifestyle were far sharper then than now; and it is difficult enough to make a mixed marriage like that work these days.

4. In the area of *intellectual scrutiny*, too, the Christian message received a lot of ridicule. It originated in the East, for one thing: Romans had a hearty contempt of religions from that quarter. It celebrated a crucified workman, for another, and that was no great attraction. There is a cartoon scratched on to the wall of the imperial palace in Rome, showing a man with an ass's head strung up on a cross, with the wording underneath, 'Alexamenos worships his god'. Clearly there was a lot of baiting of Christians for their apparently foolish faith going on in pagan circles. To suppose that this Jewish heresy could be final truth, when even mainstream Judaism repudiated it, was the height of folly. To suppose that in the one sordid instance of a crucified man the wisdom of heaven was revealed in a way unknown to Socrates and Plato was sheer lunacy.

At every level the Christians faced a path beset with obstacles. If we think that it is hard to win people to the faith of Christ today, we should be thankful that we do not live in the early days of the church, when the task was immeasurably more difficult. Instead of thinking, albeit subconsciously, 'It must have been easier for Christians in those far off days,' let us give them the honour that is their due and celebrate the astonishing dynamism and sheer heroism that enabled them to succeed to such a remarkable degree in changing the whole face of the Empire within a single generation, and to such an extent that it could never be reversed. It was a phenomenal achievement. As we reflect on the problems which face us in the twentieth century, it should be an encouragement to us that we have such magnificent predecessors in the history of the church who have already shown us that it can be done, and how it can be done, despite all the difficulties.

3

Luke and His Heroes

I wonder how much you know of St Luke, the man who wrote nearly a third of the New Testament? If you feel 'not very much' you are in good company, because nobody does for sure. This is not surprising: he says nothing about himself. He hugs the shadows, believing that he cannot at the same time both advertise himself, and persuade people that Jesus is wonderful. He is clearly consumed with wonder: as to how salvation came (the subject of the Gospel) and how salvation spread (the subject of the Acts). You could call his two volume work, 'Salvation, its root and fruit'. We have to read between the lines if we are to find out about this man and his priorities, but it will be a rewarding enterprise, a small essay in New Testament detection.

Luke in the New Testament

We begin with three references in Paul's writings, Colossians 4:10, 14, Philemon 24, and 2 Timothy 4:11. From these we glean that Luke was a doctor, a companion of St Paul, an associate of Mark, and a Gentile Christian. Luke was in prison with Paul, though apparently not compulsorily: a zealous fellow labourer with Paul in spreading the gospel, he was prepared even to go to prison with him.

Our second clue to this retiring figure comes in the Preface to his Gospel and Acts. He had a distinguished pagan acquaintance to whom he could dedicate this two volume work: and such people were very valuable, for they paid for the publication of the book. Theophilus may be his real name, or a pseudonym; at all events he was wealthy and interested. The Preface also makes it plain that Luke was not an eyewitness of the ministry of Jesus, but he was a diligent researcher into the roots of Christianity, and was concerned to produce *asphaleia*, 'confident assurance', about the reliability of his record (Luke 1:4).

The third clue to Luke and his involvement in the unfolding story of the early church comes in the so-called 'we passages'. These denote the times when the author of the Acts slips into the first person plural. By far the most reasonable explanation of this is to suppose that it is Luke's modest way of saying, 'I was there at this point in the narrative.'

There are three such 'we passages'. The first comes in Acts 16:10-17, where Luke joins Paul in Troas at a time of major frustration and confusion in the apostle's life. It turned out to be a big step forward in the mission of the early church: no less than the invasion of Europe with the gospel. Was Luke, perhaps, that 'man of Macedonia' who pleaded with the apostle Paul to 'come over and help us'? Did Paul dream about him that night? We shall never know. Conceivably Luke followed Paul in a professional capacity. At all events he accompanied the apostle as far as Philippi. And there the 'we passage' stops.

The second such passage is in Acts 20:5-21:17, in which Luke joins Paul at – Philippi! Just where we left him. But this is some six years later, in about AD 58, and together they make that baleful journey to Jerusalem, which ended in Paul very nearly being lynched. He was thrown into prison, in Jerusalem and Caesarea, and there he stayed for the next two years before being transferred to Rome on appeal to the emperor. Luke will certainly have made good use of the time in interviewing the earliest witnesses to Jesus, including his mother Mary, in preparation for the two volume work he was already planning.

The third 'we passage' comes in Acts 27:1-28:16. Luke joins Paul the prisoner in Caesarea at the end of AD 59, and goes with him through shipwreck to prison in Rome.

Having mentioned those 'we passages' we have come to the end of what we know about Luke. Or have we? The 'Western Text' (an alternative and early text of Acts, which has some striking readings, often showing local colour) of Acts 11:28 says, 'When we were gathered together at (Syrian) Antioch . . .' What is more, the Anti-Marcionite Prologue, which is a second century preface to the gospels, says, 'Luke was an Antiochene of Syria. He wrote the Gospel in Greece, and died childless at eighty-four in Boeotia.' Nobody can prove the truth of those two hints, but they fit what we do know like a glove.

Luke's home church
If Luke really came from Antioch in Syria, it would be worth a glance at his home church. That might well give us some insight into the man and his priorities.

Antioch, Queen of the East, was the third city in the Empire after Rome and Alexandria. It had a population of half a million, large for those days, including many Jews, and it cannot but have influenced Luke. Jews possessed citizen's rights in Antioch, and this was unusual. It was a large international city, and so it had been since the days when Alexander the Great swept through it in the fourth century BC. Intellectually, it rivalled Alexandria. Morally, it was a cesspool. It had a suburb, Daphne, where ritual prostitution was the order of the day, and the locals talked of *Daphnici mores* which to us would mean a 'Playboy' mentality (Juvenal *Satires* 3:62). Compare the local story of Apollo chasing the daughter of the river god and seducing her, with the pure birth story of Jesus which Luke records. The difference is startling!

The church at Antioch was founded by some homeless laymen when a cruel persecution in Jerusalem ensued after the death of Stephen; Acts 11:19-30 and 13:1-4 tell us the story. It was established by the wise leadership of Barnabas and Paul. The church grew fast, and was well taught. It had both teachers and prophets in its ranks, and its multiple leadership was so talented that Barnabas and Paul do not even head the list. It was a prayerful church: we find that emphasised again and again. It was a church devoid of class distinction. Here Jew and Gentile met on level terms. They ate at the same table, and that was regarded as newsworthy: so much so, that it caused palpitations back in the church at Jerusalem. It was a giving church: they were even concerned about what went on 300 miles away down in Jerusalem, though they might have felt that the problems there were no concern of theirs. It was a church that was passionately concerned with evangelism. People were called 'Christians' there for the first time, perhaps because they were always talking about Jesus Christ, and bringing him to mind by the quality of their lifestyle. It was a church rich in spiritual gifts. You would have seen the charismata of the Holy Spirit dynamically displayed in Antioch.

In the light of this background, it would be fair to suppose that Luke's characteristic emphases on prayer, on dedication, on prophecy, on equality for man and woman, for Jew and Gentile in Christ, on evangelism, on witness and on the Holy Spirit all fit very well with the character of his home church. How important for our churches to exhibit that quality of all-round spirituality which can be unconsciously absorbed by the members, as Luke seems to have absorbed the values and emphases of Antioch.

Luke's attitudes

Luke's attitudes are well worth pausing over.

First, *his humility*. It is perfectly astonishing that this gifted man, responsible for two of the most exciting books in the world, should have been content to say nothing at all about himself. I guess that if one of us had been the close companion of St Paul we would not have been able to maintain the same reticence. His was the modesty not of lack of talents or of self-denigration, but of self-forgetfulness. Perhaps the most amazing aspect of this humility is the fact that Luke seems to have spent six years or so at Philippi: that is where we leave him after the first of the 'we passages', and that is where we pick him up at the start of the next. But he does not tell us anything about it! The commentaries often deplore the fact that Luke seems ill informed on Paul's exploits in Asia during those years. They are quite right. He is ill informed because he was not there. He was quietly beavering away in Philippi, building up the church there from a handful of ex-mediums, gaolers and business people into the church to which Paul could write the Epistle to the Philippians. Who had been responsible for the build up of this church? Who lies behind its bishops and deacons, its love and joy and generosity? Probably none other than Luke. And he does not say a word about it! To me that is truly Christlike humility.

A second striking quality about Luke is *his professionalism*. 'Luke the beloved physician', Paul calls him. That was his job. But his job was totally at the disposal of his Master, and he was willing to sacrifice his professional prospects to go where he felt God was calling him, and to stay loyal to a friend who needed him. Humanly speaking, Luke's attitude to his medical qualifications spelt professional suicide, but what a marvellous man it made him. Here was someone who remained spiritual throughout his professional career and clearly did not allow his early zeal to be eroded by the prizes and pressures of the job.

In the strains and stresses of medicine it is very hard indeed to keep spiritually fresh: the work is so demanding, the sheer bulk of patients so great. To be sure, you have contacts galore, but no time to do anything with them. I recall one doctor friend who refused to be driven into the ground in this way and have his spiritual life squeezed out. So he embraced a simple lifestyle, took on only half the regular size of list, and therefore had only half the income – but he had the leisure to lead some of his patients to faith, right there in his surgery. That man stayed spiritually fresh as well as professionally competent. It is not easy. I know a leading psychiatrist who thinks it a bad week if he does not help two or three of his patients to Christ. Many would throw up their hands at such an idea. But why? Surely the task of the physician is to help people to wholeness and health. If it is perfectly plain to the doctor that the patient's real trouble is spiritual, and if he is equipped to deal with it, why on earth should he not do so? And if you tell me that matters of private conviction should not be brought into the market place, I have to reply that such a disjunction dates only back to the Enlightenment and has proved disastrous for our society which has kept values and facts in different compartments of life. As a matter of fact, of course, doctors and psychiatrists are making value judgments all the time – with many of which other professional colleagues would disagree. It seems to me both proper and admirable for them to use their best insights, not excluding the spiritual, for the good of their patients, where this is the done thing or not. We work not only to make money and do a useful job, but to be ambassadors of Jesus Christ. And until that happens on a large scale we shall not see a transformation of society such as was so evident in the first and second centuries. Luke quietly shows us the way.

There is another aspect to the professionalism of Luke, *his writing*. Here was an educated man with artistic gifts and literary interests. Later Christians imagined Luke as a painter. We have no idea whether or not this is so. But he was certainly a painter with words. These talents were all laid at the feet of Jesus. His literary skill produced what E. Renan called, 'the most beautiful book in the world', and he did it for Jesus. His artistry preserved and shaped the parable of the prodigal son, the good Samaritan, indeed nearly all the really memorable parables of Jesus. What an artist with words! And all the time Luke was a researcher into documents. In the writing of his Gospel he used at least the writings of Mark and the so-called 'Q' source of gospel material. In his Preface he hints that his research was more extensive than that. But the interesting thing is that in the midst of a busy life this man used his opportunities for research, limited though they were, with diligence. And at the same time he seems to have stayed fresh for Christ. Library work often dulls zeal. You can just watch the enthusiasm for Christ, so marked in freshmen at a Christian teaching institution, drop away as they dive into a world of books and libraries, research and essays. Just a few manage to retain that spiritual vitality throughout. Luke was noteworthy for it.

Another significant aspect of Luke's outlook was *his missionary concern*. He misses no opportunity to rehearse the good news afresh in one evangelistic address after another. He constantly notes some new outreach and advance of the Christian cause. He cannot keep quiet about the gospel. He is always talking about it, and always doing it. He seems to be utterly committed to Christian mission. He has more to say about salvation in his two books than has the whole of the rest of the New Testament put together. He is constantly stressing repentance, faith, baptism, and outreach to every kind of person in ever-widening circles. Obviously his intention is to draw Theophilus and readers like him into this faith which so governs his own life. His pen, his tongue and his career are at the service of the gospel. That is very challenging. These days I cannot help noticing that apart from a few gifted evangelists who are at it professionally, most conversions seem to come about through the testimony of new believers. Christians who have reached some maturity seem to retire from the front line into the structures of the church and its life, and no longer reach out beyond their comfort zone, to people who are ignorant of the gospel. Luke was not like that.

Another striking characteristic of this man is *his care for disadvantaged people*. When quoting Isaiah 40:3, the theme song of John the Baptist to which all the synoptists refer, Luke alone gives the last part of the quotation, 'and all flesh shall see the salvation of God' (Luke 3:6). Luke alone tells us that, 'the Son of man has come to seek and to save the lost' (Luke 19:10). Those two hints give us an insight into Luke's concern for 'left-over people', a concern which he displays constantly throughout his two books.

Luke manifestly had a deep interest in people: in the pages of his Gospel are rich and poor, Jew and Greek, proconsul and sorcerer, prostitute and Pharisee, beggar and rich fool, the hungry and the lonely. And in the Acts you have this outreach to the Gentiles, to the Samaritans, to the untouchables, the poor and the outcast, the tax collectors, the harlots, the penitent thief – you find them all in Luke. The women are prominent. Jews maintained that to educate a woman was to cast pearls before swine. What a contrast we find in Luke! Here it is the women who followed Jesus and even contributed to his meagre finances. It is the women who were still there at the cross when the men had run away. It is the women who were the first witnesses of the resurrection. Martha and Mary, the widow of Nain, the crippled woman, Sapphira and Rhoda, Bernice and Drusilla, Mary and Lydia – there they all are in the pages of St Luke. To preach good news to the poor, the disadvantaged, the left-over people, the women, that is the glory of the gospel, and it is important to Luke. When churches really care

about the poor, society sits up and takes notice. It does not happen
very often.

Prayer and praise are further characteristics of this remarkable man.
His two books are redolent with both. This may seem ordinary and
obvious. But it is not. There are not many churches where prayer is
a power, and where praise takes off. Luke stresses prayer in the life of
Jesus, and records him at prayer before his ministry begins. We find
Jesus praying before his healings, praying before the choosing of the
twelve, praying before the transfiguration. His example in prayer inspired his disciples to ask him to teach them how to pray, and the prayer
parables of the importunate widow, the unjust judge, the Pharisee and
the publican, all show different sides of prayer. And Jesus not only
prayed for his executioners; he died with a prayer on his lips.

In Acts prayer is crucial. When the Christians pray, the Spirit comes,
prison doors open, the place of worship is shaken, they speak with
boldness. The first Gentile mission was born in prayer, and we read
of prayer in prison, prayer in the home, prayer on the beach, prayer
in the temple. Prayer is the source of power. Luke is sure of it. I, too,
believe it, but I do not pray like that: nor, I suspect, do you. Let us
learn from Luke not simply to agree to its importance but to give it
priority in our churches and in our lives.

And Luke also wrote the Gospel of praise. The phrase 'praising God'
comes more often in Luke's writings than in the whole of the rest of
the New Testament. There are three main words which he uses. One
is to 'glorify', *doxazein*. It means to let the light of God be reflected in
the situation, and if we recall the Hebrew background of the word, to
allow its 'weight' to make its own impact for God. We find it used
most commonly after healings, when people glorified God. Another
rather general word is *ainein*, to lift your heart in praise and worship
to God. The third word is *eulogein*, to speak well of God. It means
that we often cry out, 'Lord, I love you. You are wonderful!' Luke's
Gospel begins and ends in the temple with people praising God (1:9,
24:53), and that atmosphere is carried through into the Acts.

There is a tremendous power in praise: we often rob ourselves of
its potency because our offering of praise to God is too contingent on
how we feel, or on our circumstances. We do not sufficiently honour
him for who he is and for his astounding mercy to us in adopting us
into his family. A church where praise is a way of life is a church
which exhibits the beauty, and the impact, of the Lord.

Look, too, at *Luke's loyalty*. This man had courage and stickability.
He had determined to give his life to working with this missionary

Paul, and he did. 'Only Luke is with me.' His loyalty stood out. Many will have told him he was wasting his time and his professional skills. But Luke was clear that this was God's calling to him. He was going to see it through. And that quality of loyalty is surely one of the keys to understanding the impact of the early church. Their loyalty to each other, to Jesus Christ, to the calling he had given them, forged them into a mighty task-force. By contrast, in many parts of the world today the church is only visible on Sundays. You would never know, from their conduct during the week, that its members were pledged to Jesus Christ at all. In parts of the world, however, where there is that passionate wholeheartedness – and I think of countries like Tanzania and China, Poland and Korea – the church manifests the same power as it did in the first century. In God's book there are no prizes for marginal commitment.

A final side of Luke's outlook which we would be foolish to neglect is *his spiritual expectancy*. The Holy Spirit is mentioned five times in the Gospel of Matthew, four times in Mark, and fifty-three times in Luke-Acts! That says it all. The start of the Gospel is a continuous narrative of the Spirit at work. The start of the Acts is the same. After his baptism Jesus is recorded as being full of the Holy Spirit. After Pentecost the disciples are the same. They have been 'baptised', or deeply plunged into the waters of the Holy Spirit, and 'signs and wonders' appear in their midst as a result. Luke speaks of such things far more than any other New Testament writer. He is fascinated with the work of the Spirit in the church. This is a big challenge to us. Would you be surprised if someone for whom you prayed was healed? Would you be shocked if someone next to you in church started praying in tongues, with tears of joy? We should not be surprised, if we share Luke's spiritual expectancy. That is the sort of climate when God can work – when his people are expecting and trusting him to do so.

Those are some of the characteristics, largely absent from the commentaries, which mark this amazing man Luke, explain his choice of material and his approach, and provide a beacon and a challenge to us all.

Luke's heroes

Such was the man. Who were his heroes? What was the thing that really excited Luke about this movement? Who were these people who made such an astonishing impact on the world?

The first thing to note is that they were utterly *unqualified laypeople*. That is the shock wave that reverberates from a verse like Acts 4:13: 'They were uneducated, common men.' That was amazing. People had, of course, said the same of Jesus. But if you were going to choose a revolutionary task-force of twelve men, who would you go for? Surely not unqualified laymen! They had no education apart from the basics which they gained from the synagogue school. They had no standing in the community. They had no authorisation from anyone. There was not a rabbi among them.

Is this not one of the supreme glories of the Christian church? There is no hard and fast separation between clergy and laity in Christianity. All other faiths have that distinction. There are always some special gurus, some particular holy people who stand out as separate from the common ruck. Not so among the followers of Jesus. You can go right down to the end of the second century and you find Christian writers boasting, 'We have no altars, no temple, no priesthood.' Their altar was a cross. Their temple was the body of believers. Their priesthood included the whole Christian membership. To be sure, there were those with particular gifts and functions within the body of the church, and these included gifts of leadership, of administration, of prophecy, and so forth. But it was a one class society.

In many parts of Christendom that pattern has been reversed during the past 1500 years. Christianity has become very sharply divided between clergy and laity, between those who minister and those who do not. That is a great pity. It takes away one of the special differentia of the early church. It obscures the fact that all, not some, are called to serve. And it allows churches to regard themselves as forlorn if they have no paid full-time leader. That is why it is so salutary to remember that the early churches had no paid, full-time leadership, and did not seem to manage too badly on that account! It is my conviction that God has all the necessary gifts of leadership within each congregation, if only those people could be recognised and encouraged to contribute their abilities in their own way for the good of the whole. This could be a message of profound joy and hope to small struggling churches which feel they can't go on because they cannot afford a 'minister'.

Not only were Luke's heroes unqualified laypeople. *They had no backing.* They had no power base. Indeed, most of them did not even live in Jerusalem, their first headquarters. They had no organisation, no back-up. They had no secretaries, no phones, no TV – none of the things that we regard as indispensable for outreach. There were no buildings. Many ministers find church buildings an albatross round the neck, yet they feel they cannot do without them. These people felt they could do without them. So did the law, for that matter! Christians were not permitted to own buildings until the end of the second century. This proved to be a great advantage. It kept them mobile, and it meant that they did not see their identity in buildings, and their role as curators of ancient monuments. They had no finances, just like their Master. So they got up at 4.00 a.m. and did a day's work at the tent-making business, or its equivalent, before they started preaching in the streets. They had no experience. Nobody had taught them the essentials of conducting evangelistic campaigns. And yet they won. These men are Luke's heroes. Mine, too.

The third thing about these first Christians is that they were *international and cross cultural.* You find Jews and Gentiles, Greeks and Romans, Samaritans and Africans all pulling together. You find male and female working side by side, and that was unusual in those days. You find slave and free, educated and simple. And then you find the Hellenists. They are among the most interesting people in the Acts of the Apostles. They are the cultural translators. They moved not only in Greek language but in Greek thought forms. They took from the early proclamation what was essential, as opposed to what was culture-bound, and they transposed it into another cultural key. That has not always been done by church growth movements or by missionaries. It is a matter of crucial importance, though of great difficulty: for we must not ask people to accept the eternal gospel of Christ at the same time as accepting the cultural wrappings in which we pass it on. The gospel must be the judge of culture, be it native or imported. And the cross-cultural and international emphasis among the early Christians seems to have been an enormous asset in this matter. It prevented the gospel from being identified with any particular nation or cultural pattern. It tended to show what was important in the message and what was culturally conditioned. It prevented any form of cultural imperialism. It demonstrated the international nature of the new movement. And if Europe is to be re-evangelised, it is unlikely to happen without the partnership in mission of Afro-Asian Christians, sharing their insights and enthusiasm in a continent jaded by materialism and nominal Christianity.

It was the custom of the church where I used to work to have interns from a variety of nationalities and cultures: America, Finland, Nigeria, Latin America. It made an enormous difference as these people were integrated both with the congregation at large and with the leadership. It opened the eyes of the church to the trans-national nature of the

Christian family. It fed in new insights. It showed us that some of the things which we thought important were actually trivial. It opened our eyes to a needy world. And it led to a measure of balance in our Christianity. That happened to be a large church, but I believe that the possibilities are open to many churches if they will only take them. Young people travel a great deal these days, and they are prepared to rough it and to sacrifice. All a church has to do is to find a small financial allowance for such a person from an overseas church, together with a loving Christian home into which he or she can be incorporated, and then to let them loose in the congregation. The young person offers a year of their life. The church offers an allowance and accommodation. Both home church and visitor are enormously enriched.

Another feature of these first Christians is *their cohesion*. They loved one another, and they stuck together. Think of Acts 2 and 4. Luke's admiration is evident. These early Christians did not only share income with one another – and that would have been pretty remarkable by our standards: they shared capital. It may have been crazy, but if so, what a wonderful way to be mad! They did not count their possessions their own: what a message that carries to the materialistic West. I recall, in the hippy days of the 60s, visiting a church full of this love and cohesion. About seventy of the members lived communally in shared houses. Now that may not be the final answer, and I think that when children came along it proved to be less than ideal. But what a superb example of cohesion, love and commitment to one another.

That is what the early church embodied. And one way or another, that is what we must embody today, when so many relationships are falling apart. The church must be, and must be seen to be, a body of people who love one another very much and very sacrificially. That is how the fragrance of Christ will break out. But it often is not so perceived, because of the insularity of our lifestyle. Hospitality is one of the greatest joys in life, and the early Christians used it to the full; but it is undeniably costly. It costs time, effort, trouble, money. Yet the first Christians found it absolutely central to their mission. Their hospitality to strangers and to travellers was legendary. This is how the early Christians managed to get around so much when they lacked the requisite finances. They stayed with the Christian households in that town, in that street. Indeed, that seems to have been how episcopacy originated: the chairman of the board of presbyters would tend to put up travellers from afar, and thus would gain influence by being in touch with what was happening in various parts of the Christian church worldwide. This love, this cohesiveness, this hospitality is no less vital today. Why *should* God add people to his church until there is something warm and loving for him to add them to? He does not hatch chickens in order to put them into deep freezers. I often find myself being asked by churches to speak on evangelism. And sometimes I conclude that it is premature to address the subject in that church: there is no warmth, no incandescent love in the congregation. How could newcomers survive and be nourished? The whole project would need to start much further back, by equipping the church to *be* the church of Jesus Christ, exhibiting something of his love, his compassion, his joy.

Another thing that I find striking about these people whom Luke wrote about and so clearly admired: *they were very mobile*. A family such as that of Aquila and Priscilla is at one moment in Corinth (Acts 18:2), at another in Ephesus (Acts 18:24), at another in Rome (Rom. 16:3). We have a far higher capability for mobility than they had, and yet how stuck in ruts many Christians are. We are not willing to move house and to go somewhere else if the Lord calls us. We are burdened with possessions which we deem all but indispensable. This is one of the strengths of the Roman Catholic priesthood at its best. These single men are willing at a moment's notice to drop anything and go to wherever they are directed by their superiors, and in whatever country. It is a superb example of dedicated Christian mobility. I guess we need to sit a good deal less tight to possessions, to houses, to educational facilities, to all the things which conspire to peg us down in one place. Revolutionaries do not tend to be bolted down into one place and one set of circumstances. These revolutionaries certainly were not.

Their relevance today

As we look at these early Christians, there is so much that sets them apart from us. They had the advantages of being pioneers in evangelism. Some of them were eyewitnesses. They lived before the days of printing. They were orientals. We are separated by culture and by centuries: it is not difficult to distance ourselves from them, if we are so disposed. But nevertheless there are three things in particular which they share with us.

First, *theirs was an urban milieu*, like our own. They lived in a culture which functioned round cities. Of course, there were plenty of people outside cities, pursuing an agrarian way of life. But that is not where the power and influence lay. It was the cities that the early Christians targeted. Jerusalem, Antioch, Alexandria, Philippi, Rome, Corinth:

all of these were key cities. The early Christians went for tough city
centres, and they lived and planted churches there. In our day the city
has come into its own, with a vengeance. Our lot is inescapably cast
in megalopolis. It will get bigger, and worse. It will get more concrete.
It will produce more breakdown of society, more erosion of marriage
and furtherance of crime. But that is where the gospel *won* in the
first century. I've seen in Singapore the planting of a little Christian
cell in the midst of a high-rise block that before long influenced
the whole building. I've seen a heroic little church in the slums in
Bogota, Columbia, making a dynamic impact for Christ, and another
in the gangster land of Chicago. That is where it has to happen, in
the urban centres of the world, which are growing all the time.

Second, *theirs was a multi-faith context*, like ours. I find it ironic that
people object to the proclamation of the Christian gospel these days
because so many other faiths jostle on the doorstep of our global village.
What's new? The variety of faiths in antiquity was even greater than it
is today. And the early Christians, making as they did ultimate claims
for Jesus, met the problem of other faiths head-on from the very
outset. Their approach was interesting. They did not sit down and
dialogue with other faiths very much, so far as we know. They did
not denounce other faiths. They simply proclaimed Jesus with all the
power and persuasiveness at their disposal. Naturally they had to adapt
the way they spoke to the context in which they operated, and to take
due account of the beliefs of those they spoke to. It is fascinating to see
this happening in the Acts. The Hellenists, followers of Stephen, are
engaged in it. Paul is engaged in it. It is an education to see Paul and
Barnabas at work in Lystra where a simple, bucolic paganism is about
to accord the missionaries divine status; and at Athens where a highly
sophisticated audience is handled with deftness and brilliance. But the
actual content of the good news seems to have been much the same
in both cases, and is in line with what the Acts shows us of the early
Christians spreading the gospel wherever they went. What is more,
they never syncretised with these other ideologies. They did not for
a moment deny that other faiths possessed some of the light of truth.
Of course not. But Jesus *was* the Light, and he was to be proclaimed
as such whatever the religious context of the hearers.

I think of some of my Jewish friends who have discovered their
Messiah; several of them have become missionaries. They are not in
the least embarrassed about their background: they revel in it, and
they see Jesus as its fulfilment. I think of a Hindu friend who came to
England to do a further degree. He was brought to faith in Jesus at

London University and came on to the College where I was training ordinands in order to be prepared for the Anglican ministry. He was so grateful for his Hindu past. But he wanted to make it very plain that in Jesus he found things of which he never dreamed in Hinduism. He found God as Father, a Father who cared about him personally: that was wonderful news. He found forgiveness of sins, in contrast to the cold inexorable process of *karma* where there is no forgiveness: you have to pay your debts. His love and gratitude to Jesus for dealing with his sins, of which he had been only too well aware during his Hindu days, was wonderful to see. And he found the Spirit of Jesus coming to indwell his life and start transforming him from the inside, supplying power and a joy to which he had been a total stranger. There was nothing in Hindu meditation, in which he had engaged, to even begin to compare with that.

The early Christians did not make the mistake of setting up one religion against another. They told the good news of a personal relationship with a living, loving God who accepts us although we do not in the least deserve it, and wants to enlist us as his partners. That is how the first Christians faced the multitude of faiths around them. Maybe they have something to teach our timid modern church which is often so short of a vibrant relationship with Christ, and therefore has little to declare.

A third respect in which these early Christians were like us is *that they met a wall of rejection*. Not always expressed in the same way, of course. Sometimes it was downright hostility, but amused apathy must often have met them, as it did at Athens. And the thing that really made an impact among their apathetic hearers was the difference Christ made to their lives. I think of an ex-student of mine who is currently baptising scores of Buddhists in Sri Lanka. He stands at street corners, telling passers-by about Jesus. To be sure, he faces both apathy and hostility. But what breaks through is the love and quality of life of himself and his friends, and the healings and exorcisms in the name of Jesus which are highly effective in this animist culture. People get well. People have dark forces thrown out of their lives. I recall him telling me of one spirit which possessed six members of a family in turn, giving powerful evidence of its presence as it moved from one to the other, before being finally banished. It is not to be wondered at that several people were converted to Christ as a result of that incident. Changed lives of the preachers, along with the incontrovertible power of God, transformed apathy into deep interest. I think of a couple coming to a house group in our own church one night, quite out of the blue. They had a very sick child with them. The group prayed earnestly for the child, to their amazement; and to their even greater amazement the child was dramatically healed, then and there. It is not surprising that their amused apathy, which had only brought them to that house group to see what went on and because friends pestered them to go, turned into enthusiastic discipleship, and they are now fully fledged and active members of the church. I am persuaded that nothing but transformed lives will be able to intrigue and attract a generation which is bored with religion and cynical of pious talk. Love will do it. Lifestyle will do it. The manifest power of God will do it. And so will dynamic Christian worship, where the Beyond comes into the midst and deeply touches those who would not even admit to believing there is a Beyond.

Such were some of the qualities of Luke and the men he admired, the heroes who spread good news in very unpropitious circumstances in the first few crucial decades of the church. We are deeply in their debt.

4

What of Their Approach?

I once came across the trail of a remarkable layman, Harry Denman. He remained unmarried throughout his life for Christ's sake. He had no settled home, no regular income. He had only one suit and one pair of shoes and he wore them until they were finished and then replaced them. When money came his way, he used what he needed for his very simple wants and gave the rest away. He travelled widely in the southern United States, holding meetings as he went: he rarely advertised them. People just seemed to turn up. He would talk to people on trains and in the streets about the first love in his life, Jesus Christ. In the course of his life he led many thousands of people to the Christian faith, for he was consumed with a passion to spread the good news. It was what he lived for.

Think of the cost of this sort of thing. I guess it must have been very similar for the first Christians. Many of them had no settled abode: they wandered from place to place. They spoke to people whom they met in the streets and the shops. They were grateful when someone gave them a pair of sandals or a tunic. They had no regular income. They must have slept in a different bed almost every night – except the nights when they had no beds. Of course, not all the early Christians lived like that. But some of them clearly did. And that sort of lifestyle illustrates in the most graphic way the passion to spread the gospel which was a major characteristic of the early church. They challenge us to put evangelism at the head of our list of priorities, and give ourselves to it wholeheartedly. For the church in the West has grown complacent, obese, inactive and far too respectable to do that sort of thing. The result is inevitable: almost every major denomination in the Western world, apart from the Pentecostals, is in decline. And the Pentecostals are not in decline precisely because they *do* go out fearlessly, sometimes crudely, but with passion and conviction to preach 'as dying men to dying men'.

Preconditions for outreach

We tend to think that the outreach in Acts begins in chapter 2, with the coming of the Spirit. Chapter one normally gets far less attention from Christians, with the exception of the promise of 1:8 ('You will receive power . . .') and perhaps the Lord's putting down of the date-fixers in the preceding two verses. Indeed the rest of the chapter is puzzling and apparently unhelpful. The attempt to find a replacement for Judas by drawing lots seems to have little for us these days: it may well have had little for them, because we do not hear of the method being used again – nor do we hear of Matthias! But I believe that there are some very important principles in that first chapter. Here are four which hint at what it might involve if Christians today were to have the same passion for outreach, the same fire of the Holy Spirit as the first disciples.

1. *Obedience*. In verse 4 Jesus told his disciples not to depart from Jerusalem until the Spirit came. In verse 12 we read that they did precisely that. Jesus gave them an instruction: they obeyed it promptly, exactly, and without argument. These early Christians seem to have learned the lesson of obedience to a remarkable extent, perhaps in those forty days of post-resurrection instruction by Jesus; they had not been so notable for obedience during his ministry. Those disciples discovered, in the days of waiting for the Spirit, that they had to get right and stay right with God if he was going to be able to use them. At the time I do not suppose they realised anything more than that they were doing what Jesus had told them. But in retrospect it was plain that obedience had proved the path to usefulness.

It would probably not be an exaggeration to say that disobedience is one of the main characteristics of modern Christianity. We know what Jesus teaches, but we do not do it. Disobedience in sexual morals, in relationships, in attitudes to those who make life hard for us. Disobedience in lack of hospitality, in begrudging our money, in unwillingness for change. Our disobedience is not marginal to our lives: it is central. We do not make time to spend with God, but give it all to our work and our pleasure. We do not set our affections on things above and find treasure in heaven, but are more materialistic than any previous generation has ever been. We do not obey the Lord's last command to go and make disciples. Instead we are hesitant about the content of the good news, and reluctant to talk about it.

Occasionally there may come a clear voice from God which we recognise: and it may indicate something utterly strange. I heard some time ago of a man speaking at an important Christian conference in the US. He was woken in the middle of the night by a powerful conviction that he should go to Vancouver and meet up with a well-known public figure who was a friend of his. I wonder what you or I would have done in such circumstances? This man went down to the airport and flew to Vancouver. He found his friend was in a critical decision-making meeting, and he slunk into the back of the room. He only heard the last ten minutes of the meeting, but what he gleaned in those minutes and the time alone which he had afterwards with his friend, were absolutely life-changing. He was used, because he obeyed.

But at least as important as responding to unusual impulses like that, is the settled habit of obeying whatever we conscientiously believe to be the will of God. God can do wonders through an obedient person, however limited his capacities. God cannot and will not use a disobedient person, however great her talents. The obedience of these first disciples in that hard matter of waiting, the obedience of Philip the evangelist going out into the burning desert of the Gaza strip, the deep-seated obedience of Paul to the call to go to Jerusalem, to imprisonment and ultimately to death, was one of the main reasons for the spread of the early church.

2. *Prayer*. 'All of these with one accord devoted themselves to prayer' (1:14). Prayer is almost as difficult, almost as unfashionable, as obedience. It was in prayer that they drew lots over Matthias (1:24). They were at prayer when the day of Pentecost dawned and the Spirit fell (2:1). They made prayer a top priority. And it was prayer among people who did not really like each other: I do not imagine that the family of Jesus and his disciples found it very easy to pray together after the strained relationships between them during the ministry of Jesus. The family, remember, had thought Jesus mad (Mark 3:21). But that did not stop them uniting in prayer.

3. *Unity*. Acts 1:14 and 2:1 stress the togetherness of the disciples before the Spirit came. God's Spirit comes upon those who are united: those are the people he uses. And the churches in the West have been bedevilled by individualism and disunity. So much so that we do not even notice our own arrogance in the way we unchurch others. We are oblivious of our failings and our blindness, but very strong on some

aspects of the truth which we are confident that we have and others do not. But the division frequently comes not from doctrinal roots but from personal. People leave churches, whole congregations split up, because of a change in the church furniture or some equally trivial reason. The sheer conservatism of the church, that most radical society which Jesus sent to bring in his kingdom, tends to create division over even the most minimal changes. Most Christians are not even bothered by the divided state of the church. Some Christians are convinced that only they constitute the church. Other Christians feel that it is sufficient to have 'spiritual unity', which means little more than amiable good will towards other believers. And the secularised modern world watches cynically at this supposed embodiment of God's kingly rule, torn apart by different emphases and policies of mutual distrust and exclusion. God cannot bless disunity, and he will not. For then the church would be proclaiming a lie: maintaining the reconciliation Christ came to bring to all who trust him, yet manifesting nothing but division. It is only when men and women are clearly being reconciled with one another despite all their differences that sceptics will stop and take note of the Reconciler.

In recent years I have found great joy in taking teams of Christians away for an evangelistic outreach in some town or city. The team is comprised of many different denominations and nationalities. The receiving town sinks its differences, and all the churches come together to back the campaign. Then the town really does sit up and take notice. They see the unity of reconciled Christians, and they are open to at least listen to what they have to say. It may be difficult, but it is vital. Those early disciples, too, found it difficult, but they knew it to be vital. What had a freedom fighter like Simon the Zealot in common with a collaborator like Matthew? What had a dreamer like John in common with a hotheaded man of action like Peter? Precious little – except Jesus. He had reconciled each of them to himself, and he had reconciled them to each other. They preserved that God-given unity to a remarkable extent. They manifestly belonged together. And the Lord was able to pour his Spirit upon them and use them mightily.

4. *There was openness to the Holy Spirit.* Unless we are in vibrant touch with the Holy Spirit, little of his character will be seen in us, and our impact will be negligible. I do not imagine the disciples awaiting the Holy Spirit before Pentecost knew quite what they were waiting for. They had read of some of his manifestations in the Old Testament,

through prophecy, through strong men, through craftsmen, through kings. They had seen one outstanding life which seemed to them to be full of that great Spirit of God, the life of Jesus. They had his promise that the Spirit would be passed on to them. They did not know quite what to expect. But they were open. They did not deny the possibility of some ways of the Spirit becoming real to them, while welcoming others.

This openness, this gentle willingness to have whatever good gift the heavenly Father decides to lavish on us, is such an important condition of receiving anything. It is sad to find Christians today maintaining that the Spirit can only be received in such and such a way; that he always (or never) gives initial indications of his presence through tongues; that signs and wonders are (or are not) palpable evidence of the Spirit at work; that the Spirit is (or cannot be) discerned in the resolutions of the World Council of Churches. Christians get very worked up about these things. There is not the openness that there should be. We cannot tell God what gifts he should give us. We cannot judge the reality of other people's gifts by those we have ourselves. An attitude of openness is an important avenue to reception and to growth. The Spirit is sovereign in his world and in his church. The last thing we want to do is to grieve him and to get in his way.

So let us resolve to emulate the prayerfulness, obedience, unity and openness to the Spirit's direction which marked the first Christians. If those four preconditions for effective ministry were necessary for them, it would be rash to suppose we can ignore them with impunity.

Approaches to outreach: a study in contrasts

When we turn to look at the actual way in which these early Christians went about their outreach with the gospel, once the Spirit came upon them, we see some very remarkable contrasts with the way we do things in the modern church.

1. First, they seem consistently to have *worked outwards from a warm centre*. This may seem obvious, but it is not normally the way modern churches operate. We do not tend to do much evangelism at all, in our local churches, until falling numbers and finance drive us to realise that the congregation is declining and cannot manage the upkeep of the church. Then we might look at the lists of those who used to come to the church, or who were baptised or married

here, and try to interest them afresh. We call it 'outreach'. But it is really 'in-drag'. And it is not greatly appreciated by those who are targeted. It is usually fruitless.

The approach of the first Christians was strikingly different. It was a totally opposite strategy. They learned it from Jesus. He had spent much quality time with three men, Peter, James and John. Beyond that had been the circle of the twelve, then of the seventy, then of the crowds. Jesus had concentrated on getting the centre of his little band hot and well informed, and he moved out from there. And that is what the disciples did. They gave attention to their own unity and prayerfulness, obedience and expectancy. And they were able to move out from that hot centre on to the streets with enormous effect on the day of Pentecost and in the months that followed. In obedience to Jesus they began to be his witnesses in Jerusalem first, then Judaea, then Samaria, and then to the uttermost ends of the earth. It was an effective strategy. Their fellowship was so vibrant, their lifestyle so attractive, their warmth so great that it was infectious. People were drawn in, as to a vortex. God added daily to the church those who were being saved.

I have to say that in my own ministry I have known periods like that. I wish I understood how to bring them about. I wish they happened all the time. They do not. But there have been times when strangers from the streets have come knocking on the door and saying, 'Excuse me, but can you tell me how to become a Christian?' It was a joy to be able to say to them, 'Come in. Yes, I can. Come along to the study.' I think, on reflection, that those were times when the vitality of the church was such that people were challenged, intrigued, attracted. The love, the praise and prayer and the relationships were in place: this enabled the light of the gospel to shine out almost despite ourselves. But it underlines the principle: once get the centre of the fire hot, and people will be warmed on its outskirts, and drawn in. If we want the gospel to spread in the community of which we are a part, we would be unwise to start with some evangelistic outreach. We would be much better employed in paying attention to the quality of our church life. That is going to be the magnet to draw others to the Jesus who has made us into his body. But if our fellowship is cold, if nobody stays behind after the services because they are, frankly, ready to get away, if the music is dominated by an ogre, if the minister is too fond of his own voice, if people are made to feel of a consumer mentality, rather than participants, if joy is frowned on, then we are unlikely to see significant growth.

2. Second, these disciples of Jesus *believed in every member minis-try*. As we were reminded in the last chapter, all these men were unqualified, ordinary people. They talked to ordinary people. And ordinary people got converted. Think of the Hellenists of Acts 8. After Stephen's murder they put their haversacks on their backs and set out. And they went everywhere chattering the message, we are told (Acts 8:4). That is how the early church spread. They really believed in the ministry of every member. They were not all Pauls and Peters. They were just witnesses. And witnesses do not preach. They simply tell what they have seen. In this way evangelism was engaged in continually, naturally, joyfully by Christians wherever they went. Harnack, one of the great historians of the early church, says that the mission of the church was in fact accomplished by informal missionaries. Christians would wander from hamlet to hamlet, from village to village, said Eusebius, in order to win fresh converts for their Lord.

Is that not strikingly different from today? These days evangelism is spasmodic, if it happens at all. It is expensive. It is minister dominated. It is usually dependent upon the skills of the resident evangelist, if a church has one, or else of the visiting specialist. But if you want to see fruit, a three-week campaign run by visitors is not the best way. Equip the members of your church to be witnesses to Jesus. They do not need to be able to say much. All they really need to say is, 'Jesus Christ is alive, and I know him.' That is quite sufficient to be a conversation stopper in most company. And after the stoppage, there is a chance for it to become a conversation starter. It is not difficult. You do not need to know a lot. You just need to know Jesus and to love him. Christians are not all supposed to be brilliant evangelists. They are just supposed to be witnesses. And the Greek word *martus* meant 'witness' long be-fore it came to mean 'martyr', someone who was killed for his witness. I saw this repeatedly in the church where I have recently ministered, and where several scores of people came to a living faith in the course of each year. The best evangelists were the new believers. They had so many unbelievers as friends. And when they mentioned that they had been to some Christian meeting or other, and their friends expressed amazement, they replied, 'Yes of course I went. And I have found the most wonderful treasure in the world.' That is what stimulated their friends to seek, and a good many of them found. If every member ministry is inculcated in a church, that church will grow.

3. Another characteristic of these early Christians, is that *they worked most effectively on the Godfearing fringe of the synagogue*. What the Jews called the *phoboumenoi*, the 'Godfearers', had been attracted by the worship, the monotheism, the ethics, the Scriptures of the Jews. They had been impressed, as we saw in chapter 2, but they had not become part of Judaism. That fringe became the most fertile field for evangelism.

All churches have a fringe: those who are married to believers but do not themselves worship the Lord – except on high days and holidays. Every church has its complement of such rare winter migrants. Well, how are you going to operate on the occasions when they come to church; Easter, Christmas, Harvest Festival or Thanksgiving? If you are wise you will let down the nets. You will preach the gospel very directly. Paul did. Acts 13 is a good example of his preaching to such people.

He started exactly where they were (13:16). He addressed them courteously, the regulars and the Godfearers alike: 'Men of Israel, and you that fear God, listen.' And then he showed how relevant Scripture was, and how up to date (v 17). He gave them a potted history of the people of Israel and then applied it to them personally: 'To us has been given the message of salvation.' He told them how this scripture had come true. He told them of a God who was at work in the contemporary situation (v 23): 'Of this man's posterity God has brought to Israel a Saviour, Jesus, as he promised.' The Bible's promises are true. This book is relevant. It is not dusty and out of date. Paul preached Jesus, not a doctrine (v 38): 'Through this man forgiveness of sins is proclaimed to you.' He showed how Jesus could meet their deepest needs in a way nobody else could (v 39): 'Every one that believes is freed from everything from which you could not be freed by the law of Moses.' That got to them at gut level. They had tried to keep the Law, and they had failed, every one of them. And here was the offer of forgiveness, which was simply not available under the Law of Moses. The offer of a new start gripped people who were plagued by a bad conscience. It was attractive. There was a touch of personal testimony in the address (v 31ff), but not enough to be sickly. He moved into a gentle appeal to his listeners: 'Brethren, sons of the family of Abraham, and those among you that fear God, to us has been sent the message of this salvation' (v 26). Don't miss it! He warned them about the seriousness of the issues involved (v 41). And as people went out, we read that they begged that these things might be told them afresh the next sabbath.

That's not surprising. It took them by storm. They sensed the reality of it. They wanted to know more.

Opportunities among our Godfearing fringe are considerable. Think of Christmas and Easter, for a start. One festival proclaims that the Lord God has come among us, the other that even death cannot keep him down. He is the God who is here, the God who is alive and in business. Is that message really heard in our churches? Some time ago I wrote a book, *The Day Death Died*, about the resurrection of Jesus. I received this letter from a reader: 'Why is not the resurrection shouted from the housetops in our churches every Sunday? I have been in church for years, but I have never heard it − at all events, in any way that made sense.' Isn't that tragic? It is so important to make the most of these opportunities to influence fringe attenders at church. Plan for them. Visit for them. And make sure it is something worth *hearing* when they get there, and worth *sensing* when they get there; for the worship is as important as the preaching.

But there are other ways in which we can reach the fringe. What about a Christian Business Men's Luncheon? I know of a town where this became so high profile that there was a waiting list of people wanting to join because all the key people in the town were there! When they joined, they got hard hit with the love and challenge of Jesus, as some business man came and told them about Jesus and the difference he had made in his life. Wine and cheese parties in the home can be a great draw. So can a church houseparty holiday, to which all sorts of fellow travellers will come. It is a marvellous milieu in which to lead some of them to Christ. Meetings for sportspeople are extremely profitable. There are now Christian sports ministries in over 100 countries, and people in the close-knit sports circle are coming to Christ all over the world. You can have a group for politicians or trades unionists, or any manner of interest. And it is perfectly possible, given prayer and commitment, to make a substantial impact there for Jesus Christ. But it is important to make a serious effort to reach the *men*. This is not a chauvinist sentiment. It is simply to say that if you want to win families, you would be wise to go for the men. If you gauge your work towards women and children you are unlikely to attract the men. You will confirm them in their belief that this is a matter for the distaff side of the family. And you will convince the kids that as soon as they are old enough to register effective dissent, they will join Dad and stay away.

4. Another characteristic of the first Christians is *that they had joyful*

worship. That comes as something of a shock, for the Christian image is not one of joyful worship. It is one of decorum, and predictability. The music may be good. The preaching may be good. But we expect the whole thing to be over in an hour, and joy is not one of the marks we normally associate with it. But our Christian forebears were very exciting in their gatherings for worship. You might find them worshipping in the open air, as for example at Philippi. The worship might well be accompanied, as there, by an exorcism, which would stir up the inhabitants pretty effectively. There would be praise to the Lord, testimony as Lydia told of what God had done in her life, prayer and proclamation. It was certainly neither joyless nor dull. Sometimes their worship was conducted in the streets: it was on the Day of Pentecost, and nobody could have accused them of lack of life and joy on that occasion. Their services embodied the contributions of many: one would bring his hymn, one his lesson, his revelation, his tongue, or his interpretation. That is how Paul describes early meetings for worship, as if it was the most natural thing in the world, needing no further explanation (1 Cor. 14:26). I fancy he would be very surprised indeed at the sameness, the unimaginativeness, the control by the minister or choir that marks many churches today and turns them into places from which happy people want to keep away.

But why should we be surprised by Christian joy? I think of an Easter celebration in a church where I used to work. And celebration is the right word: it was an overflow of the joy brought by the risen Christ. Here are some of the ingredients in this service, which lasted about three hours. The outline was the Holy Communion according to the Alternative Service Book of the Church of England. There were about twenty minutes of praise. There was a dramatic reading of Scripture. There was biblical preaching, but the preaching was not the main fare, although some people did come to faith that night. It was just part of the ensemble. There were two adult baptisms, each candidate telling of what Christ had come to mean to him. This was followed by more songs of worship, then liturgical dance. After that we shared the peace, and people greeted one another with great joy all over the church. We then broke up for a meal, which was brought by all the members and set out on trestles at the side of the church. The Communion was, of course, first celebrated at a meal, and this went on for many years until abuses led to its discontinuance. So we included it on high days and holidays like this. Supper was a joyful occasion, all under a beautiful wall banner featuring the resurrection, made by one of the congregation. We then had a slide-tape sequence drawing us to consider the cross of Jesus, his body broken and his blood shed for us. Then came the prayer time led by the young people in the church, culminating in the Communion. And during the Communion there was opportunity for people, after having received the bread and the wine, to ask for personal ministry. Someone was moved to give a prophetic utterance which was full of encouragement, and the service ended with a time of totally spontaneous worship: people just started singing from their hearts to the Lord, and it took off round the church. Not surprisingly, nobody realised that it had taken three hours until they looked at their watches. Not surprisingly, several people were drawn to Christ that night. For when Christian worship shows reality and joy it is immensely attractive even to people who, like not a few of that Easter evening congregation, had not been in church for many a long year. We must let the joy of Christ shine out. We must value and allow spontaneity. We must foster gifts of music, drama, banner-making and dance, photography and cooking, visiting and testimony. All these were used in this one service. Christian worship should be profoundly joyous. It was in the early church. It needs to be today.

5. Furthermore, I am fascinated by the way these first Christians *used such influence as they had.* Look at Paul in Acts 20:31. He is saying goodbye to the Ephesian elders, and says, 'Be alert. Remember that for three years I did not cease night or day to admonish every one of you with tears.' Here is a man with a passionate attitude towards the use of time. He planned his time and his influence with care. He was well aware that he had only one life, and he wanted it to tell. He was not, however, consumed by activism or individualism: there is a strong mystical and corporate side to Paul's Christianity. Yet these emphases do not prevent him from taking very seriously the responsibility that his life, his circumstances and his abilities gave him. Notice the cities that he went to: Antioch, the third city in the Empire; Philippi, a Roman colony and administrative capital of a province; Thessalonica, the administrative capital of Macedonia; Athens, the cultural centre of Greece; Corinth the capital city of Greece at that time, where he spent eighteen months; and Ephesus, the great metropolis of Asia, where he spent three years. How shrewd. It was from Ephesus that the word of God spread out into the whole province of Asia. This is the centre from which churches like Laodicea, Hierapolis and Colossae were reached. Of course, detailed planning can easily degenerate into an unspiritual attitude, into manipulating the Holy Spirit of God. And this is ugly

where it occurs. But if, deep down in the heart, there is a great passion to use your own life for God and the advance of his kingdom, there is not likely to be much manipulation, for that motive is very cathartic. And if you remember that there is a Lord of the harvest, and you personally are not meant to be carrying responsibility for the whole enterprise, that is very liberating, and further removes the dangers of organising the Holy Spirit out of the picture. And that will bring a marvellous balance to life, a naturalness, a joy, a relaxation, that will save you from the dangers of religious mania.

One of the most remarkable passages in the Acts on the use of influence is 19:31ff. Paul was in danger of being lynched – not for the first time! And so 'the Asiarchs, who were friends of Paul, sent to him and begged him not to venture into the theatre' where the angry crowd was demonstrating. These men saved his life. Who were they? The Asiarchs were officials whose duty it was to enforce the imperial cult, which required all the inhabitants of a province to make a gesture of loyalty to Rome and Augustus by sprinkling incense before the statue of the Emperor. Can you imagine Paul consenting to do that? By no means. He would not engage in something that smacked of idolatry, even if it cost him his life. It actually cost the life of Antipas, a courageous Christian in first century Pergamum who refused to participate in the ceremony (Rev. 2:13). No, Paul would be totally opposed to all the Asiarchs stood for. Yet he had befriended these men. He was regarded so warmly by them that they warned him not to go and risk his life in that theatre.

I think this is an astounding example of a great man using his influence to the maximum. He had befriended these folk, he had tried to win them for Christ. And although he had not succeeded, they re-spected him and liked him. It is a magnificent example to us of how we should use our business contacts, our sporting contacts, our leisure time contacts to build up the sort of relationships out of which thoughtful and honest conversation about Jesus Christ might emerge. There are, however, twin risks which the modern church is running.

Some, conscious of the purity of the gospel, are very particular about whom they spend time with; Jesus was not. As a result, people in a non-favoured category, perhaps women or blacks, criminals or homosexuals, have gained a bad impression of the Christian church. They find it cold and judgmental, and they do not want to know any more about it.

The other extreme is for churchpeople to be so broad and liberal, so accepting of every activity and every lifestyle that they have plenty of contacts, but do nothing with them. They never speak of Jesus, and their lives do little to commend him. We need Christians who are fearless in making Jesus known, and extremely broad in the range of their contacts. If the church used the vast influence in society represented by literally millions of contacts between Christian and non-Christian, the impact would be incalculable. I find it encouraging that God has made me my shape, with my strengths and weaknesses, my range of friends and contacts, and invited me to be his ambassador there. It is as if he has lit each of us up as a candle, and told us to go and shine. Our reaction is, 'Lord, it is dark out there.' But his reply is unanswerable, 'I know it is dark. I have been the same route. But what is the point of a candle unless it shines in the dark? That is what it is made for.'

6. A forgotten aspect of these first Christians, as they advanced so boldly with the gospel in the face of immense difficulties was this. They concentrated on *oversight*. They took great care of those they led to faith.

Not for them the hit-and-run tactics of some modern evangelists who seem to be interested in the numbers who make an overt response, rather than in the ensuing growth of disciples. Aftercare was of the highest importance to the early church. They soon developed quite an elaborate catechumenate, or programme of instruction. And from the Day of Pentecost onwards we read that the new Christians devoted themselves to the apostles' teaching and fellowship, the breaking of bread and the prayers (2:42). The quality of this care must have contributed enormously to the stability and cohesion of the young church. Its members knew that they were loved and cared for. They were taught and trained. They were strengthened in their commitment and in their understanding of the faith. And so they grew. It is plain from the pages of the Acts that this oversight was seen by the leadership as an absolutely vital ingredient in the spread of the church. References such as 14:22, 15:32, 41, 16:5, 18:23 make that very plain. The apostle Paul kept retracing his steps among the churches he had founded, strengthening them. He ensured that elders were appointed to look after them (14:23, 20:28). He and his colleagues wrote letters to build them up in the Christian life and to sort out problems. They prayed for the converts. They taught them. They baptised them. They loved them. These new converts became not simply believers, but brethren (6:3, 9:17). The leaders shared their belongings with them. They cared for the needy (4:32-5). They looked after widows (6:1-6). They provided relief for those in danger of famine (11:27ff). The apostles invested their time, their influence, their love, their very lives in these newcomers to the kingdom.

We have much to learn from them. A friend of mine visiting a church recently, offered prayer for any who so wished after the service was over. Two ladies well into their seventies availed themselves of the offer. After the time of prayer, they said to him with tears in their eyes, 'Nobody has ever prayed for us in church during the whole of our lives.' And they must have been attending for half a century! I fear that faithful members of many a congregation would have to say the same. Nobody had ever taken care of them. Nobody had shown them how to grow in grace. Nobody had loved them through difficult times. Nobody had prayed for them and with them in the crises of their lives. There had been no proper nurture.

No wonder so many of our churchpeople have no sense of personal value, of being loved for themselves irrespective of the work they do. No wonder many are unable to pray, let alone share their faith with others. They have never been nurtured. Whether they were cradle churchpeople or whether they were converted to the faith at some time in their lives, there has been no adequate follow-through, no oversight. It is not surprising that many churches in the West in our day experience so little growth. God sees fit to entrust new members only to churches who know how to care for them, to incorporate them, and above all to love them.

It seems to me that we have a good deal to learn from the way the first Christians approached their mission.

5

What of Their Lifestyle?

The first century world was accustomed to the dedication of the Stoics, the travelling groups of Cynic and Epicurean teachers, the dying and rising deities of the mystery religions. There must have been something very different and special about the lives of the Christians which added credibility to their words. Let us look at some of the facets of their lives as recorded in the Acts. That record is, of course, fragmentary. There must have been omissions, and by its own admission, in the case of Ananias and Sapphira, we know there were terrible failures. Yet the total impression of the lives of the Christians clearly commended their message in a way which we have failed to emulate in the West.

Maybe chapter 11 is the place to begin, at verse 26. It was in Antioch that the disciples were for the first time called 'Christians'. That was not the name they gave themselves. They called themselves simply disciples, or followers of the Way. It was those observing them who gave them the name which has stuck ever since. The origin of the term is obviously related to Christ, but its form is interesting. There was an enormous extension of the Imperial household, almost an Imperial civil service, all over the Empire. Its officials originated in the household of the Emperor Augustus. They represented him. They reported to him what was going on as they administered his lands and preserved his interests. They were called *Augustiani*, and this title proved an apt precedent for naming the followers of Jesus. When others saw the parallel and gave them the nickname of *Christiani*, they did not disclaim it. I fancy they were proud to bear it. Clearly their speech, their behaviour, their way of life reminded people of the relationship between the *Augustiani* and the Emperor. That was a compliment: they were indeed Christ's civil service, the members of

his extended household, scattered increasingly widely over the Empire.
They did represent his interests; they were charged with his message;
they did report back to him; and they sought to live in such a way that
people's eyes were directed not to themselves but to him whose name
they bore. The title was given, no doubt, partly in jest and mockery.
It was intended to hurt. And yet it would not have been given at all
had there not been some noticeable parallel between their lives and
that of Jesus. To put it bluntly, they reminded people of Jesus. As 4:13
expresses it, people 'recognised that they had been with Jesus'.

When you are struck by something new and unfamiliar, it often
prompts three questions. Is it true? Does it matter? Does it work?
The first question encourages the enquirer to look into the evidence
for the new phenomenon and check it out. The second encourages
a comparison with his present knowledge or lifestyle. The third is
the most important of all to the casual passer-by. He may well not
be sufficiently motivated to enquire at all deeply into evidence. He
may not want to face the comparison of his own life with what it
might become. But if he sees something that makes a joyful and
radical difference to someone else, he is likely to stop and take a
good long look at it. And therefore although the logical order of
those three questions is as I have described, that is not the order
in which most people approach them. They are only arrested when
they see something that clearly works. They wonder why it is that it
makes a difference. Only then do they bother to examine the claims.
That shows how important the lives of those who call themselves
Christians are. They constitute the only gospel that many people
ever read. If the print is blurred, if the message of those lives is
ambiguous, who is going to ask if what they say is true? For they
have not been persuaded that it matters. This puts the emphasis fairly
and squarely on our lifestyle, whether we live in the first century
or the twentieth. There are many aspects of lifestyle that will differ
among Christians, depending on the communities in which they live.
But there are a number of stable qualities that always mark authentic
Christian lifestyle, and always make their own strong impact. Let us
look a little more closely at some of them.

Dedication.   Dedication is perhaps the first quality which strikes us.
The disciples seriously set out to obey their Lord, whatever it might
cost. 9:17 is a graphic example of that obedience. It shines out from
Peter and John when, arraigned before the Sanhedrin and forbidden
to preach in the name of Jesus (4:18), they simply took no notice!

It blazes out from chapter 5 where the apostles were arrested for their preaching and imprisoned: in some way of which we have no details God set them free, with the commission, 'Go and stand in the temple and speak to the people all the words of this life' (5:20). Or think of the dedication of Stephen, who remained steadfast in the face of certain death. Think of the dedication of his followers as they cheerfully set out from a Jerusalem that was too hostile to hold them, without employment, without family, without home, to proclaim Christ wherever they went.

Think of the dedication of Paul, in prison for his faith and preaching, spurning any opportunity of release through recantation, and repeatedly attempting to reach his judges with the gospel (chs 24-6). And at the end of his life, under house arrest in Rome, he is still to be found proclaiming the gospel to all comers (28:30f). There is no slackening of zeal, no hanging on to creature comforts as age catches up with him. He still burns with the desire to make Christ known even to those around him who were most antagonistic. Such zeal, such dedication was noted by Athenagoras in the second century:

> Among us you will find uneducated persons and artisans and old women, who, if they are unable to prove the benefits of our doctrine, yet by their deeds they exhibit the benefits arising from their persuasion of its truth. They do not practise great speeches, but they exhibit good works. When struck, they do not strike back. When robbed, they do not go to law. They give to those that ask of them. And they love their neighbours as themselves (*Embassy*, 11).

That is a delightful description not of famous apostles but of nameless Christians who were fulfilling the first and greatest of all God's commandments and loving and serving him with wholehearted devotion. A life like that shows.

Enthusiasm. The burning enthusiasm of the disciples on that amazing day of Pentecost led them to do the unthinkable and proclaim Jesus on the streets to an international crowd from all over the world (2:14ff). It led them to the most courageous witness. It led them joyfully to claim the fulfilment of the ancient prophecies (2:16ff). And once attempted, it became infectious. You find that same enthusiasm bubbling out in Jerusalem as they graciously but powerfully witnessed to the resurrection (4:33). You find it inducing a church leader to run

after a chariot in the desert in temperatures that do not bear thinking of
(8:30). You find it in Saul of Tarsus, returning to preach the gospel in
Jerusalem so soon after he had set out from that very city to quell the
Christian movement (9:31). You find it in the first missionary journey,
as Barnabas, Saul and John Mark launch out into totally uncharted
waters with the good news which was too good to keep to the Jews
(13:4ff). You find it in Athens, where Paul cannot bear to keep silent
amidst the idolatry and sophistication of that pagan city, but bursts out
with his emphasis on Jesus and the resurrection (17:18).

Enthusiasm is often suspect in our 'cool' society; yet it is mag-
netic. When people have really found something to be enthusiastic
about in our blasé culture, others stop and wonder. But enthusiasm
alone may be shallow: it may simply derive from words, or some
fleshly energy of the moment. The energy which the first Christians embodied came from a much deeper source. It derived from
a deep compassion, knowing the need of men and women who
were alienated from God. And it was backed by a lifestyle which
commended it even to the most sceptical.

Joy.   Joy erupts from the pages of Acts. It is to be found in people,
many of whom had little to be joyful about. 2:46 shows such folk
praising God daily as they share food in homes, and enjoy the favour
of the people, while their numbers are continually being enlarged.
I wonder what impact this made on the measured worship of the
temple! But that same joy was to be seen when persecution and hard
times set in. It flows through the defence which Peter and John give
in chapter 4. It flows through the time of prayer and praise which the
apostles enjoy among their friends as soon as they are released. It flows
from Stephen, even as the rocks crash in to extinguish his life. There
was great joy in Samaria once they found the Lord Jesus: the city
overflowed with it (8:8). You might persecute Saul and Barnabas and
kick them out of Pisidian Antioch, but you could not rob them of their
joy (13:52). And there was no joy like hearing of other people coming
to faith (15:3). No wonder some manuscripts of 20:24 read, 'finish my
course *with joy*' in Paul's anticipation of his coming hardships and
death: the words are so characteristic, even though they do not belong
in the best manuscripts. Had not Paul and Silas been found singing
hymns to God at midnight in the jail at Philippi when their backs were
raw with the cat o'nine tails, and their feet fast in the stocks (16:42f)? It
was very much in character. Jesus had promised to leave his joy with his
disciples, and it had come true. Tertullian, who was well aware of

hard times in his own day in North Africa, after a remarkable eruption of the gospel there, writes like this about the Christians and their joy: 'We are not ashamed of Christ. We rejoice to be his disciples, and in his name to suffer' (*Apologeticus*, 21).

Until very recently it has been illegal, in Nepal, to change your faith. Even so, many have been fearless in responding to and sharing the gospel. Often they went to prison, and then the gospel spread behind bars. This is by no means all a matter of talk: it is the sheer joy of these impoverished Christians which makes such an impact, along with their praise, which it seems impossible to douse. As they face death, people have been known to have been so attracted by the joy of these believers that they have asked, 'Can you tell me about the rising God, please?' It is this joyous confidence which lies behind the spread of the good news in Nepal today, just as it did in Judaea and Samaria in the early days.

Faith.   Another quality which stands out is the faith of these be-lievers. It took tremendous faith to cry out on the day of Pentecost in the very centre of Judaism, 'Repent and be baptised, every one of you, in the name of Jesus Christ for the forgiveness of your sins, and you shall receive the gift of the Holy Spirit.' One of the qualities needed in an evangelist is the conviction that when the gospel is preached, people will come to the Lord, and some of them will do it then and there. Peter was one such person. Philip provides another example of this faith. He is persuaded that the despised Samaritans can receive this gospel (8:4f); and the apostles have the faith to send Peter and John to confirm the reconciliation of Jew and Samaritan into the one body of Christ which emerged from his preaching (8:14). Such action required tremendous faith that God was doing a new thing and undoing centuries of hatred and mistrust. And of course the same was true of Peter's historic visit to Cornelius in chapter 10, to lead a man who was not only a despised Gentile but also an officer in the hated army of occupation, into the family of God.

These men showed amazing faith in the living God who was always leading them on to the new and unexpected. In hostile Jerusalem, in despised Samaria, among the hated Gentiles, the Spirit and his gifts had been poured out, and the apostles believed and affirmed God's sovereign control of these most unexpected and, frankly, unwelcome happenings. It is only in the context of faith that the Spirit's gifts can be poured out, as they were in Jerusalem (2:43), in Samaria (8:7) and in the Gentile world (10:44ff). The *Apostolic Constitutions* (8:1) makes an interesting comment on this faith, attested by signs following:

These gifts were first bestowed upon us the apostles, when
we were about to preach the gospel to every creature, and
afterwards were necessarily provided to those who had come
to faith through our agency; not for the advantage of those
who performed them, but for the conviction of the believers,
that those whom the word did not persuade, the power of signs
might put to shame.

The signs of repentance and faith, of healing and exorcism, of prophecy
and tongues did shame a sceptical world and did establish the faith,
as intrepid disciples launched out against all the odds to bring the
gospel to the most unlikely places. That barrier-breaking faith is
very much needed in the modern church. The walls of caste, of
race, of class, of respectability, of culture often appear to be so
high that our puny faith does not dare to try to scale them. It
was not thus that the ancient world was won by the gospel.

Endurance. A fifth quality which was very evident among the first
Christians is endurance. In our highly mobile and consumer-oriented
society there is a strong tendency, if you do not much like the situation
in a neighbourhood or church, to drive away and try somewhere
else. That does not seem to have been characteristic of the first
Christians' approach to difficulties. Of course, there were times, as
in the persecutions in Jerusalem and the pogroms in the missionary
journeys, when they had to move on after being ejected, but this
was not their way if they could help it. You find Peter and John
firmly defying the leaders of their church and nation: 'We must obey
God rather than men' (5:29). And when, after the wise intervention
of Gamaliel, they were given a conditional discharge, 'they left the
council, rejoicing that they were counted worthy to suffer dishonour
for that name. And every day in the temple and at home they
did not cease teaching and preaching Jesus as the Christ' (5:42).
Would it not be marvellous if courage and consistency in the face
of opposition became as much a mark of our church life as it was of
theirs? We are so timid in the face of the least whisper of disapproval.
It was the same endurance that marked the Hellenists after Stephen's
death. 'Saul was ravaging the church, and entering house after house he
dragged off men and women and committed them to prison' (8:3). But
did that change them? Not at all. We find them scattered, to be sure,
but the very next verse shows how they turned that to good account,
and went on consistently and steadily with what they had been doing

before, sharing the message with all and sundry. As so often, the supreme example is Paul, who after years of persecutions, whippings, shipwrecks, attacks by robbers and betrayals by false brethren could say to his friends at Ephesus as he went up to what seemed certain death at Jerusalem, 'Imprisonment and afflictions await me. But I do not account my life of any value, nor as precious to myself, if only I may accomplish my course and the ministry which I received from the Lord Jesus, to testify to the gospel of the grace of God' (20:23f).

You can't defeat men like this. Tell them to keep quiet, and they disobey you. Throw them into prison, and they convert the jailer. Whip them, and they rejoice to be allowed to suffer for Christ. Stone them to within an inch of their lives in one city, and they carry on with just the same message in the next. Kill them, and others arise to take their place. Endurance like that simply has to win in the long run. But we do not see enough of it in our Western church. There is plenty of obstinacy, to be sure; but usually about the wrong things: church property, ministers who are not liked, or style of services. But go to Kenya, for example, learn of the unbelievable courage displayed by Christians in the Mau Mau persecutions, and you will discover the secret of the greatness of that largely Christian nation. Clement of Alexandria offers a moving postscript to the death of the apostle James, whom Herod beheaded as part of his harassment of the church (12:1f). The man whose denunciation of James had led to his arrest was so impressed by his testimony to Christ at his trial before Herod Agrippa, that he himself became a Christian, and was led away to execution along with James. 'On the way he asked James for forgiveness. James looked at him for a moment and said, "Peace be to you" and kissed him. So both were beheaded at the same time' (recorded in Eusebius *HE* 2:8). We have no means of checking that story. Clement was much closer to the events than we are. But it is the sort of thing which seems constantly to have taken place in the steady, costly endurance of the early Christians. They knew that the blood of the martyrs was seed, and they were prepared if necessary to sow that seed. It would become a mighty harvest.

Holiness. A sixth quality is holiness. Look at the qualifications that were needed to serve tables: you needed to be 'of good repute, full of the Spirit and wisdom' (6:3). And if that seems a demanding set of qualifications, it could be because the general standard of ethics in the early Christian community was so high. Seven men were chosen to serve in chapter 6; those seven men are examples of Christian holiness. They needed to be. To handle money and defuse suspicion requires utter integrity. The only thing that will counter 'murmurings' is holiness. When leadership falls into the hands of people who are beyond reproach, then you can get back from the squabbles to love and trust.

Acts contains many other examples of holiness. Clearly Stephen is one. Just as Jesus glowed with the radiance of his Father's glory at the transfiguration, so did Stephen at his trial (6:15). That man was in touch with God, and it showed. In 15:29 we see another, surprising aspect of holiness in the 'Apostolic Decree' which the leaders at Jerusalem gave to new Gentile Christians. It may have looked like legalism, which the Judaisers would have loved to impose: 'Get circumcised, keep the Law of Moses, and you can't go wrong.' But that is what the apostles and elders declined to countenance. They refused to give a long list of prohibitions. Instead, they offered shrewd advice to Gentile Christians on how they could live in peace, freedom and purity without offending their Christian brethren from a strict Jewish background.

In our own day, we have seen a holiness movement which has produced much disenchantment when it has failed, and when it has succeeded has tended to be highly legalistic. The early Christians managed to maintain a relaxed attitude which was clear on the freedom we have in Christ, but was equally clear on the self-denial that was necessary if fellowship across the board was to be maintained. The modern church needs to discover how it can lay stress on holiness of life without relapsing into legalism. The early Christians managed to discover a wise balance between legalism and licence, and they found it in the principle of seeking to please Christ and submit every doubtful practice to his Lordship. It is this principle, more than any specifics, which dominates the ethics of the Acts, and indeed of the whole New Testament. Theophilus of Antioch, writing in the second century, puts it like this, as he refutes the charges of incest and cannibalism which were commonly brought against the Christians (because they talked about love and feeding on Christ):

Believers are forbidden even to go to gladiatorial shows, lest they become hardened to cruelty and condone murder. Be it far from Christians to conceive any such deeds, for with them temperance dwells, self-restraint is practised, monogamy observed, chastity guarded, righteousness exercised, worship performed, God acknowledged. Truth governs them, grace guards them, peace screens them, and the holy word guides (*Ad Autolochum*, 15).

What a beautiful description of holy living. These Christian people managed to remain pure in the cesspit of the ancient world. Holiness cannot effectively be gainsaid.

Spiritual power.   Another notable characteristic of the early Christians was spiritual power. And in this they offer the most marked contrast with the modern church. They may not have owned any money to give beggars, but they did have the power of the Holy Spirit, and in that power they healed a cripple (3:1ff). That healing had repercussions through the next two chapters of the book. They were demonstrating the same power that Jesus had exercised during the days of his flesh. What Jesus had begun to do then, he was continuing now, through his apostles. You do not need many healed cripples to amaze the authorities!

The Acts is full of demonstrations of spiritual power. I think of the supernatural blindness that fell upon Elymas at Paul's word (13:11f). I think of the amazing recall to life of Tabitha (9:40) when Peter ejected the mourners and said to this Christian woman who had just died, 'Tabitha, arise!' She did. There are very rare contemporary examples of even so remarkable a miracle as this. I recall the amazement of an acquaintance of mine when he went to visit a patient in hospital and discovered that she had just been pronounced dead. He had a profound sense that this was wrong. And so he called on God for the same life-giving power that Peter had tapped into, and prayed for her restoration. In this particular instance it was granted. You can imagine the shock waves it made around the hospital!

Philippi provided another example of the Lord's power. We read there of an encounter with the dark spirits (16:16ff). A slave girl who had 'the spirit of divination' and brought her owners a fortune through it, kept annoying Paul with unwelcome publicity. She maintained, 'These men are servants of the most High God, who proclaim to you the way of salvation.' This went on for a good while, and Paul, irritated, said to the spirit which was gripping her, 'I charge you in the name of Jesus Christ to come out of her.' It did. This was a notable example of God's light banishing the darkness. It was an exercise of power in the name of the Lord. The ancient world was full of black magic, necromancy, and astrology, but this was such a different phenomenon. Justin Martyr tells us how this ministry of power was still active in the second century. He is very explicit:

Though the demons will not yield to exorcism in the name of
other men, every demon, when exorcised in the name of this
true Son of God, who is the firstborn of every creature, who
became man by the Virgin, who suffered and was crucified under
Pontius Pilate, who rose again from the dead and ascended into
heaven, is overcome and subdued (2 *Apology*, 6).

Exorcism in the name of Jesus was a vital and continuing part of the
Christian armoury. It still happens today. I recall the banishing of an
evil force that had held a young man in bondage to homosexuality for
many years. He was filled with immediate joy, and within six months
was engaged. I recall, very recently, the liberation of a woman affected
since childhood by obscure but debilitating ailments, who had not
been helped by a multitude of medical practitioners, but was set free
by the power of the Holy Spirit. This is not make-believe. It is real.
There *are* dark forces which hold human beings in bondage. And Jesus
is the Liberator, if only we will call on him.

Courage.   Another characteristic of these first Christians was courage. It took incredible courage to go out and preach the gospel in
the light of all the attacks they suffered. There is a good example
in the early part of Acts (3:11ff). There was a man who had been
astonishingly healed. He clung to Peter and John. And what next?
Peter grasps the unexpected opportunity that had come his way.
He makes a bold and extempore proclamation of the good news.
This must have been difficult and dangerous to do in the face
of the passionate convictions held by the leaders of his nation.
    Another example of apostolic courage comes in 15:36. It stands out
in high relief after the account of the beatings and stoning which Paul
and Barnabas had already endured in southern Turkey. Paul suggests,
with incredible bravery, 'Come let us return and visit the brethren
in every city where we proclaimed the word of the Lord, and see
how they are.' They might well have thanked God that they had
emerged with their lives from the persecutions they had faced in
these unfriendly cities; yet here they are proposing to return! Hear
what Ignatius had to say a few years later, in advocating the same
courage: 'Allow them to learn a lesson that leads from your works.
Be meek when they break out in anger. Be humble against their
arrogant words. Set your prayers against their blasphemies. Do not
try to copy them in requital. Let us show ourselves their brethren
by our forbearance, and let us be zealous to be imitators of the

Lord' (*Ephesians,* 10). There are few things so moving as to see new Christians setting out bravely on the streets for Jesus Christ. It makes an indelible impression for the Master. It challenges those who have been Christians longer. And it is a wonderful means of growth for those who engage in it. Does it happen in your church?

Generosity.   A ninth feature of the lifestyle of these early Christians was their generosity. The gospel made an enormous difference to their bank balance; and people in Western culture sit up and take notice when they see Christians making major financial sacrifices for Jesus Christ. 'They sold their possessions and goods, and they distributed them to all, as any had need', we are told (2:45).

I well remember a Gift Day in our church when one person placed her jewels into the offering, and another contributed his fine stereo system. That sort of generosity is rare and attractive. It speaks loud and clear. But it was not unusual in the early church. Barnabas 'sold a field which belonged to him and brought the money and laid it at the apostles' feet' (4:37). That was a costly and generous gesture. Agabus predicted a famine; at once the disciples at Antioch had a quick whip-round and produced a wonderful gift to send to the impoverished church at Jerusalem through the personal agency of Barnabas and Saul (11:27-30). That generosity was eloquent. It was the sort of thing Tertullian wrote about in his day:

> Contributions are voluntary, and proportionate to each one's income. They are used to support and bury poor people, to supply the wants of boys and girls who are destitute of means and parents, and of old people, now confined to the house, and such as have suffered shipwreck, or any who are in the mines, or banished to the islands, or shut up in prison for their fidelity to God's church (*Apologeticus,* 39).

The early Christians had a deep care for their fellows who were undergoing hard times. Generosity was a way of life.

Prayer.   It would be impossible to conclude this list of qualities of the first Christians without paying some attention to their prayer life. We shall be examining it in more detail in chapter 14. But it was a notable aspect of the lifestyle of the early church. It confronts us at the very beginning of the story. The apostles all devoted themselves to prayer, we read, together with the women, and Mary the mother of Jesus, and his brothers (1:14). That commitment to prayer seems to have been a characteristic of the earliest believers. In 4:24, for example, when they know they are in trouble, they do not complain, but commit themselves in total surrender to their sovereign Lord. That is a classic example of prayer in a tight spot. Their prayer for Peter in 12:5 is another: we shall examine it later. Prayer was clearly a way of life for them, and it is not surprising to read this commendation of the church by the second century bishop and theologian, Irenaeus:

> The church does not perform anything by means of angelic inter-
> vention, or by invocations, or by any other wicked or curious art;
> but by directing her prayers to the Lord, who has made all things
> in a pure, sincere, and straightforward spirit, and calling on the
> name of our Lord Jesus Christ, she has been accustomed to work
> miracles, for the advantage of mankind (*Adversus Haereses*, 2:32).

Transformation.   One of the best ways of realising the impact of the early Christians is to glance briefly at the transformation in their lives. Take Simon Peter, for example. In the Gospels we see a mercurial character, as notable for massive error as for shrewd insight. But in the Acts, from the very first chapter we find a confident leader who stands and speaks on behalf of all the apostles. Something life-changing has happened.

It is the same in the life of Saul of Tarsus. In 9:1 he is breathing out threats and murder against the Christians; but by 9:20 he is proclaiming Jesus as Messiah in the synagogue, with all his powers. What an astonishing transformation!

Or think of Barnabas. In 4:36 he is described as Joseph, an aristo-cratic, land-owning Levite. But in the very next verse we read of him giving his patrimony away, and becoming noted as a generous 'son of encouragement'.

Philip is a similar example of transformation. In 6:5 he is simply a quiet social worker. But by 8:5 he is an outstanding preacher, leading an evangelistic outreach in the hotbed of Samaria.

Or think of James. In Mark 6:3 he is mentioned as a brother of Jesus; and John 7:5 makes it clear that none of Jesus' brothers believed in him. Yet by Acts 15:13 this same man is the wise leader of the Jerusalem church, brilliantly handling the first and most difficult Christian Council.

Another example of this remarkable change is Cornelius (10:1). He meets us first as a Roman soldier who is a devout Godfearer. He is trying hard to do his best by giving alms and praying regularly. But in 10:44 we find a changed man, full of the Holy Spirit, praising God for all he is worth, and getting baptised, along with all his household.

Stephen is one of the outstanding examples of transformation. He is already full of faith and the Holy Spirit as he launches out on the humble ministry of serving tables (6:5). But he shows himself an articulate and courageous apologist (7:51). He lays out the most coherent explanation we find anywhere in the New Testament of the way in which Jesus fits into and brings to a climax all that God had been doing over the centuries of his dealings with Israel.

Apollos is another man wonderfully transformed by God's Spirit. In 18:25 we see him as an eloquent but slightly unbalanced teacher. He is accurate in what he says about Jesus, but he only knows about the baptism of John. In 18:28 we see him grown into a powerful and effective preacher who is underwritten by the local community and sent across from Ephesus to Greece.

Priscilla and Aquila serve as a further example. In 18:2 they are dispirited refugees, ejected from Rome in AD 49 by Claudius' edict. But by 18:26 they are concerned counsellors who took Apollos into their house church and gave him deeper instruction about the Christian life.

This transformation which we see in different ways and in different lives throughout the pages of the Acts, continues in the Christian family today. It is one of the most powerful evidences for the truth of the gospel. The writers of the ancient world were well aware of this, and some of them were sceptical. Origen tells of the pagan philosopher Celsus' comment, 'Nobody could entirely change people who sin by nature and habit, not even by punishment, much less by mercy.' But let the *Epistle to Diognetus* (7) supply the terse refutation, as he rehearses some of the transformation in life and character among the Christians: 'This does not look like the work of man. This is the power of God.'

These qualities which went to make up the lifestyle of at least a sizeable proportion of the first Christians are very attractive. Lives marked by dedication, enthusiasm, joy, faith, endurance, holiness, power, generosity and prayer will make a great impact in any culture. They constitute a totally international language. If they are present they will act as a great model and encouragement to young Christians and will prove an intriguing indicator to those who are not yet Christians but cannot deny the spiritual vacuum within their own hearts. One thing is certain: unless people are impressed by the Christian lives they

see, they are not going to want to go further and examine the truth of
the Christian message we proclaim. Clement puts it succinctly:

> For when unbelievers hear from our mouth the oracles of God,
> they wonder at their beauty and greatness. Then, discover-
> ing that our deeds are not worthy of the words we utter,
> they turn from their wonder to blasphemy, saying it is all a
> myth and delusion (2 *Clement* 13:3).

In the case of the first disciples, this was a charge that could not be
levelled!

> They dwell in their own countries, but simply as sojourners. As
> citizens they share in all things with others, yet endure all things
> as if foreigners . . . They marry, as do all. They beget children,
> but they do not destroy their offspring. They have a common
> table but not a common bed . . . They pass their days on earth,
> but they are citizens of heaven . . . They obey the prescribed
> laws and at the same time surpass the laws by their lives . . .
> They are poor, yet make many rich. They are in lack of all
> things, yet abound in all. They are dishonoured, and yet in their
> very dishonour are glorified. They are evil spoken of, yet they are
> justified. They are reviled, and bless. They are insulted and pay
> back the insult with honour. They do good, yet are punished as
> evil doers. When punished, they rejoice as if quickened into life.
> They are assailed by the Jews as foreigners, and are persecuted
> by the Greeks. Yet those who hate them are unable to assign
> any reason for their hatred (*Epistle to Diognetus* 5).

Such was the lifestyle that won the ancient world!

6

What of Their Message?

On any showing, the preaching of the first disciples was electrifying. It won converts to the new movement from every people group in the ancient world. There had never been anything like it before. What were they trying to do? Why was it so effective? What did they actually say? These are questions to which we would dearly love an exhaustive answer. That may be beyond us, separated as we are by two millennia, but there is fortunately no doubt about the main outlines of their message.

What was their aim?

Without clarity of aim, one achieves nothing. These men and women had great clarity of aim: they wanted to see people from every background in antiquity won to the exclusive allegiance of Jesus Christ. By 'exclusive' I do not, of course, mean the elimination of all the normal relationships of life: rather, the elimination of any other object of worship than the God who had revealed himself in the coming and dying and rising of Jesus. And that was quite without parallel.

The notion of conversion was strange to the ancient world. We use the word either to mean that someone has left one religion (or none) for exclusive attachment to another; or else we use it of someone who has hitherto been a merely nominal adherent of some faith but has then awoken to its significance with enthusiasm and insight. And that simply did not happen in the Graeco-Roman world. That world was polytheist. It recognised all manner of gods. If you liked to take on the worship of a few more, that was your business; the others got rearranged, not wiped off. Some of the philosophers, it is true, spoke of 'awakening' to Stoicism or Cynicism in terms reminiscent of Christian conversion, but the parallel is more apparent than real. These noble pagans like Cicero, Seneca and Marcus Aurelius have left us detailed reflections on their life and beliefs, their struggles and attainments. And all of them end up in agnosticism, confessing that they have no compelling reasons for believing that the gods even exist. Moreover, for all their claims to transformation of life through adherence to the new philosophy, the gap between precept and practice in these men was enormous. Marcus Aurelius came out with some of the most Christlike talk, but was the most bitter persecutor of Christians during the first two centuries. Seneca claimed he was 'not only being improved but being transformed' (*Epist.* 6:1), but his life showed no signs of it. He claimed to be totally uninterested in whether he was rich or poor, yet hung assiduously on to his vast wealth, after acquiring much of it by questionable means. His ruthlessness to his creditors was one of the economic reasons behind the Boadicea Revolt in Britain, which cost the Empire one of its best legions. He proclaimed noble truths about the equality of slaves and freemen as human beings, but did nothing to set any of his own slaves free. Men came to philosophers like these for advice, not for example. The separation between belief and behaviour was one of the fundamental differences between the best of philosophical religion and Christian conversion.

If conversion was unknown in pagan society, what of the Jews? They alone of all nations refused to worship gods other than their own Yawheh, and thereby they evoked the interest, amazement, hatred and fascination of the Roman world. It was possible to join the Jews, by becoming a proselyte. But it was rare. How hard for those who had achieved the highest ranking in the world, that of Roman citizens, to demean themselves by joining in the exclusive worship and lifestyle of a strange little subject nation which had long ago yielded to Roman arms. So while Judaism had indeed introduced the idea of conversion to antiquity, they never looked like making any major advances in the Roman world, and frankly, did not try very hard to proselytise, any more than they do today.

It was totally different with the Christian preachers. They had a deep assurance of the truth of what they were saying, supremely of the reality and relevance of the living God about whom the pagan philosophers were so agnostic. They had a passionate longing, absent from Judaism, to share their own dynamic experience with others of all races and bring them to the same allegiance. And this was novel for Jew as well as Greek. For the Jew was being asked for conversion *within* the faith he had been nourished, rather than *to* a new faith:

Christ was proclaimed as the summit and the crown of Judaism. But conversion would have been just as unacceptable for the Jew as for the Gentile. Both would have to be baptised into the church of the Messiah, and whereas for the Gentile that would be preferable to circumcision, to the Jew it was an enormous hurdle. It meant renouncing all claim to being God's elect simply on the grounds of birth and circumcision. It meant becoming like a newborn child, and washing away all impurities in the bath of baptism – which is what they were accustomed to think took place when a proselyte was baptised into Israel. A more humbling renunciation of all privilege, all acquired or inherited merit and standing before God, could not be imagined. The stumbling block of conversion to Christianity was absolute.

What, then, were the early disciples trying to achieve when they called for conversion? There is no better place to find an answer to that question than in the case of Saul of Tarsus. For one thing his story is so well documented, being recounted no less than three times in the Acts, not to mention allusions in various places in his own correspondence. For another, his is such a clear and prominent example of conversion. And above all, perhaps, because he tells us that his conversion, despite its peculiarities, is a pattern for those who will come to faith subsequently (1 Tim. 1:16).

How, then, did the Christian proclamation percolate to this most hostile opponent? And how could it possibly form a pattern for the future? The answer lies in the following four ways.

First, it touched his *conscience*. 'Saul, Saul, why do you persecute me?' was the question he could not evade on the Damascus Road (Acts 9:4). Saul had struggled with a bad conscience ever since he assisted in the murder of Stephen. He must have had a shrewd idea that he was persecuting both love and truth when he continued to drive Christians to their death. Behind the Christians themselves he was launching the attack of his hurt pride against a shadowy figure of whom he was only partly aware. And now that figure caught up with him. He knew it in his conscience.

That always happens, does it not? I do not mean that everybody comes to Christ through a bad conscience. There are many gateways into Christ. But I do mean that whenever anyone comes face to face with Jesus, he is driven to the conviction that he is unworthy, and that Jesus is supremely worthy. One of the surest signs of an authentic conversion is a conscience that has become sensitised.

Second, it illuminated his *mind*. 'Who are you, Lord?' he asks. 'I am Jesus' (9:5). It must have been shattering for the proud Pharisee, who had found the claims of Jesus such a stumbling block, to realise that he had been exalted to the place where the word 'Lord' is appropriate. 'Jesus' and 'Lord': in those two words we see to the heart of the early Christian confession, and the essence of what they preached. The condemned, crucified peasant has the right to the name Adonai, Lord, the word often used of God himself in the Old Testament. It is hardly surprising that these two words became the centrepiece of the short creed used by early Christians at their baptism: 'Jesus is Lord'.

It was not long afterwards that Paul the apostle filled out the content of those two words in a lyrical passage which he may have composed, or may perhaps have drawn from a current hymn or credal fragment:

> Jesus . . . did not count equality with God a thing to be grasped, but emptied himself, taking the form of a servant, being born in the likeness of men. And being found in human form he humbled himself and became obedient unto death, even death on a cross. Therefore God has highly exalted him, and given him the name which is above every name, that at the name of Jesus every knee should bow, in heaven, and on earth, and under the earth, and every tongue confess that Jesus is Lord, to the glory of God the Father (Phil. 2:6ff).

Even in its longer form, that is not a very full doctrinal statement. Not nearly as full as many Christians would like to make it. But it was enough to bring Saul of Tarsus to the feet of Jesus. I do not see how it is possible to become a Christian on less in terms of doctrine than the conviction that Jesus is Lord. Unless I believe that Jesus came into this world, died and rose again, and has the right to share God's name and throne − then it is hard to see how I could properly be called a Christian. But Saul's conversion makes it plain that it is not necessary to believe a great deal more than this in order to become a Christian! When helping people come in from the outside to Christian faith we have no right to ask for a more detailed understanding than this. It will grow in due course as people develop their relationship with Christ, but at the outset it is sufficiently staggering to recognise that the unknown, despised Jesus is no less than God Almighty.

Notice how that conviction does and does not come about. Saul did not discover it by earnest struggles in the library under Gamaliel. God showed the truth to Saul in God's own way and in God's own time. 'God was pleased to reveal his Son to me' was how Saul put it later (Gal. 1:16). The intellectual content of Christian believing can be as small as those two words, 'Jesus' and 'Lord', but the mystery of conversion is that they are a divine disclosure. Only God can reveal God. An evangelist is a partner with God in seeking to facilitate among his hearers a situation where that disclosure can most readily take place.

Third, conversion reached his *will*. Saul acknowledged the Lordship of Jesus. That was the nub of it. He allowed himself to go where Jesus indicated, into the city of Damascus – but for a very different mission than that on which he had set out! The Lord had 'converted' or turned to Saul with a most gracious self-disclosure. He had showed his willingness to receive his rebel subject. Now Saul turns, or 'converts' to God, and grasps the proffered hand in awed gratitude at such unexpected grace. His will was bent to seek and follow the will of God.

That lies at the heart of every true conversion. Incidentally, it explains to some degree the phenomenon of false conversion, the person who has 'tried it all and it does not work'. My experience with many such people is that they have not 'tried it all'. What they have done is to confuse emotion with commitment, ardour with discipleship. They may have made some kind of overt response in days gone by, but on reflection they will agree that it was no wholehearted turning to God, no handing over to him their entire future. The citadel of their will remained unstormed by the divine Spirit. They were not converted.

Fourthly, conversion changed Saul's *life*. His whole behaviour pattern changed. 'He is a chosen instrument of mine to carry my name before the Gentiles and kings and the sons of Israel: for I will show him how much he must suffer for the sake of my name' (9:15). All very different from the career and the lifestyle which Saul had planned for himself. The whole subsequent direction of his life was transformed by this encounter with the risen Jesus. The changes were stupendous, some of them apparent in this very chapter.

We find him now revelling in Christian company (v 19) as enthusiastically as he had once detested and despised it. I well recall how it was like that with me!

We find him anxious to share what he has discovered about Jesus with others. 'In the synagogues immediately he proclaimed Jesus' (v 20). That is one of the surest signs of genuine conversion. A good many new believers simply can't wait to tell their friends about the discovery they have begun to make, however incoherently they explain it! And this happens without any prompting. It is the natural outworking of the beginnings of new life stirring within.

We find him keen to grow. He is not satisfied with what he has already taken in of Christ. He longs to go further. 'He increased all the more in strength' (v 22). As in physical life, so in spiritual, appetite is one of the surest signs of health.

Saul becomes increasingly bold. He is willing to face opposition and court mockery for his change of stance, both from within and from outside the circle of his new companions (vv 21, 23). That is a sign of life. So is his readiness to accept ministry from others (v 18f). Previously this proud, independent man would have shied away from any such thing. But now we find him willing to be ministered to by Ananias, fed and taught by the Christians, and rescued from acute danger by their intervention in lowering him over the town wall to safety in a basket. No one can become a Christian without letting Christ serve him. This usually has the effect of opening the new Christian up to receive help and love from others. I recall one young man telling me that he disliked and despised the Christians in his university, until he came face to face with Christ. The very next day he went to them and asked them to help him with his new faith. There was a new openness to receive, as well as to give. Christ had softened up his heart. None of this is surprising really, if conversion places us into a new family where we are all brothers and sisters, all interdependent. It is the very antithesis of the Western myth of macho independence!

Of course the greatest mark of the reality of Saul's conversion was his welcoming of the Holy Spirit into his heart and life (9:17). The big difference in Saul was not his turning towards God but God's filling him with the Holy Spirit. This divine gift was in fact the source of all the other changes which flowed from the conversion of this remarkable man. He now had a new life. Inevitably, and naturally, it produced an entirely new lifestyle. It still does.

Those four aspects of Saul's conversion are true of every person who turns to Christ, are they not? They are by no means exhaustive indicators of new life. But they are always present: a newly sensitised conscience with a tendency now towards repentance, rather than self-justification; a rudimentary understanding of who Jesus is and what he has achieved for us; a determination to surrender the will to him, which is at once matched by God's infusion of his Holy Spirit; and a changed life which flows from that encounter with Jesus.

That, and nothing less, is what the first Christians were seeking to do when they preached the gospel.

What was their content?

They adopted a flexible approach

The first Christians did not give a well-prepared address that had little to do with the situation of their hearers. That is very obvious on the Day of Pentecost, when they began with the charge of drunken behaviour and moved into a powerful presentation of the gospel. At Athens it was the brilliant discovery of an inscription to an unknown god that triggered off the sermon. In a word, the approach of the first Christians was flexible. It was determined by the needs of the hearers.

Stephen is a good example. He is handling the regular church-goers of official Judaism, and he shows them in his long speech that throughout the history of their nation God has been moving them on, but that, through refusing to listen to Christ, the climax of God's revelation, they were in fact resisting the Spirit. Solomon built God a house . . . and from that house they were not prepared to budge!

Or think of Philip dealing with the eunuch, a man in search of meaning, scanning the prophet Isaiah to see if he could find some (8:30ff). That proved to be the right way in for Philip.

But it was a different matter with the proconsul, Sergius Paulus. He was a very modern man, who was only interested, it would seem, in what really worked (13:7ff). So Paul called upon the mighty power of God that works – and he was not disappointed.

It was different again in Pisidian Antioch. Paul spoke directly to the conscience of the Jewish inhabitants there. They were well aware of their need. They knew God's law, but were quite unable to keep it. That is why they had such a bad conscience, and why Paul preached to them release from guilt through what Christ had done (13:39ff).

At Caesarea it was different again. Peter began by laying aside the prejudice with which Jew and Gentile regarded each other, and confessing his own guilt in the matter. Then he gave a simple summary of the good news, starting from the very beginning. Before he had finished, the Holy Spirit had come upon the gathering in his own inimitable way (11:34ff).

The message of these early Christians was always directed to the needs of the hearers. Sometimes the preachers were shameless oppor-tunists. Think of the Philippian jailer, terrified, flustered, wondering how he could get out of so difficult a situation and keep his job – and his head. Paul humorously takes his phrase 'be saved' in a very different sense, and leads the man to a security he could never have dreamed possible.

Or think of the rather more extended approach which the Christians took to the polytheism and atheism all round them. (Polytheism and atheism are almost the same.) They did not talk about Christ and sin. To do so would have been meaningless. They generally made a threefold approach, not only in the days of the first Christians but for a long time to come. You see it in the account of evangelism at Lystra (ch 14), at Athens (ch 17) and in the Letter to Rome (ch 1). You see it in Christian apologetics in the second and third centuries.

They addressed the *mind* of the polytheist, and argued for the existence of one God, Creator both of the world and of mankind. He provides. He cares. In the past, unbelief may have been understandable, but not now, since God has shed such abundant light on his nature through the coming of Jesus. No doubt they adduced the evidence for who Jesus was: his matchless teaching, his miracles, his quality of life, the prophecies pointing to him, his sacrificial death, his mighty resurrection, and the visible power and presence of his Spirit.

Equally, they addressed the *heart* of the polytheist. They poured scorn on the stories of the amours and battles of the gods as narrated by Homer and the poets. Scorn is a powerful weapon, especially when the other person's heart supports your ridicule of the idols he somewhat ruefully honours in his own life. As we saw in chapter 2, the Greek philosophers had already prepared the way for this Christian scorn, and so had some Jewish writings. But nobody carried it home to the hearers with positive content and personal challenge until the Christians came along.

Nor did they leave it there. The first Christians challenged the *conscience* of the polytheist. They set out to attack immorality, and show how wrong belief led inevitably to wrong conduct. They laid stress on man's accountability to the God he has spurned. They made it plain that everyone had to choose.

In all these ways, we see the first disciples seeking to discover the needs of those to whom they preached; only when they had done that did they feel they had a platform for the gospel.

In today's world the hunger for freedom, the disenchantment with authority, the absence of meaning and purpose, the quest for satisfaction, the emptiness of existentialism and the perplexing nature of spirituality, rediscovered in the New Age, all require distinct approaches. I have tried to suggest a number in my book, *Evangelism Through the Local Church*.

Some people are enslaved through occult involvement. This is an increasing phenomenon in our post-Christian society. They need the liberating power of Jesus to set them free.

A lonely widow, on the other hand, calls for a very gentle approach. She needs to discover the compassionate Jesus, who weeps in empathy with Martha and Mary over the death of Lazarus. She needs, moreover, to discover Jesus as the resurrection and the life, and she is likely to do that by seeing deep Christian compassion in those who try to help her.

The hard-headed scientist is most likely to be brought to faith through the resurrection, too. He is used to the empirical method: so feed it to him! Tell him that you are going to face him with a piece of evidence which will not fit in with his materialistic world-view, and ask him to assess the evidence carefully and come up, if he can, with a watertight alternative to the resurrection of Jesus Christ. Many scientists come to the Lord through examining the evidence critically, weighing it up, and then committing themselves to the Christian hypothesis on the strength of it – only to find it works!

Those who are proud of their high moral standards, on the other hand, are open to the approach of Paul at Pisidian Antioch. They know full well that they have not and cannot live up to their own standards, let alone those of a holy God. And the offer of free pardon and forgiveness through what God himself has done for us in Christ is a breathtaking mystery which is likely to prove deeply attractive.

At all events, if we are to learn from the early Christians, we must discover the appropriate way in to the real situation of those we are seeking to help, and relate the good news, that many splendoured thing, to it.

They concentrated on the person of Jesus

No philosophy of life, no system of morals, engaged the attention of the first preachers, but only the living, loving person of Jesus. I cannot help being struck by their concentration on the person of Jesus – the one who can still troubled consciences (13:39), fill an empty life (2:38), restore a paralysed man (3:6), exorcise a demonised girl (16:18) or rescue sailors in a storm (27:21ff). It is the person of Jesus which has a supreme fascination. He, and he alone, has that endless power to attract people of all types and backgrounds. We must, therefore, keep the spotlight on him. Be Christ-centred, however flexible your presentation, if you want to follow the example of the earliest missionaries.

It would be worth our while to pause and consider some aspects of what the disciples considered important about Jesus; and what better place to examine than the first Christian evangelistic address on the day of Pentecost?

They spoke of Jesus as *fulfilment* (2:16ff cf, and ch 7). Jesus is no mere contingent figure through whom God arbitrarily decreed salvation. All the Old Testament story and the whole history of salvation point to him. The ideal no longer lies beyond us. The ideal has lived; and his name is Jesus. People often think of Christianity as backward looking, in an age when everyone else is looking forward to the future. It is our fault that they have got that impression. Jesus came not so much in the past as at the mid-point of time. He encapsulates the past and prefigures the search for the highest. I remember a university lecturer coming up to me at the conclusion of a mission address at a university, and saying, 'Thank you. I teach English in this university. You have shown me that Jesus is the fulfilment of the existentialist quest.' Or I think of a Jewess whom I took through some of the major prophecies in the Old Testament. She saw how those prophecies fitted Jesus in the way they fitted nobody else, and she put her trust in Israel's Messiah – and now is a missionary overseas.

They spoke of Jesus *the man*. Jesus of Nazareth was 'a man attested to you by God with mighty works and wonders and signs' (2:22). We need a delicate balance in the way we make Christ known. In the past the church has majored too much on the divinity of Jesus, and perhaps given the impression that he is so entirely God that he is scarcely one of us. That is dangerously wide of the mark. It leads to Jesus worship, with scant attention to the Father and the Holy Spirit. It also accounts for the tendency at a popular level, particularly in Catholic countries, to regard Jesus as so far out of reach that you need the assistance of the Blessed Virgin or St Christopher if you are to gain his ear.

On the other hand, if we regard Jesus too exclusively as 'a man for others' and no more, there can be no salvation, no way back to God. We are driven to paradox whenever we seriously consider the person of Jesus. He is both divine and human. He is the bridge that is firmly anchored on our side of the river, and yet reaches equally firmly to God's side. In this way alone can he be a reliable interpreter of God to us, and a sure route back to God. A bridge that does not reach both sides of the river is not a bridge at all, but a folly. The earliest evangelists instinctively managed to keep that balance and face that paradox. Read a really earthy Gospel like Mark's, which begins, 'The beginning of the gospel of Jesus Christ, the Son of God' and then proceeds to show how firmly Jesus is one of us! Or consider how Peter in this very sermon matches the humanity of Jesus in 2:22 with a firm declaration of his deity in 2:36: 'God has made him both Lord and Christ'. And he uses Psalm 110:1 to stress that this Jesus who comes as a man to us is none other than the Lord who shares the throne of Almighty God. Such balance is enviable – and rare.

They spoke of Jesus *crucified*. Unlike some Christians, they did not seem to stress, at any rate universally, any particular doctrine of the atonement. But they did make it plain that their hearers were implicated in the human guilt of putting Christ on the cross: it was their fault that he hung there. What is more, they spoke of this Jesus offering people forgiveness (2:38). They sometimes spoke of him as the passover lamb (20:28), sometimes as the Suffering Servant (8:32-5), and sometimes as the one exposed on the wooden stake of Deuteronomy 21:22, the place of curse (Acts 5:30). The rare word used there, *xulon*, is applied to the cross only in those few New Testament passages which refer to Deuteronomy 21:22. Paul highlights the significance of it in Galatians 3:10 and 13. He was struggling to understand how God's Messiah could have ended up not only in the place of impotence and failure, but of divine curse: had not Deuteronomy declared, 'Cursed is everyone who hangs upon a tree'? And then he saw it. Christ had indeed endured the place of cursing; but the curse he bore was not for any misdeeds of his own, but for us – who have failed to keep God's law and are therefore liable to its penalties (Gal. 3:10). In varied ways like these, the early Christians tried to help people see what Jesus had done for them in Calvary. They were clear that the cross did not save anyone. It was Jesus who saved, the Jesus who had gone to that bitter cross gladly for sinners. We might profitably emulate their flexibility, Christ-centredness and reserve.

They spoke of Jesus *risen*. The major emphasis of their preaching was on the one who broke the power of death and rose on the first Easter day. 'We are all witnesses', they insisted (2:32). This confident assertion both of the resurrection of Jesus and of their relationship with him runs throughout the Acts. It comes in every evangelistic address recorded in the book. It is a major theme. I wonder if our contemporaries would say the same about our preaching? Are we always indicating that Jesus is not dead but alive, and that we know him? The churches which are growing these days are churches like that.

I recall a few years ago seeing written all over the walls of Oxford, 'Ché lives'. He didn't, of course. Ché Guevara, the self-sacrificing leader, was dead, even though his fame and ideology lived on in Bolivia and more widely in Latin America. The Messianic myth, for such it was, proved fragile at its most crucial point. The man was dead, and he did not rise. But since then many thousands of people have turned to Christ in Bolivia where Ché used to operate. And on the walls of Oxford you can often see scrawled a different legend: 'Jesus lives'.

They spoke of Jesus *reigning*. The one who had embodied God's sacrificial love now shared the throne of God (2:34). They were persuaded of it. There is nothing more regal in the whole universe than the self-sacrificial love of God. We have spurned it, but it will not let us go. That is the principle which people at their best most admire – in the mother sacrificing herself for her children, or the captain for his ship. And that is the principle which God rates most highly. I think it is important for us in evangelism to help people escape from their childhood image of 'gentle Jesus meek and mild' and realise that in him they are confronting the very essence of the universe, a God who gives and gives, whatever our response – or lack of it. He is enthroned on high, and he awaits our loyal allegiance. The only indestructible thing in the whole cosmos is this self-abandoning love. Unless we are touched by it, respond to it, and begin to model it, we are ultimately on the road to destruction.

They spoke of a *contemporary* Jesus. He is no mere figure of long ago, but our contemporary. That is how they understood the Holy Spirit who was so manifestly among them (2:33). He is the presence of Jesus for today, released from the limitations of a physical body. The early Christians seem to have recognised from the outset that their experience of the Spirit was a continuation of their experience of Jesus. The Spirit was the means by which their Master kept them company. No longer was he the fitful, subpersonal manifestation of the naked might of God, as so often in Old Testament days. He was God's mighty presence, brought to them in Jesus. 'The Spirit,' they maintained, 'has come and changed our lives. He can do it for you.' Had all Christian evangelists given this stress on the person and work of the third person of the Trinity, there would have been less talk of the 'baptism of the Holy Spirit' as a second initiatory experience, and less confusion over his gifts and graces.

Such was the wonderfully rounded picture of Jesus which we find in the very first Christian sermon. It is faithfully portrayed in all the addresses that follow it.

They offered a gift

Most religions tell you of something you must do. This one tells of
something God has done. He did it through Jesus Christ, on the
cross. Acts 2:38 puts it very plainly. When his hearers wanted to
know what they should do in the light of Peter's preaching, he told
them to do nothing at all, but rather receive what God had done
for them. He sketched a picture of God approaching them with
two gifts in his hand. They could never earn them. They could
only accept them or reject them.

God proffers us the gift of *forgiveness*: complete cleansing from
whatever we have done in the past. That is unimaginable mercy.
And it is possible only because of what Jesus achieved on the cross.
In other words, forgiveness is nothing to do with the good life we
think we have lived or the kind deeds we pride ourselves on having
done. How could these things buy God's favour? It took the cross
– no less – to make possible man's full and free acceptance. The
sinbearing which Jesus underwent upon the cross meant that 'through
this man forgiveness of sins is proclaimed to you, and by him every
one who believes is freed from everything from which you could
not be freed by the law of Moses'. Grace is entirely free for us –
but was infinitely costly for him.

God proffers us another gift, *the Holy Spirit*. In days of old, as
we have seen, he was confined to special people; perhaps a king
or a prophet might expect from time to time to be touched by
the Spirit of the Lord. But he was not generally available. Indeed,
in the centuries immediately preceding Jesus, people had ceased to
expect the presence of the Spirit of God. He went out, they reckoned,
with the last of the prophets. They had to satisfy themselves at
best with the *bath qol*, the 'daughter of the voice', the spoken word
from God such as at the baptism of Jesus.

But Jesus was the man full of the Spirit. He was the last and
greatest of the prophets, and he was more. He both embodied the
Spirit of God in every way of which a human being was capable,
and promised to dispense the Spirit to his followers. On the Day of
Pentecost it began to happen. And it has been happening ever since.
The Spirit of Jesus was poured out upon the disciples, making Jesus
real to them though they could no longer see him, and changing them
into his likeness as he equipped them for the service of others and the
proclamation of the good news.

And all this was sheer gift! I wonder if most people outside the
church today see Christianity as a gift? Do they not have the image of

the church which is always appealing for money to mend its leaking roof, or do this or that improvement? Do they not see Christianity as a threat to their joys rather than the fulfilment of their identity? Do they not see it as a dreary attempt to be good rather than a dynamic experience of the love and power of Jesus? Have they any idea that God is willing to justify the utterly undeserving? Do they realise that it is not a question of grim duty but of generous gift? I doubt it. And to the extent that they fail to see this (whether they respond to it or not), we Christians show ourselves to be false witnesses to Christ's good news.

They expected a response

Like their Master before them, who changed the whole direction of people's lives as he looked into their eyes and said, 'Come, follow me,' the early missionaries never tired of challenging their hearers to accept the gift that God proffered them, and to begin in earnest the life of following Jesus.

They expressed this challenge in different ways. Sometimes the thrust was to repent, sometimes to believe, sometimes to be baptised (2:38f, 16:31). All three strands are connected. All three are necessary. They saw that people could not come to receive God's gifts with dirty hands. They needed to drop the mud with which they were playing, and come with empty hands to be washed and receive the gift of God. Repentance is not primarily an exercise in remorse about the past. It is an attitude of turning back to God. It is a change of mind, resulting in a change of direction. And Paul urged his hearers to 'repentance towards God' as well as 'faith in our Lord Jesus Christ' (20:21). The basic human failure lies not in our peccadilloes but in our relationship with God, ruptured through many years, decades even, of rebellion and neglect. Repentance is the willingness to have this put right, and the determination to remove any hindrance on our part to its repair.

Faith has two sides, a cognitive and a volitional. It does involve some *understanding*, but not necessarily a great deal, to begin with. To believe that in Jesus Christ God has done all that is needful to restore the broken relationship is, I suppose, the bare minimum content of faith. As we have seen, 'Jesus is Lord' seems to have been the earliest baptismal confession of faith. It centres in *Jesus*, the historical figure; and the meaning of that word is 'Yahweh saves'. So in making that confession, the candidate is recognising that through Jesus God is becoming his Saviour. And *Lord* takes us back to Psalm 110:1: Jesus is seen to fulfil the role of the 'Lord' who sits at God's right hand. Jesus is the Saviour, the Fulfiller, the Lord. The intellectual framework thus outlined will need to be enlarged throughout the years of Christian discipleship, but it all begins with those two words.

The other side of faith concerns the *will*, and this is most important. When a meal is laid before me, I act in faith. I have some (vague) idea of the ingredients: that is the cognitive side. But unless that intellectual appreciation leads to action I shall remain hungry! It is only when I take that meal into myself and make it my own that I shall benefit from it. And it is an act of faith. I cannot be sure before I eat it that it will not poison me. Of course, such faith is well grounded, especially when I know the one who provides the meal! In the case of Christian beginnings we can be very sure that the heavenly Father will not poison us. 'He who did not spare his own Son, but gave him up for us all, will he not also give us all things with him?' (Rom. 8:32). How wise, then, to 'taste and see that the Lord is good. Happy is the man who takes refuge in him' (Ps. 34:8).

Baptism is the physical expression of response to the gospel. We shall look more carefully into it in chapter 9. But it has at least two sides. It is the embodiment of our response to the good news. It is also the sacrament of God's part in the whole transaction. Not only does it make over to us, like a will, all that Christ did for us upon the cross (without our co-operation or even consent); it symbolises, and may convey, the outpouring of God's Holy Spirit into our lives. If the person has already been baptised but has never repented and believed the gospel, then he or she needs to welcome the Spirit into their heart with joy and gratitude. If they have never been baptised, baptism should follow speedily. It belongs to the act of commitment as surely as the wedding ring does to the vows!

The point is this. The Christian life is a relationship. And it takes two to make a relationship. God approaches us with his arms held out in love, proffering us forgiveness for the past and his Holy Spirit as guardian of the present and pledge of the future. We have to make up our minds whether to say 'Yes' to his offer and challenge. To make no response is, for the present at least, to say 'No'. That is why a demand for response is an essential part of proclaiming the good news.

These elements which we have been looking at in the apostolic preaching are not an arbitrary selection on my part. One of the most seminal New Testament studies in this century has been conducted by Professor C.H. Dodd, in *The Apostolic Preaching and its Developments*. It dealt with the preaching in the earliest church. Dodd finds

two ways to reconstruct it. One is to ransack the Epistles of Paul:
embedded within them are traditional statements whose wording
and style shows that Paul did not formulate them but took them
over from the earliest preachers. From these Dodd summarises the
Pauline *kerygma*, or gospel, as follows:

> The prophecies are fulfilled, and the new Age is inaugurated
> by the coming of Christ. He was born of the seed of David.
> He died according to the scriptures, to deliver us out of this
> present evil Age. He was buried. He rose again on the third
> day according to the scriptures. He is exalted at the right hand
> of God, as Son of God and Lord of quick and dead. He will
> come again as Judge and Saviour of men.

It concludes with a challenge to repentance, faith and baptism into
Christ.

Paul's testimony is very important, because it takes us back to
within a very few years of the death of Jesus and gives us the
apostolic message which Paul heard from the church and proclaimed
alongside the other early preachers.

The other way Dodd seeks to get back to the earliest preaching is to examine the sermons in Acts. He does this with care,
and his conclusions are as follows. The characteristic *kerygma* recorded in Acts proclaimed that,

> The age of fulfilment has dawned. This has taken place through
> the ministry, death and resurrection of Jesus of Nazareth. In
> virtue of that resurrection Jesus has been exalted to the right
> hand of God, as Messianic head over the new Israel. The Holy
> Spirit in the church is the sign of Christ's present power and
> glory. The Messianic age will shortly reach its climax in the
> return of Christ.

This proclamation always closed with an appeal for repentance, and
the offer of forgiveness and of the Holy Spirit. This follows closely the
summary of the preaching of Jesus, given in Mark 1:14,15: 'Jesus came
into Galilee preaching the gospel of God, and saying "The time is fulfilled, and the kingdom of God has drawn near: repent and believe the
gospel."' While not identical, there is substantial agreement between
the gospel as reconstructed from a study of the Acts and the Pauline
letters. So we can be confident that we have the essential content of

what the first Christians preached. It is our responsibility to interpret it faithfully within the culture of our own day.

What can we learn from them?

There are a number of characteristics of the early preaching which stand out in sharp contrast to contemporary presentations.

1. I am struck by the *seriousness* with which the early preachers went about their task. There was nothing casual about it. It consumed their lives. They passionately believed it. They used every means at their disposal to share it. The very words used for imparting the gospel are significant. *Euaggelizomai* suggests there is good news to share. *Kerusso* indicates that it needs to be shared from the housetops: a *keryx* is a herald! There was nothing timid or hole-in-the-corner about that sort of preaching. *Laleo* is another common but more informal word for their preaching: sometimes you could almost translate it 'to chatter'. But there was nothing shallow about their message. It was something we find them witnessing to most thoroughly (*diamarturesthai*, e.g. 2:40, 18:5). They were prepared not to speak six feet above contradiction but to dialogue (*dialogizesthai* 19:8). They gave themselves to serious teaching (*didaskein*, e.g. 11:26). They put together texts from the Old Testament along with their fulfilment in Jesus: that is the meaning of *symbibazein* (e.g. 9:22). They forcefully sought to persuade people (*peithein*, 28:23). They used the resources of the Old Testament, scraps of Greek poetry, insights derived from the philosophers to supplement their proclamation of Jesus and to drive it home to their hearers.

I do not always see that measure of commitment in contemporary preachers. We make preaching dull and lifeless. We are even glad to dispense with it in a service. It will certainly not be the major theme that occupies our waking hours as it did theirs. They had a commitment to this message in terms of time, content and priorities which shows me the poverty of my own Christian faith and work.

2. A second thing that stands out is their refusal to have anything to do with *syncretism*, or relativism, which were as seductive in the culture of the first century as they are today. For the first time for centuries the world was united under one rule, one ideology, almost one language. The pressures to conform were enormous, especially when so little was asked of you. Just a touch of incense in front of the Emperor's

statue – a mere political gesture. Just a broadminded recognition of other people's views, an openness to other high-minded faiths like Judaism and Stoicism, equally valid ways to God. It was very tempting. It seemed very reasonable. But they resolutely refused to do it.

They were very willing to dialogue, that most fashionable word which has replaced mission in many circles these days. But they dialogued in order to give the grounds for their belief and to persuade others to join it. Modern dialogue, on the contrary, is simply the exchange of views about faiths without any attempt to persuade. But if you have come to the conclusion that Jesus is both divine and atoning, there is no way in which you can put him on a shelf alongside other deities. You have to say, like Peter, 'There is salvation in no one else, for there is no other name under heaven given among men by which we must be saved' (4:12). You have to say, like Paul (in response to Agrippa's quip, 'In a short time you think to make me a Christian'), 'Whether short or long, I would to God that not only you but all who hear me this day become such as I – except for these chains!' (26:29f).

There is nothing petulant or obscurantist about such intransigence. These men believed that the Absolute had come into the world of the relative, and they were not prepared to abdicate that claim. The pluralism all round them was even more pervasive than it is today. The temptation to syncretism was even more appealing then than now. But they would have nothing of it. And I can just imagine what they would say about our inter-faith services, our massive syncretism, our willingness to compromise on the essentials of the faith, and our lack of conviction about what we believe and why.

3. A third area that strikes me is their *flexibility* over methods, allied to firmness about the content of evangelising. The relative fixity of the *kerygma* they preached is in striking contrast to the flexibility with which they went about it. They had no desire to keep talk about Jesus to the synagogue. They did it on the streets, in the court rooms, on board ship, in prison, in front of the high and mighty or the beggars by the kerbside. In our own day, however, I see almost a reversal of their approach – great fixity about how preaching is done, and great flexibility about its content. The Western church at large has lost the certainty and New Testament content from its gospel: but it always does its 'preaching thing' in much the same way. It will be done in church, as a monologue, for between fifteen and thirty minutes, by a clergyman. Our Christian forefathers would be amazed that we have both lost the heart of the

gospel they took such pains to conserve and that we have become so unimaginative and inflexible in its presentation, neglecting almost entirely neutral ground in favour of ecclesiastical turf, and personal testimony in favour of clerical composition.

4. This brings me to another fascinating element in the good news as we read of it in Acts. It is the word '*witness*'. The Greek root comes eighteen times in Acts. It is clearly very important. The word is used alongside *kerusso* and *euaggelizomai* as one of the main words for telling the gospel. The content of 'witnessing' is just the same as of 'proclaiming' or 'telling good news'. It is no puny self-centred thing as so often today when someone is put up to tell you how bad they were before they met Christ and how great the difference has been since then! No, it was an unambiguously Christ-centred word. They were bearing witness to him – his person, his life, his death and his resurrection. But the distinctive flavour about the 'witness' language is the note of personal experience. Jesus envisaged this in the seminal passages about the witness they would bring in Luke 24:48 and Acts 1:8. The content would be about him. The overtones would be about their discovery of him. It is as if the good news about Jesus is a lovely rich cake; and the note of personal witness is the icing on the cake. Cake without icing can be dull. Icing without cake can be sickly.

I miss this note of witness-bearing in contemporary Christianity. Many preachers bring carefully prepared scripts which they read with greater or lesser skill and conviction. But rarely do they let you know that this stuff is their very life blood. Rarely do they allow their own discovery of Jesus, their own profound convictions about him, the difference he has made to their own lives, to surface in their address. I do not know whether they think this is out of date, or embarrassing. I do know that sermons devoid of witness are drearily boring. I want to hear what Jesus can do to men of flesh and blood like me. I want it from the Scriptures, but I want it from the life too, and that is why witness is such an important part of the proclamation of the gospel. Often two minutes of honest testimony, the more broken and unschooled the better, is worth twenty minutes of eloquent discourse by some silver-tongued preacher. The early Christians knew this. They were not all preachers, but they were all witnesses. And they expected every Christian to have something to say about Jesus and the difference that Jesus makes to life. And where that happens in the world today, the church grows and people come to faith. People can see that it makes a difference to Mr and Mrs Ordinary Citizen – and they take notice.

5. This note of witness leads naturally into another characteristic which marked the first Christians. We have seen that the person of *Jesus* dominated their sermons. It was him they proclaimed, with all the conviction, intelligence and passion of which they were capable. That is not often the case today. You can hear many an address in a church without a single mention of the name of Jesus in it. And you can listen to many more which would give you the impression that Jesus was just a good teacher who lived a long time ago. Where is the Christ-centred passion which lit these first disciples? Where is the balance between his humanity and his deity? Where is the fearless challenge over the sin of neglecting him, or crucifying him afresh? Where is the assurance that through the cross forgiveness of sins is available? The resurrection of Jesus is the most staggering truth in the history of the world, and yet it is rarely talked about except at Easter: and even then the resurrection appears to many as a myth which no intelligent person can be expected to believe, instead of the bedrock on which the Christian faith stands or falls.

Where, in contemporary preaching, do you hear of the palpable presence of the Holy Spirit attesting the reality of Jesus' ascension, and presaging his return at the end of history? When, indeed, do you hear anything at all about the Christian hope, be it at the end of life or at the end of history? The modern church really is like the Laodicean church in Revelation: lukewarm, because it has kept Jesus outside: outside the mainstream of its life and teaching, outside the hearts of its members. We in the West may pride ourselves on being 'rich, prosperous and in need of nothing', but the Jesus we have kept out, the Jesus we have misrepresented, has eyes like a laser, and his assessment is that we are 'wretched, pitiable, poor, blind and naked'.

6. Because we are so weak on Jesus, his incarnation, atonement and resurrection, we are inevitably reluctant to *challenge* men and women with him. The absence of challenge is one of the most notable marks of modern preaching, and is in starkest contrast with the apostles. They fearlessly challenged all and sundry with this despised Jesus whom they loved and who had made such a difference to them. They had no qualms at all about calling on men and women of all ranks in life, from kings to magicians, to repent, to believe and to receive the gift of the Holy Spirit and of baptism. We have come to feel that to challenge others is almost indecent. It is an unwarranted invasion of their private space. But do we feel that about people perishing in

the sea or in a burning house? We invade their space with enthusiasm then! But that is the situation, spiritually speaking, that the apostles saw men and women to be in – in deep need of rescue, without which they would perish. They saw Jesus as the Lifeguard, the Fireman, and they therefore challenged people unashamedly to allow themselves to be rescued by him into a new and fuller life.

Is this not something we need to recover? It is very evidently part of the thrust in Third World Christianity. Some churchmen from Argentina came on an exchange visit to Vancouver not long ago, and were duly impressed by the social work of the church among the poor. But they asked in amazement at the end of their visit, after allowing the full enormity of it to sink into them, 'But do you never tell them about Jesus and challenge them to respond to him?'

7. A final reflection on the difference between their preaching then and ours today is the matter of *conviction* and confidence. These men and women preached with conviction. There were no 'maybes', no 'ifs' and 'buts' about their proclamation. They were not naïve. Their preaching rested on prolonged study of the Scriptures, deep wrestling over its fulfilment in Jesus, and carefully calculated application. The result was confident powerful stuff. Here were men who knew God and wanted above all to make the way back to him plain to all who heard them.

Think of the final cameo in Luke's story, Paul in prison in Rome – and needless to say locked in dialogue with people about Jesus! We find him 'expounding', 'testifying', 'trying to convince' them about Jesus both from the Law of Moses and from the prophets. It went on from morning to night. It was divisive: some were convinced, and some disbelieved. And the crowd went out, to carry on the debate in the Jewish ghetto, with these astonishing words ringing in their ears:

'The Holy Spirit was right in saying to your fathers through Isaiah the prophet:

Go to this people and say, "You shall indeed hear but never understand,
and you shall indeed see but never perceive.
For this people's heart has grown dull,
and their ears are heavy of hearing,
and their eyes they have closed;
lest they should perceive with their eyes,

    and hear with their ears,
    and understand with their heart,
    and turn for me to heal them"' (28:25-7).

Was that tactful? No. Was it combative? Yes. Was it in line with the
teaching of Jesus (cf Mark 4:12)? Yes. But the overwhelming thing I
see in this tailpiece to the Acts is the immense confidence Paul has in
the unpalatable Scripture which he quotes and the truth it embodies.
He himself explains it thus, when writing to the Thessalonians: 'Our
gospel came to you not only in word but also in power and in the
Holy Spirit and with full conviction' (1 Thess. 1:5). That was it.
The first Christians were faithful to the 'word', the revelation they
had been given in Jesus. They looked to the Holy Spirit to give
wings to their words. They were so persuaded of that word, and
so full of that Spirit, that they came across with 'full conviction'.
That is the sort of Christian proclamation that packs power in the
twentieth century, as it did in the first.

7

What of Their Methods?

How did these few men, with their pitiful lack of education and resources, make such an effective impact on their civilisation with the gospel while we, with far more going for us, are on the whole making so little? It is an intriguing question when you reflect that the two most natural ways for Christians to spread these days are through activities based on church buildings and through large rallies or crusades held in public places by famous preachers. Both of these expedients were denied the early Christians. The imperial government was very allergic to large meetings in public places; these could so easily take on a political dimension – or so the emperors feared. As for church buildings, the Christians did not own any until the third century, and by that time their advance was virtually unstoppable. Robbed, then, of these two obvious ways to share their message, how did they do it?

The following pages will outline some of the ways they did it. These stand out in fairly sharp contrast to the procedures most modern churches are disposed to favour. But I have a feeling we could learn from them.

The gospel in the open air

These early Christians majored in open air ministry, just as their Master had done. The church was born in the open air on the day of Pentecost. They followed the greatest open air preacher ever, Jesus. It is salutary to remember this, imprisoned as most of us are in our ecclesiastical buildings. Christianity has been from the start a faith for the ordinary people, a faith to be proclaimed in the open air and among the non-religious. There are several ways of doing it.

One is to make a city-wide celebration. I think of an occasion in England, when a team under the leadership of my colleague Bruce Gillingham, initiated just such an outreach in Bradford. Most of the churches of the city joined in to celebrate their common faith. A great marquee was produced and the gifts and talents of the local Christians were the main feature, with some input from the visitors. Drama, dance, music, orchestra, banner-making were all part of it, and there was something for every sector of the community: the disabled, the elderly, the children, the mentally handicapped, business people and so on. Every church put on its own exhibition. And every night for a week they held major presentations in the marquee, with about 1000 people coming most nights. This grew as the week went on and people brought friends. It culminated on the last Sunday evening with Christians marching on all the available roads to the city centre, in such numbers that the flaps of the tent had to be raised as overspill crowds gathered round. In that context of loving trust and unity, there was much praise, much ministry, many needs opened up, and some healings. Nobody was bludgeoned into it. They were drawn into it, by the supreme attraction of Jesus at the centre of the whole enterprise.

There is a lot to be said for such meetings of celebration, involving real contact with ordinary people on the streets. I think of an occasion in South Africa when I and some friends (who had been studying issues concerning the gospel and race, up in the mountains) came to the nearby town, announced ourselves in the shops and then started proclaiming Jesus Christ the reconciler outside the main store of the town. A crowd gathered and was very appreciative. We knew that these people would be very poor blacks, so we had made a picnic lunch to which we invited the crowd. Some hundreds decamped to a local park and the conversation about the free grace of God went on, with real impact. They had never seen anything like that before. Surprise, the use of the unconventional, and demonstrable caring are important aspects of open air ministry.

When you go out on a limb and really trust Christ in an unknown situation out of obedience to his call, you should not be surprised to see the Lord working in power. I think of an occasion when I was due to speak at a large open air gathering in Nigeria. Thousands of people were there. It was Palm Sunday, and the Bishop and the choir were dancing in the arena with palms. They even persuaded a (reluctant) bench of judges to join in! But then it came to the time for people to sit in the burning sun and listen to the preaching. An archdeacon led in prayer, and besought the Lord for some cloud cover so that people should not get ill from sunstroke. I looked through my hands as I joined in the prayer, but I doubted. There was not a cloud in the sky. It was burning brass. But within ten minutes the cloud had come, mild cirrus cloud which shielded people from the most potent rays of the sun.

I think of another open air situation in England when that same archdeacon came to Britain for further studies, and was with us in a mission to a northern city. He and a group of students were due to proclaim the gospel in drama, dance and preaching in the local shopping centre. But when they got there it was pelting with rain. So he got the team into a corner and they prayed. They then sang 'Our God Reigns' (which doubtless some of them spelt 'rains') and by the time they had finished singing the rain had stopped and a very powerful open air ministry began. If God really means you to proclaim him in this way, you can expect his intervention. This is what happened in Acts 3. There was a remarkable healing, which acted as a powerful visual aid to the preaching which followed. It was the same at Lystra. Paul's healing of a man who had been a cripple from birth was the crucial element in a dynamic open air ministry. And from time to time it still happens today, especially when his people really trust their God to act.

Of course, nobody can organise divine intervention like that. But there are other ways of using visuals in open air ministry. One way is simply to hold up visual material which bears on what you are saying. Another is to take posters with you, which you gradually unveil. A series of short testimonies by real people who know the power of Christ in their life is very useful: this can be conducted either as a monologue or, better, as a brief question and answer occasion. I worked with a man once who could gather a crowd simply by standing up on a chair and spouting rubbish, but such amusing rubbish that the inhabitants of the local pub crowded round to see what would happen next. It was, of course, the good news that happened next! I have found circle-dancing to Israeli folk tunes a marvellous way of drawing a crowd. The medium *is* the message, and the sheer joy of the circle dance poses the question, 'What have these people got to be so happy about?' When people are asking that sort of question, it is very easy for the speaker. I have also found some good jugglers are a magnificent way of drawing a crowd, especially if they can use the ups and downs of their balls to explain something of the ups and downs of life and how Christ can catch you in any situation.

It is worth spending a bit of space on open air ministry, because it is so rarely done well. The key is confidence, confidence in God's

approval and confidence in the power of the gospel. This can lead
to a barbecue on the beach, when people gather round, and the
strumming guitars can lead into a gentle and honest proclamation
of the good news. It helps if there is some Coke and good food on
free offer. After all, the gospel is free. All this helps to create a mood,
and the mood facilitates people hearing the message.

The use of drama teams in the streets is another way of reaching
people on appropriate occasions, when folk have time and are not
in a rush. The team needs to have worked together over a period
of time. You need several sketches, and a compère who can link
them, speak the good news between them, and then mount a challenge at the end of the presentation. Some excellent books on street
theatre, which include some outstanding short sketches, are to be
found in *Time to Act, Lightning Sketches* and *Laughter in Heaven* by
Paul Burbridge and Murray Watts.

A sketchboard is another sure way of drawing a crowd, and is
very useful when the outreach is being made by only one or two
people. The Village Evangelists specialise in this work. It is basically
the drawing of some aspect of the good news with appropriate
wording by somebody who has some rudimentary artistic gifts. He
talks as he goes along. And invariably a crowd gathers, as they do to
watch a pavement artist. I have just read of a remarkable man who
went round the pavements of Sydney writing a one-word sermon,
'Eternity'. Just that. Arthur Stuce did it until he died at eighty-three.
The number of people who came to faith in Christ by facing and
acting upon that challenge was considerable. It shows that what we
do is a lot less important than the fact that we do something, in
reaching out to people who have no idea of Christ and bringing some
aspect of his person before them.

It is a help to prepare some succinct and challenging leaflet before
going out on these open air ventures which offer an explanation of
who we are and why we are there, moving on into a brief and highly
contemporary outline of the good news. These are then distributed by
the Christians in the team who mingle with the crowd, and ask them
what they make of all that is going on. You do not have to be a skilled
apologist in order to hand out such literature effectively. All you need
is the courage to do it, a smile, and the willingness if challenged to say
a word of the difference Christ has made to your life. That is more
than enough to get a profitable conversation going.

You could even include a prayer of commitment on that brochure.
I think of one occasion when Bruce Gillingham did that, and at the

end of the open air meeting he simply said, 'As you can see, we are Christians, and we believe that Christ is alive and it is possible to meet him today and start a new friendship with God. There may be those of you who have been looking for something like this all your lives. So how about reading through this prayer on the pamphlet and see if it sums up your hopes and aspirations? If it does, let's pray this together. If it doesn't, screw it up and throw it away – and have a good day!' Four people entrusted their lives to Jesus Christ there and then. If we had not been out on the streets, they might never have found the Saviour they had been blindly looking for. Of course, they were given New Testaments to celebrate the occasion and linked up with vital churches. What a joy for all concerned. The good news is too good to keep in the churches. It must erupt on to the streets.

This open air work is great fun once you lose your inhibitions. I took a drama team from our church to Germany some time ago. We went to Stuttgart, and trained up some Germans to do drama and dance in the streets. This was eminently non-Teutonic! But it had an electric effect. Soon the German team was much better at it than we were, and on a subsequent visit we worked with them in the streets. We found that they were highly disciplined, but instead of chatting with people in the crowd after the sketches they were back in line waiting for the next sketch, and waiting, incidentally, for our team to rejoin them; whereas we were following through the thrust of the sketches with the large crowd that had gathered! We were surprised that they did not do any preaching with their dramatic sketches. They simply left these rather enigmatic pieces to be understood as people could. I wanted to change that. So I went down one afternoon, determined to preach, to show that it could be done. Everyone was gardening in Stuttgart that weekend, and that seemed an obvious lead. So I took one empty flowerpot, and one with a lovely plant in it, another with a cactus. You do not need to speak for long on these occasions. I spoke a bit about gardening! I held up the empty flowerpot (upside down) and said, 'Without Christ your life is like that, ladies and gentlemen. Empty, upside down, and dark.' I went on, 'Now look at this one. It has a beautiful flower growing from it. And that flower springs from the union of the seed and the soil. God has the seed. You are the earth. Let new life germinate!' Then I showed them the cactus: 'Some Christians are a bit like this. They are prickly, but at all events they have life. Have you?' The crucial thing in open air work is to see something visual and speak the good news from it. That not only shows the vitality and relevance of the gospel, but it attaches it to a physical object, and that physical object reminds people of the message each time they look at it.

There is, of course, an entirely different way of doing open air work. You can, like Paul at Athens, start by speaking from the express objections of the crowd. There is a fine man in the United States, Cliffe Knechtle, who goes round the universities in that great nation telling the good news of Jesus in the most populous area of the campus. He only speaks for ten minutes at the most, and then allows the questions and objections to flow. He is a genius at dealing with them. And he sees a steady flow of people coming to faith in Jesus Christ.

Open air witness for Christ is one of the most neglected aspects of evangelism today. Either it does not happen at all, or there is the courageous but mildly mad character with billboards about him who recites in stentorian tones, 'Repent, and meet thy God.' There is a crying need for the church to regain confidence in the good news entrusted to it, and to get out into the streets with it. The early Christians did it, including the intellectuals and the bishops. Why not us? We have become too respectable. That is the trouble. And respectability and Christianity are bad bedfellows. Until we take to the open air, we may not be taken seriously by the man in the street.

But we must move on from the open air to the home. That, too, was enormously used by the early Christians, as they sought to spread the good news of Jesus.

The gospel in the home

The Acts give high priority to the home. It was the central pivot for the Christian advance. They met, for example, in Jason's house (17:5), or in Justus' house (18:7), in Philip's house (21:8) and so on. Sometimes it was a meeting for prayer (12:12), sometimes a fellowship meeting (20:7), sometimes a Holy Communion (2:46), sometimes it was an evangelistic day study conference (28:17ff). Sometimes it was an impromptu gathering (16:32). Occasionally they found a house full of seekers who were just waiting to hear the good news (10:22).

Yes, in the Acts they went for many house meetings. And the fact that they could not have public meetings is beside the point. They would have gone for house meetings anyway. For the home is a priceless asset. It is informal and relaxed. It makes participation easy. The leader is not distant, but approachable. There is no temptation to put on a performance. How important, therefore, for us to use the homes of the congregation. Use them for Bible studies, for fellowship groups, for prayer meetings, for evangelistic outreach, for baptism groups, for anything.

I recall a situation which emerged from my preaching one Christmas Day. A 'once a year' visitor turned up, and was touched by the challenge of the incarnation. He made some comment to me as he left, and I invited myself to his house in the following week. When I arrived at the prearranged time, I found a houseful of his adult family sitting round the table, fortified by onions and plentiful supplies of beer. Four hours later I had moved from the creation of the world to the step of personal response to Christ. I left, exhausted, at midnight. Next time I came round, a week later, I found the man had come to Christ, and his wife and brother were on the way. His brother's wife too, was not far off. It was a very interesting situation. One by one most of those people came to Christ. The original man, who had in fact put his faith in Christ that very night after the four-hour marathon, told me of the difference it made to him, a building contractor, as he went through his yard the next morning. He found himself turning to the Lord and asking his help in the problems of the job, which of course he had never done before in his life. Nobody had told him how to do this. It was an instinctive reaction of the new birth. At all events, before long he wanted to show his gratitude to God, so he threw a party for all his pagan friends, and asked me to speak. I did, on the Great Supper, the Christian life which God designed not to be a funeral but a feast. I told them about the Jesus who loved parties. I told them about the great supper party of the Christian life. I told them about the folly of complacent people who turned down the invitation. I told them that one day the door would be shut; but that in the meantime anyone, yes anyone, could come into the feast, whatever the mess in their lives.

I think of a particularly well-organised meeting in Birmingham, England, when a large house meeting had been arranged. The place was packed with people: they even extended up the stairs and into the bedrooms (where a relay system had been set up). I spoke, and took a small team with me to share their experience of the living Christ. There was a bookstall, and people made for that afterwards. All over the room and up the stairs, the conversation was about Jesus. Many people came to the start of a lifetime of discipleship that night. I can recall one of them, a garage owner, who was absolutely bowled over by the good news of Jesus which had come to him so freshly. People may come to house meetings who would not be seen dead at any Christian church. If we wish to spread the gospel, the home is one of the best ways to do it.

There are many ways to use the home: it is such a flexible asset. I think of a church in Canada that was born in a home like this, and has since spawned three additional churches. It all began with three couples who visited in their area, and said something like this: 'Some of us are thinking of doing an interesting little project. We want to get to the root of Christianity, and so we are going to read the oldest Gospel, and see if it has anything to say to us. A man called Mark wrote it. Would you care to come along for the next eight evenings? No strings attached: we don't have to believe it, but it would be very interesting to discuss it. Supper first. Do come.' And a number of people did. The result? A vigorous Bible study, conversions, expansion, and growth into an entirely new church. As I write on one of the Pacific Islands, I attend a dynamic church. How was that started eight years ago? Simply by a couple of business people who were champion surfers, and they asked among other surfers to see who would like to come to a house Bible study. That is where it began. Now that Bible study has become a church of 200 members with missionaries in two continents.

When inviting people to such an event, it is important to be relaxed and low key, and not to make great claims for Scripture as an authoritative book. It is much better, as Paul did in Rome (28:17ff), to expose people to it and let it make its own impact upon them. They will not believe its authority and power until they discover it for themselves.

Another very obvious way of doing it is to invite two couples to supper. This is an informal evening among friends, and you can afford to be gently direct. Pray for a suitable opportunity to bring conversation on to a spiritual level. It may be helpful to inaugurate some discussion of the most important discovery each person present has made in their lives. And you can simply tell them that the most vital and life-changing discovery you have ever made is that Jesus Christ is alive, and that it is possible to know him. You will be assured of a very interesting evening's discussion! It could lead to the conversion of somebody else at that meal table. You see, in a situation like that everyone is relaxed: nobody is trying to prove anything. It is just friends sharing experience. And friendship and experience are the best way to interest others in Christ and show that it is not religious humbug, but truth.

I have spent a lot of this chapter on just two ways in which the early church concentrated their efforts. They made much of the open air, and they made much of the home. On the whole we choose to neglect their emphases. And we are the poorer for it. But it is time to turn to some of their other approaches.

The use of neutral ground

The early Christians liked to debate the content of their faith on neutral ground, whereas we are rather shy of it. It might be with Jews, in a hired house in Rome (28:17). It might be when on trial in court (25:23ff). In our own day the heroic Russian Christian Georgi Vins, when arraigned under Stalin for his Christian involvement, took the opportunity afforded by his trial to bear eloquent testimony to the court in general and the public prosecutor in particular. It might be when shipwreck was pending, or when sitting around a fire after the shipwreck, as in Malta (27:21-44, 28:1-10). It might be before the full Areopagus on Mars Hill in Athens, debating the unknown God (17:16-34). But one of the most interesting examples given in Acts is Paul taking over the school of Tyrannus at Ephesus (19:9,10). One wonders who this man was, and whether his name really was 'Tyrant' or whether that is what his students called him. One wonders how Paul got to know him and got to use his school. The most likely explanation, and one suggested by the Western text of the verse, is that Paul took over between 'the fifth hour and the tenth' (i.e. between 11 a.m. and 4 p.m.). This was siesta time, the time when teachers did not need their premises, because they reckoned they would not be able to teach their pupils much or even keep them awake at that time in the heat of the day. So Paul was glad to get the hall. And I have no doubt that he kept wide awake the crowds of Jews and Greeks who grasped their lunchtime hamburger and Coke and came in to argue and to enjoy themselves. He took on all comers daily in the school of Tyrannus. And the result, Luke goes on to tell us, was that 'this continued for two years, so that all the residents of Asia heard the word of the Lord, both Jews and Greeks'. We shall have more to say about this in a later chapter. But one thing is certain: this public arguing about the truth of the gospel had an enormous impact on the many visitors to the great city of Ephesus, and was taken back home by them all over the province.

You have to get the right speaker for that sort of thing, otherwise the enterprise is counter-productive. But given the right person, the impact of such ministry is great. Who, of those who knew him, could forget Dr Francis Schaeffer in the 60s and 70s, arguing the faith against all comers from his base in Huemoz in Switzerland, and moving round many of the universities and large churches in the English-speaking world? He gathered round him intellectual opponents, communists and anarchists, atheists and far-out artists and musicians. And beginning from where they were, he drew many of them to a thoroughly thought-out Christianity. Another man who comes to mind is Lance Shilton, the Dean of the Anglican Cathedral in Sydney. Each Friday lunch hour you would find him at an outdoor pulpit in the square outside the cathedral, contending for the truth of the gospel against all comers. He was greatly respected in Sydney, and many came and were touched by this regular 'School of Tyrannus' type of ministry. He has recently retired, and you do not easily find Deans who can be replacements in that sort of work.

In my small way, I too have found how valuable it is to argue the truth of the faith in non-ecclesiastical places. The most obvious context is a formal debate. For several years when I was rector of an Oxford church, the Debating Union would, on occasion, ask me to take the floor against some well-known opponent of the Christian faith. And when the speeches from the platform were over, there was ample opportunity for Christians from the floor of the house to join in and make their contribution for Christ. I recall one such debate where discussion went on all night: the subject was the very heart of the Christian position – the resurrection of Jesus Christ. On another occasion a teller at one of these formal debates was converted and became a full-time Christian worker in due course. That person was so far away from Christian belief that you would never have found her at any ordinary Christian meeting. But she came to the debate!

In a recent city-wide mission, the organisers got hold of a big shop and used this for mission headquarters, the place from which we shared the faith using debate, music and questions, while people were able to move in and out, and take free refreshments and buy books and records that might help them. For the main meetings at such a venture I prefer not to use one of the churches, although they would be free, but rather to hire the town hall or sports arena. That somehow gives the impression that the gospel is not just for churchmen, but for everybody, and it makes it a lot easier for people who are uneasy about going into a church to take part.

Occasionally I have found bars are both welcoming and appropriate: often not! But if the goodwill of the bartender can be gained, it is a marvellous milieu in which to find people relaxed and open. There is usually some barracking and jostling, but if you take that with a smile, they are generally willing to give you a hearing, and then energetically to debate with you. I have actually known one man come to faith in the course of a long evening in the bar, where everyone was caught up in the discussion. He gave his life to Christ then and there, sitting on his bar stool. That is unusual. But if you are at ease in a pub, it is a very promising place in which to put the good news before people who normally would never give it a thought. I am sure that 'the friend of publicans and sinners' would go into bars without the least lowering his own personal standards. In some circumstances it could be good for his disciples to follow suit.

Music has a universal appeal, and the common ground of music is easy to exploit for the gospel. It may be with teenagers and a Christian pop musician. If so, it is easy to get young people in, but every care must be taken to avoid cheap evangelism which fails to give the young people an idea of what it will cost to follow Jesus when the musician has departed. Classical singers or pianists who are Christians can also be a great draw to a wider constituency. The personality concerned will mingle autobiographical elements with his performance, and among them will be reference to the difference Christ has made. It is then up to the Christians in the audience to take matters further, if appropriate, with the friends they have invited.

Sport rivals music for the hearts of most people. And although leading athletes and sportspeople are no more valuable than anyone else in the kingdom of God, their influence is, or can be, much greater because they are looked up to as role models by many in the community, and they cause a ripple of interest among everyone. A sporting fixture between the locals and a visiting Christian team can be intriguing, especially if it is followed by a barbecue where plenty of personal conversation and interchange can take place. Or a meeting organised to meet a sporting star who is willing to speak about Christ. Then either he can lead into a challenge at the end, or, if he does not have those particular finishing skills, some other suitable person can do it.

But we must not forget the opportunities provided by the workplace. They are great. Quite apart from the impact that attractive Christian living, coupled with the willingness to speak about Christ personally, can have, it may well be possible from time to time to arrange a meeting for teachers, lawyers, builders and so forth in a relaxed surrounding when a well-known speaker from that particular discipline can be asked to speak. I shall never forget a crammed hotel room full of builders and architects, and Sir John Laing, the creator of the first motorway in England, speaking with dignity and assurance that only an elderly person commands, on the importance of laying the right foundation in life, and building on the rock that is Christ. Opportunities for this sort of thing are plentiful once we get into the habit of looking for them. Where there is a will there is a way. But generally, in the church, there is not much of a will, and no imagination has been expended on a possible way. We have abandoned the common ground.

Visiting

Visiting is another way the early Christians used to spread the word. The most notable example in Acts must be that memorable occasion when God prompted Ananias to visit Saul of Tarsus (9:10ff). It was, as we all know, most fruitful. But Ananias did not want to go, any more than we modern churchpeople want to go. He was afraid of what he would find on the other side of the door in Straight Street. He argued about going. But in the end he went. It is interesting to find a man so like us. When the Lord spoke to him in a vision and called his name, Ananias immediately expressed his availability: 'Here I am, Lord.' But when he realised what the assignment entailed, he was much more reluctant. Nevertheless he went, his knees knocking, and his mind sceptical about whether such an enemy of the faith could possibly have become a believer. But his approach was warm and conciliatory. There is a wealth of meaning in those two astonishing words, 'Brother Saul.' Somehow he believed the best about Saul, despite his doubts. And he let his Christian love flow out not only in the words he used, so remarkable as a greeting to one who had Christian blood on his hands, but in his affectionate embrace as 'he laid his hands on him'. That astonishing house visit ended with a miraculous healing of Saul's blindness and his baptism, followed by a meal, which was, no doubt, a time of overwhelming joy and gratitude.

When all allowance is made for the exceptional nature of this particular visit, it is plain that God relies on his people to visit. He is not bound to work through us, but he generally does, and I suspect that the virtual abandonment of visiting in the modern church has contributed considerably to our decline. Church members need to be visited: not to remain nameless parts of a congregation on Sundays. Occasional church-goers need to be visited: the fact that they have taken the unusual step of coming may well mean that they are reaching out hopefully to the church, to see if it can meet their needs. Complete strangers to the church need to be visited: their first visit to church should be followed up by somebody (not necessarily the minister) coming from the church, to express welcome and find out in a relaxed way about them, their interests, where they have come from and what the church could do for them. People who never darken the doors of a church need to be visited. If someone does not show the love of Christ for them by coming to tell them of it and, in part, to embody it, how will they ever find out? The disaffected need to be visited: many leave the church for a variety of reasons, and they are often written off as difficult and intractable: nobody spends time listening to them and allowing the hurts to surface and to be talked over. Only two weeks ago a whole town was visited by the combined local churches, with a specially made magazine promoting both the gospel and the city-wide mission that was about to begin.

Visiting is a vital part of outreach. Churches which practise it find how valuable it is, and so they train teams of people from the congregation to visit the sick, visit the whole area once or twice a year, visit promising contacts, and visit to inform people of specific projects the church is putting on. It is unspectacular. It is often frustrating. The temptation to drop it is great. But it remains for us, as for the early church, the human face of Christianity. Christianity is a shamelessly incarnational religion. That is why visiting cannot be sidestepped.

Good news through literature

The early Christians used literature. Luke's own Gospel is an example of superbly crafted outreach material. It is intended to bring Theophilus and people like him to discover in Christ what Luke had found him to be. All the Gospels are designed for outreach, either directly or, like Matthew, to equip the Christians for that outreach. The Acts' speeches make it plain that these first Christians used also the appropriate texts of the Old Testament. Of course, Christians and Jews held its authority in common, so it was a great meeting ground. But it is clear from the way the Scriptures are used (less frequently, to be sure, but still used) when dealing with a totally Gentile constituency, that the first Christians were confident of their ring of truth and wanted not so much to defend them as to let them loose. Naturally, at times, they moved from attack to defence of the gospel. The second century has a rising tide of apologetic material which may well go back to Luke. Luke's emphasis on fulfilled prophecy, the miracles which abound both in the Gospel and in the Acts, and the sheer success of the movement, are three of the major themes which occur in second and third century writers to validate the Christian claims. Naturally, too, they wrote other material, such as the Epistles of the New Testament: but these were intended for internal consumption within the church rather than for outreach. It is, at all events, abundantly plain that these first Christians recognised the value of quality literary output as a means of spreading the gospel, and that they were highly innovative and took great pains about it. They even invented a totally new literary form, the Gospel.

Missionary journeys

Another thing which is so impressive about these first Christians is their missionary journeys. Some of us have groaned in our youth at having to memorise the direction taken by the missionary journeys of St Paul: they have been spoiled for us. But when you consider them coolly, they must have contributed enormously to the church's advance, and they have a lot to teach us. Sometimes it was all very spontaneous, like the evangelisation of the Phoenician coast and Antioch by the evicted Hellenists after the death of Stephen. Sometimes it gives the impression of having considerable organisation behind it, as in the first missionary journey from Antioch. Sometimes it was involuntary, either because of inner divine constraint (e.g. 20:22-25) or external captivity (e.g. 27:1ff). But always the first Christians seem to have had an outward orientation to their church life. And it is here that we are so unlike them. It has been calculated that today over 95% of Christian money is devoted to the maintenance of existing Christian institutions rather than looking towards outreach. So long as that maintenance mentality grips us, rather than mission, we shall shrink, and deservedly so.

It is noteworthy that these missions seem to have begun in hot centres of life, like Jerusalem in the earliest days, Samaria, Antioch, Ephesus. This is another most important principle. You will not get vital outreach unless it comes from a vital home church situation. Many churches have a steady trickle of ordinands and missionaries coming from them: these are churches where there is a real vision and a real warmth, accompanied by challenges to sacrificial service and the example of others who have gone before. By contrast, there are vast numbers of churches who have never bred an ordinand or a minister, and never look like doing so, because the necessary preconditions are not there. If outreach is our goal it does not begin there, but with a church life which the Holy Spirit is allowed to warm with his love.

The importance of teams

Nor did these first missionaries go out alone. There were usually at least two of them, and frequently there was a Timothy, a Titus, a

Silvanus, or a Mark who accompanied them and learnt while on the job. This is another area where we tend to make big mistakes. In our missionary work, our evangelism, our church leadership, we go for the model of the one-man minister, and that produces its own bitter fruits of loneliness, frustration, authoritarianism and burn-out. God believes in teams. Jesus chose, and left behind, a team. When he sent them out, he sent them two by two. The Mormons and the Jehovah's Witnesses have learned that truth. It is important for mutual encouragement, prayer, complementarity, and imagination. I now hardly ever accept a speaking engagement on my own. I always want to take a small team, so that we can tackle the enterprise together, pray and plan together, enjoy Christian fellowship together, which is always at its best in outreach, and train on the job. The outreach may be for a single meeting. It may be for a weekend, or a week's mission. But the principle of going out together stands in all those circumstances. If nothing else, it is an eloquent example of 'body life'. In a world that is divided and individualistic, it speaks of love and partnership.

It is instructive to notice that they reported back. There is a good deal of coming back to the Twelve by the various missionaries in the Acts, including Paul. They formed the inalienable centre of the moment. And it is very noticeable in the first missionary journey, where Paul and Barnabas are sent out from Antioch (13:4ff). It is to Antioch they return, and are strengthened, encouraged and renewed for future ministry (14:26f); while on their side, the home church is enormously encouraged by what God has achieved through the missionaries. Mission is a partnership between those who stay, pray, and give, and those who go. There needs to be time spent sharing news. There needs to be mutual accountability. And that is one of the things that is very lacking in many modern churches: accountability. Ministers do their own thing without anyone calling them to account. Missionaries, once sent out, may well take a leaf out of the same book. Rarely does anyone sit down with them and assess what has been attempted, what has been achieved, and where alterations need to be made in future. If we were to stick to the principles of no leadership without delegation, and no delegation without accountability, there might be a new seriousness in many a Christian church.

Two other things fascinate me about these missionary trips. One is that those concerned seem to have returned, if it was at all possible, to see how the new believers were doing; to encourage them, and to establish leadership among them (cf 14:21-3, 15:36f and probably 19:1). This is all part of the strategy of nurture which we noted earlier.

But it does not chime in with a good deal of today's evangelism, which tends to make over-confident claims for response, and to give less than desirable attention to aftercare.

The other is that these evangelistic teams generally seem to have moved on so fast. To be sure, Paul stayed for upwards of eighteen months in Corinth (18:11) and longer still in Ephesus (19:10), but on the whole, the impression we gain is of speedy moving on. Paphos, Perga, Pisidian Antioch, Iconium, Lystra, Derbe follow one another in quick succession. It appears from 13:14 and 44 that they spent only two weeks in Pisidian Antioch; and in the Second Missionary Journey apparently only three weeks were spent at Thessalonica (17:2). This shows up an important principle of trusting the initiative of the new Christians. Trust them into leadership soon – shared leadership of course. And let them have the joys, and pains, of Christian mission and Christian nurturing.

I shall never forget the time I spent with the Canadian who had been the pioneer in mission among the Kechua Indians, who are in three countries in Latin America. None had been converted before his ministry in the 1950s. Under his ministry, many were; soon there were thousands of Christians. He told me that one of the hardest things he ever did was to attend their gatherings for planning and leadership, *and say nothing*! He knew he had to leave it to them, to make their own plans and their own mistakes. And this they did! But they grew. And the church was indigenous from the outset as a result.

So much for 'missionary journeys' in teams. Any church can, if it will pay the price, follow the example of the early Christians. It can begin by ensuring that the minister never goes out on a speaking engagement alone, but always with a little team. It will grow from there.

Overseas ministry

It is easy to overlook how much the first Christians valued overseas people. They might be Ethiopian eunuchs, or Samaritan magicians, or Roman proconsuls, or Godfearers like Cornelius. But they were valued, and the good news was put to them in terms they could understand. From the first, the Christians seem to have understood that none of the national and social barriers common in antiquity had any validity in the kingdom of God. There is no hint of racial prejudice, class distinction or social snobbery in the church, no differentiation between slave and slave owner, between black and white, between rich and poor, Gentile and Jew. All the nationalities and stations of life seem to have been woven together pretty effectively from the start. And what variety there was in this overseas contingent: you have only to read where the people on the streets on the day of Pentecost came from (2:9-11). Again, 13:1 shows us a remarkable racial mix in the leadership of Antioch – from Palestine, Asia Minor, North Africa and Cyprus. It may have been fortuitous, but it almost seems as if the early Christians realised that when people of other cultures and nationalities came across their path, these were key people to evangelise.

It is thrilling to see what is happening among the ethnic Chinese in San Francisco, the Jews in Los Angeles, the Koreans in Vancouver. I think of a church in Melbourne which has over seventy satellite congregations – of different nationalities. We must pay attention to the ethnic minorities in our midst. But alas, we do not do it. Instead, many Christians bewail the fact that they would love to be missionaries, but cannot leave home for one of a number of good reasons. They fail to understand that the mission field is everywhere about us, particularly in those members of other races and faiths who have come to study in our midst. The missionary force is not only the expatriate missionary, but the local church itself, through its hospitality and friendships. The opportunities for many a congregation in Britain and North America to influence the world by loving and caring for ethnic minorities in their midst is phenomenal. I think the earliest Christians would greatly envy us the opportunities that lie unheeded on our doorstep. We do not have to go to them. They come to us.

Surprise

Another interesting thing about these early missionaries is this: they knew the value of surprise. Surprise in the streets at Pentecost. Surprise for the beggar who thought he might get a few coins, and he got healed (ch 3). Surprise when Philip went to the hated Samaritans (8:4f). Surprise when Paul started to evangelise his captor (26:24-30), and on many other occasions. In the modern world, the non-Christians think they know what Christianity is. But they often make a great mistake. They think it is a religion, whereas actually it is a relationship. And the difference between the two is the difference between night and day.

We need constantly to keep surprising people, and showing them that what they think they need may well not be their primary problem. The Philippian jailer thought that he needed to be 'saved' or rescued from the appalling mess he would be in with his superiors when they found out that an earthquake had hit the jail, and his prisoners had gone. Paul humorously picks up his problem and translates it into another key: 'Do you want to know how to get saved? I shall be delighted to tell you' (16:30f). When the great storm at sea was obviously going to end in shipwreck, and the sailors were assembled on deck, what they thought they needed was a lesson on lifejackets: what they got from their prisoner, of all people, was an assurance that their lives would be safe, followed by a quick meal in the presence of God! (27:23ff). I find myself constantly seeking to approach people about the faith in a way that they do not anticipate. Their guard is down, and the chance of honest interplay is great. The more we can cultivate the value of surprise, the better. A colleague of mine organised a 'crucifixion' of a member of the congregation in a local shopping mall on Good Friday. The man was hoisted up on a cross. It was easy to speak to that! And the crowd that gathered around was immediate, large, and ready to listen. On the whole, the Christian churches commit the unpardonable sin of making Jesus dull, or leaving him unknown.

Personal conversation

But most of all, the early Christians had each learned to be witnesses for Jesus, and to be ready and willing to undertake a conversation about him with enquirers. And that is where the modern church falls down so disastrously. We are not willing to talk to people about our Jesus, and we do not know how to go about it. Maybe we can learn from Philip in Acts 8:26-40. This man from Caesarea was one of the seven set aside by the apostles for work in the soup kitchens (6:5), but he soon displayed notable evangelistic gifts and went to bring the gospel to the Samaritans. It was a highly successful enterprise, and it says much for Philip that he was willing to leave it all for an undisclosed rendezvous in the south of the country, following an inner hunch which must have seemed crazy to him and to his friends, but which he sensed was the voice of the Lord. I love the way that Philip was sensitive enough to hear that voice. I love the way that he was obedient enough to follow it. I love the way he was so humble that he was willing to leave a revival in Samaria (where he was the preacher) in order, as it turned out, to help one black man in the desert. I'm struck by the importance which God clearly assigns to personal evangelism if he calls one of his prime evangelists out of the extremely fruitful work in which he was engaged, and into the desert to meet just one man in a chariot. If Philip had not obeyed, that Ethiopian official would never have been evangelised, and the gospel would not have reached his country as early as it did.

I love the way Philip was so sensitive to God, knowing when the Ethiopian came by that this must be the reason for his call into that apparently barren desert. I love his humility in running alongside the chariot and asking if he could be of any service. No wonder he was invited up! Yes, and I love his enthusiasm, running in the blazing heat of that desert. I have done it, and people thought me mad. I only did it to get a photo of a shepherd leading his sheep. Philip did it in order to bring one lost sheep back to the shepherd. Although people laugh at enthusiasm it is an enormously attractive trait, and we have no need to be embarrassed about it. Indeed, it is only when people see we are hopelessly in love with Jesus and that it has obviously had a beneficial influence on our lives, that they may be prompted to consider him for themselves.

There are other things that excite me. I am delighted by the way he asked a leading question, 'Do you understand what you are reading?' and then sat listening, instead of barging in with some prepared harangue. We need more *listeners* in the church: there is a hurting world out there, and most people do not give the time to listen to the pains and questions of others. This man was reading Isaiah 53 – a real gift to any evangelist! But wait a moment. Could *you* tell someone the good news starting from Isaiah 53? Philip could. You see, he knew his way around at least key passages like that, in the Old Testament. How many Christian laypeople in the twentieth century would be able to do that? It is not very difficult, in all conscience, but we are becoming biblically illiterate in the Western church. We need to begin to regain our grip upon the title-deeds of our inheritance, so that we can share its splendours with others. Not much is being asked. If you have half a dozen verses that can lead someone simply to commitment, that will suffice. Your expertise will grow with time and experience. But we need at least to have a basic outline of how to help someone else to faith, as Philip did. And we need to be willing to start from his or her starting point, not our own.

And don't you love the way Philip majors on the person of Jesus? 'Beginning with this scripture, he told him the good news of Jesus' (8:35). What other good news is there, but Jesus incarnate, Jesus crucified for us, Jesus alive and inviting us to come and follow him? Yet you can go into many churches for a long time without realising that Christianity is all about Jesus and your relationship to him.

Going for commitment

Perhaps the last point about this conversation is the hardest for us. Notice the way Philip clinches it. He brings the man to commitment, to the point where he asks for baptism. The same forceful challenge for commitment forms the climax of all the evangelistic addresses in Acts. We, too, need to get to that point. Once we have done it with one person, we will be into it for life. It is not very difficult, if the Holy Spirit is leading the conversation. The time will come when the friend says, 'What am I supposed to do about it all?' And you reply something like this: 'If you see that Jesus is no less than God, who has come to your rescue; if you believe he is alive and in business – then come to him just as you are, and ask him to take control of your life.' And have the courage, then and there, to ask your friend to pray with you, and to clinch this most important decision of his or her whole life. So many Christians fluff it at this point. They duck out of this culminating moment of encounter. It is time to burn your boats. If your relationship with the other person is strong, you will not offend him or her by asking, 'Would you not love to get this settled once and for all this evening? It is very simple, but very profound. You need to surrender your life, the best way you know how, to Jesus Christ. Ask him to come into your life and take control.'

It is a great joy, and privilege, to kneel and pray with a friend as they entrust their life to Christ after you have been telling them about what he can do for them. And once you have tasted that joy, you will be voracious to taste it again! That is above all how the early church grew, by personal conversation. If we could instil into our congregations the responsibility, the basic knowledge and the motivation for personal sharing of the good news, we would be well on the way to regaining Christendom in the Western world, just as it is expanding in Latin America, Africa, and Asia.

8

What of Their Church Planting?

In this chapter I propose to look at seven examples of how the early Christians actually founded churches, where there were no churches previously. More could have been selected, but these seven will suffice to show something of the variety of the ways they went about it, and the broad spectrum of spiritual resources which they drew upon.

In many parts of the Western world, church planting seems an irrelevance. The countryside has been planted with an excess of churches, over many centuries. True enough. But the vitality of those same churches has been gravely eroded over a process of time; they have suffered attrition by apathy, scepticism, division, and other factors. People have voted with their feet. They will not return to such churches, however hallowed they may be by tradition – unless it be for a white wedding, or a funeral. Does this mean then, that such people, who constitute by far the majority of the population in Europe, are to be denied the chance to hear the gospel in terms they understand? The whole history of the church says a resounding 'No' to that. If the wine-skins are so brittle that they have to be broken, so be it. The wine of the gospel must be served in more flexible wine-skins. That is what happened in Europe at the Reformation. It happened in England again at the Great Ejectment, when more than 1600 of the best clergy in the land went over to Nonconformity. It happened again in the Evangelical Revival. Whereas many won to Christ through that great movement stayed within the established church, thousands moved out with John Wesley, to form a church life which made evangelism, worship and pastoral care more real to ordinary people. In our own day the House Church movement has despaired of sufficient new life coming fast enough in the mainline churches and has started up a remarkable network of new churches, initially in homes, but subsequently meeting in cinemas and other public places; they are even building their own schools for the raising of their young.

Church planting will never be out of date. It will never be irrelevant. Circumstances will always arise where it is vital, and my years spent recently in North America have given me a fresh understanding of the need for it, and a fresh admiration for those who go out on a limb, without prospects, salary, or housing, to found a new church for God. In Britain some of the lively churches within the Anglican fold are refounding other Anglican churches which had died and been closed. This is not always appreciated by the hierarchy; it rather cuts against the traditional policy of inviolate parochial boundaries. But it is happening, and the proof of the pudding is in the eating. It works. Church planting is taking place even within the heart of that most overchurched (but underevangelised) nation, England, and with the tolerance of its bishops. In the light of this, it will be valuable to glean some principles from the Acts which could be useful in our day. Of course, the circumstances are utterly different. I am not for one moment suggesting that we can simply take over wholesale the methods of the early Christians. I am suggesting that it would not be a waste of time for us, who are so unsuccessful at it, to see how they, who were so successful, went about it.

Before we look at individual churches, one or two general observations are perhaps in place.

First, it is undeniable that the early Christians thought that founding churches was part of their commission. They were in the propagation business. They realised that they needed to export, or die. The churches I admire most are those which share that outlook, firmly rooted as it is in the express command of Jesus to his disciples (see Matt. 28:18-20). I was much struck, when visiting Guatemala a few years ago, to find a very lively church which over the past twenty-five years had founded *over 800 churches*! What a rebuke, what a challenge! Incidentally, the evangelistic zeal of that chain of churches did not eclipse social concern. They were the first to bring help and rehabilitation when a terrible earthquake devastated a sector of the country and evoked subsequent world support. Part of that international aid was used to provide people with temporary new housing, but as is the way with temporary encampments, they tended to become rather permanent. Round the two open air washing stations, one for men and one for women, in the centre of the camp, were the most densely packed dormitory-type buildings that you could imagine. I found that the colporteurs from the Bible Society of Guatemala had gone round the camp, and had started what became several new churches in that complex. That is the sort of thing the early church did. They saw it as part of their calling.

To put it another way, they took seriously the outward orientation of the church. Different denominations, over the course of time, settle down into prevailing characteristics. And for most denominations it would be fair to say that the prevailing orientation of the church is inward-looking: their leadership, their organisation, their finances, their buildings, and their special projects. We have become introverted. Church looks like a club for the pious, rather than the Jesus revolution breaking out.

The second general observation is this. The early Christians did not await consolidation, and train leaders, before moving out further. We tend, if we are ever engaged in church planting, to pay inordinate care to education, financing, and future leadership. We may stifle the project by over-protectiveness. But it is apparent from the Acts that churches like Thessalonica, Philippi, Lystra, and others were founded after the apostles had been with them for a comparatively short time. After that they moved on. Sure, they came back when they could, and wrote when they could, and commended another travelling teacher when he was heading that way. But on the whole they expected the God who had brought the little congregation into being to sustain it by providing adequate leadership. Their leaders would never have passed our Selection Boards, but they seem to have done what was required of them!

Again, as you look broadly over the Acts, I think you will not be able to discern any very highly structured church growth programme. There was no overarching body determining how it should all happen. Evangelism and church planting on the whole seem to have happened spontaneously without heavy planning. I am not denigrating planning: there needs to be proper planning behind any work for God if it is to take root and grow. But there was no monolithic, preconceived outreach plan. The planning was done by the Holy Spirit, and he seems to have guided the Christians into the appropriate approach for different situations. This meant that they needed to keep depending on him, and could not degenerate into producing a technique. Had the apostles sat down to plan the outreach in Acts, it would have looked very different from what actually happened, and it would have been microscopic in scope compared with the breadth it attained when the Holy Spirit led them in their ways.

Let us look, then, at these seven churches in Acts, taking note of just
a few factors in each one which seem to have contributed towards the
foundation of a church in their city.

Jerusalem

We have seen some of the preconditions for outreach in an earlier
chapter. Here I want to stress three factors which were significant in
the growth of the Jerusalem church. They could be equally significant
in the growth of any congregation which took them seriously. All
of them are extremely costly, as you would expect in the place
where Christianity was born. They all look simple. They are easy
to understand. They are hard to achieve.

The first is their *infectious joy on the streets*. That is manifest in
chapter 2. There was an undeniable radiance and joy about these
people, whatever you made of them. People could not help sensing
that these people had got something, and that it was very attractive.
And remember, all this took place not in the safe confines of some
hallowed building, but on the streets. What about *your* infectious
joy on the streets? There will be few things that make a greater
impact than that, for the gospel.

I first worked in a seaside parish, and we used to do open air
meetings by the sea on a summer evening. It drew large crowds, for
the simple reason that holidaymakers had nothing better to do than
to stroll along the front after their evening meal. They were relaxed.
If there was anything to arrest their attention, they might well stay and
watch. If it was no good, they would pass on. This was the challenge
that confronted us. We met in privacy to pray. We had already
planned the approach. We went out with singers and welcomers,
testimony-givers and preachers, visual aids and faith. We saw hundreds
of people stopping. The police who came to check us out used to join
the good-natured crowd. We had to put up a notice saying, 'This is the
Church of England' because nobody believed it! They simply could
not believe that this was the established church of the land, so strong
was their image of a church aloof and bound within its buildings. But
the Christian church was born in the streets, with an infectious joy
about it. And when we bring that same joy to public notice, and
particularly into the streets, it does draw people and it does produce
results. I think of a carpenter who passed by one evening: he had not
been in church for thirty-five years. But Jesus gripped him that night,
and he gave his life to Christ and became a committed Christian. That

man would never have been touched, were it not for happy Christians on the streets. It is something we dare not neglect. It is great to see its recent re-emergence in the peaceful Christian demonstrations in the East, and Graham Kendrick's Marches for Jesus in the West.

The second factor in their growth was their *utterly alternative lifestyle*. Look at chapter 2: 'They were all together' (v 1). They loved each other's company. That is a very significant thing about any church. Do they want to stay together, or are they itching to leave? How soon does the place empty after the service? 'They had all things in common' (v 44). Most Christians have very few things in common. 'They sold their possessions and goods, and distributed to all as they had need' (v 45). Maybe that was an idealism which could not be repeated. Once the capital was gone, it was gone. But what a magnificent gesture this exercise in community living was! That generosity of spirit is rare and precious, and an outstanding alternative to the normal way most people behave. It makes people stop and wonder. And such wonder is next-door-neighbour to faith. 'They distributed their goods to all as any had need'. Our distribution of goods these days is according to the political or social clout of those distributing or demanding resources. The way of the world is, 'to each according to his power'. The Christian way is, 'to each according to his need', and that is the source, incidentally, of the Communist ideal. For Communism is a Christian heresy. And it runs very much against the acquisitive ethos of Europe, America and other developed countries. But it is a principle that is vital in a world where the population will double in the next twenty-six years, where there is a strictly limited cake, of which everybody wants ever larger slices. We are heading for Doomsday if we continue with our policies of economic growth and greed. Most young couples today reckon to start where their parents have got to after a lifetime of labour, and it is absolute folly: the world will not be able to sustain it. Our assumption that this is our right is simply an expression of how deeply we are 'conformed to the pattern of this world'. We may *talk* about Jesus as a Saviour, but he sounds like a lucky charm, a talisman, if we continue to behave like this. Only an alternative lifestyle carries the credibility that draws others into the kingdom. These people 'attended the temple daily' and 'broke bread in homes' (v 46). They had hilarious meals together, rocking with laughter and joy, 'praising God, and having favour with all the people – and the Lord added to their number daily those who were being saved' (v 47). That was the undeniable flavour of the early Christian church.

A third factor was their *thoughtful reinterpretation of the good news*. This was brought about by the Hellenists, Stephen and his friends (6:1ff). They spoke Greek. They thought in Greek. And whereas Jewish Christians saw God as primarily the God of the Law, the Temple, and Israel, these people thought otherwise. They realised that the customs delivered by Moses could not measure up to Christian freedom in the age of the Spirit. The centre of their vision was no longer Israel, but Jesus, supreme in the whole world. They are the only people, outside Jesus' own words in the Gospels, who ever talk about the Son of Man. And the Son of Man is the one for whom Daniel predicted kingdom, power and glory (Dan. 7:14f).

It is significant that these Hellenists, holding such views, were kicked out from Jerusalem, while the conservative Christians of Jerusalem, including the apostles, were given a safe ride (8:1f). James the Just and the others stayed on unmolested in the Holy City, but the teachings of these Hellenists led to their banishment. Listen to what people said about Stephen; much the same must have been said about his friends: 'This man never ceases to speak words against this holy place and the Law. We have heard him say that this Jesus of Nazareth will destroy this place, and change the customs which Moses delivered to us' (6:13f). Isn't that just like the reactions today? 'He is going to change the interior of the church! He is going to change the service!' It is salutary to recall that the future lay with these Hellenistic 'extremists', not with the 'conservatives' at Jerusalem. It was they who translated the gospel into terms which secular people of the day understood. They had a big enough conception of Jesus to be emancipated from the shackles of attempting only what had been done before. They saw static religion as a betrayal of the God of Abraham. That God was always moving forward: but 'Solomon built him a house' (7:47). That is the nub of the complaint in Stephen's speech: the God who was always on the move had been shackled into a building when 'Solomon built him a house' (7:47)! That was when the rot started, according to Stephen. The Almighty cannot be caged in buildings made with hands. And these Hellenists realised it. They saw that the future lay not in sacred Jerusalem with its temple, but in the secular Roman Empire with its teeming millions. It was in this spirit that they set out. They saw Jesus not as the Messiah of Israel only, but as the Alpha and Omega of the whole world (Col. 1:15f). They saw him not as a cult figure for Sundays, but as the source of the solar system, the power behind the atom, the one who paints the beauty of the sunrise. Such was the amazing Christology with which they went out to conquer the world.

Samaria

Much could be said about church planting in Samaria (8:1f), but two principles in particular seem to emerge from the account in Acts, and once again, neither of them is very characteristic of the contemporary church.

The first one is *spiritual gifts*. Few subjects so polarise Christian opinion as this. At Samaria people saw the signs that Philip did; for 'unclean spirits came out of many who were possessed, crying with a loud voice, and many who were paralysed were healed. So there was much joy in that city' (8:7). These gifts were real. These gifts have not died. God does entrust them to Christians who really want them, and are prepared to exercise them. Very often a healing or deliverance leaves people wide open for the gospel in our own day, as it did in Samaria. I think of a colleague of mine, who would never think of himself as a church planter. But that is what John was. A whimsical upper-class person who collected butterflies – who more unlikely to be a church planter? I well recall the day he took over a tiny church, where nothing whatever was happening. It was sustained by a small group of elderly ladies praying God to restore what it had been. But through John people in that parish saw healings, and some were converted by them. They saw exorcisms, and some were converted by them. We must neither be afraid of these gifts, nor go hunting them: gift-hunting is an unattractive facet of some aspects of modern Christianity. The Lord will give gifts, when we will give ourselves to his Holy Spirit, and allow him to flood us. I do believe that when the Lord commanded his followers to go, preach and heal, he meant it, and that this was to be a paradigm for Christians. To be sure, healing is never guaranteed in this life: but neither is new birth, when we preach the gospel. The whole thing is provisional, in our fallen world. But that is no reason to attempt nothing!

The second thing which fired the mission at Samaria was *costly reconciliation*. That is a major help in mission. Why did these people have to come from Jerusalem and lay hands upon the Samaritans? 'Aha,' say the Pentecostals, 'in order that they might receive the baptism of the Holy Spirit.' 'Aha,' say the Episcopalians, 'in order that they might be confirmed.' The very same passage is adduced to support two utterly incompatible theologies! It could be that both sides have a little bit to learn.

Reflect for a moment. There had been a mighty chasm between Samaria and Jerusalem for hundreds of years. So what would have happened if the Holy Spirit fell on these new believers at Samaria? There would have been an apartheid church at Samaria, growing up in separate development from the Jerusalem church. Then there would have been another one for 'Godfearers', based on a famous church in Caesarea, perhaps led by Cornelius. And then there would have been another for Gentiles. And so it would have gone on. And the pagans would have seen precious little reconciliation, which was supposed to lie at the heart of the gospel message. So what God ordained was for some of the leaders of the Jerusalem church to come to Samaria and say, 'The apartheid is over. We all belong together in the family of Jesus.' And they laid their hands on them – worse than touching a leper in the pre-Jesus days! Jesus touched lepers. The Jerusalem church touched Samaritans. That was electric. No wonder the Holy Spirit fell on them in a big way. Everybody started praising the Lord. For the heart of that gesture is neither confirmation nor some second blessing: it is costly reconciliation. It is burying the hatchet after all those centuries of strife. And when you see that happen, the Spirit is released and the church grows.

I think of a mission that I led in the University of Rhodesia, as it was in 1974. It was the only place in the whole educational system of the country where blacks and whites learnt together. At first I was not heard at all. The whites were all talking about those terrible guerillas, while the blacks were talking about the whites who had repressed them all these years, and the privilege of being freedom fighters. I saw that the key issue there was violence. There were two sorts of violence in operation: restrictive violence which kept the blacks in bondage, and revolutionary violence which kicked against that. Two sorts of violence, locked in mortal combat. How do you preach Christ into that situation? I preached about violence all the week. What did Jesus do with the violence? Jesus ended up, most bloodily, in the place where violence terminated upon him, but in so doing, he made possible our reconciliation with God. Christians are called to follow him. The whites had to realise that if they were going to be Christians, it would mean protecting the blacks, here and now. And the blacks had to realise that if they were going to be Christians, it would mean protecting the whites, in the coming days of black rule. That was incredibly costly for both parties. But it was part of the calling to follow Christ. By the end of the week we partially won through. There was not a vast amount of fruit, but there were two or three score of people who came to that costly reconciliation. And that is a way of church founding. They discovered it in Samaria.

Caesarea

Let us move on to Caesarea. Caesarea is important in Acts. Chapters 10 and 11 are all about it. The events in chapter 10 are replayed in chapter 11 so that, right in the middle of Acts, you could not possibly fail to take note of the first time the gospel moved out of Judaism. It had already reached the Samaritans, but they were considerably nearer to God – and to Judaism – than the Godfearers were. They were at least half Jewish. But to share Jesus with a Roman officer in the occupying army, even if he did come to your synagogue, was a pretty shocking thing. So how did it happen at Caesarea?

First, there was *prayer and vision* (10:2). The remarkable soldier, Cornelius, was a man of prayer: 'He prayed constantly to God.' And while at prayer, God gave him a vision. It was very specific. He was to send men to a particular house in Joppa to bring Simon Peter, who was lodging there, to see him. Such was the vision; and being a military man, accustomed to giving and receiving orders, he obeyed at once. Meanwhile, in the amazing timing of God, Peter, way down in Joppa, was also at prayer, filling in a spare hour before lunch. And God gave him a vision, too. He saw in his vision a great sheet let down from heaven. It was full of all the animals that he had been taught to regard as unclean. A voice said, 'Rise, Peter, kill and eat.' At once he replies, 'No, Lord; for I have never eaten anything that is common or unclean.' Peter is a deeply prejudiced man. Even when God gives him a vision to break a long-standing custom, Peter contradicts, saying, 'No, Lord.' The breakthrough in this situation, so vital for the spread of the gospel into a totally new constituency (for Cornelius was the first of the 'Godfearers' to be converted), was going to be difficult. It needed two men at prayer, two separate visions, and plenty of struggles after that. But the prejudice was broken. Peter and Cornelius met. The gospel had its own mighty effect in that soldier's life, and the Holy Spirit fell in a very recognisable way upon Cornelius and the others gathered in that house in Caesarea. A fresh step had been taken in the evangelisation of the ancient world.

If churches are to be founded, it will not happen without prayer. A classic example is St Cuthbert's church in York, where David and Anne Watson were appointed to supervise the last twelve months before it closed. There were, I think, about ten people in the congregation. It was not many years before the church was one of the most celebrated in Britain, and the congregation outgrew the building and moved into its present home in St Michael's, York. What was the key to that amazing turnround, the effectual refounding of St Cuthbert's? Prayer. Every Wednesday David and Anne spent the morning in fasting and prayer. They besought God to pour out his Spirit and renew that church which was ready to perish. God did. He loves to answer prayer. And yet we find prayer the hardest thing to do. We would rather do any amount of active work instead of getting apart with God to seek his face and pray. But until that tendency is reversed, we shall not see much church founding.

It may well be that God guides you through visions, as you pray. Do not think that visions went out with the apostolic age. God can and does still guide through this medium. But it is very easy to be mistaken, so visions need to be checked out to see whether there are other indicators pointing in the same direction, and whether what seems a vision to you commends itself as authentic to other trusted Christian friends when you tell them. But these visions can be both real and exceedingly specific. I think of a Nigerian friend who had a vision one night of a dangerous journey he was due to take the next morning. He saw a group of brigands emerging from behind some rocks to kill him. When he took that journey in the morning, he was particularly vigilant when he got to the place indicated by his vision. Sure enough, the men did jump out at him, but he got away – because he was forewarned through his vision.

Not long ago Bill Bright, the president of Campus Crusade International, told me that the whole of his work sprang from a vision God gave him one day when he had surrendered every aspect of his life to Christ's direction. That work is now operating in well over one hundred countries. Prayer and vision were the preconditions of that very effective parachurch ministry. The vision does not need to be visual. It may be a deep longing for some sort of ministry, welling up within you. That could be part of God's guidance to you for the task he plans for you, however improbable it may seem at this juncture.

A second lesson I learn from Caesarea is to *expect the unexpected*. Few things could be more unexpected than for a sophisticated Roman officer to send a detachment of men off to find a Jewish fisherman to instruct him about God! It was totally unexpected, too, for Peter to be sitting on a roof-top waiting for his meal, and instead getting a vision of just what he did not want to eat! It was totally unexpected that Peter should find a houseful of people waiting for him at Cornelius' house. Utterly astonished by this chain of events, Peter began to tell them the gospel, and before he had finished, before he had even got to the point of how they might respond, the Holy Spirit fell upon them. I have twice seen that happen, when I have been seeking to lead an individual to faith. Before I had begun to talk of repentance and faith and baptism, the Spirit of God very evidently fell upon these people and they were filled with joy. It was totally unexpected! But then God is the source of the unexpected, and he can never be put away in a box labelled 'Predictable'. The Spirit of God is so much bigger than any of our systems, and will often act in ways which trample on our prejudices and call forth our awe. We need to be on tiptoe with expectancy. God is freed up to act, when we are. But many of our churches show little expectancy. I dare say that if someone were converted in half the churches of the land, it would amaze the minister! Expectancy lies very near the heart of church growth.

Household evangelism is a third feature which stands out clearly in Caesarea. There was no public proclamation: it all took place in a household. And that is a wonderful situation, when it happens. From time to time one discovers a household of people who are ripe for hearing the good news: it may be a time of celebration or of mourning. Great sensitivity is called for. But it can be a most fruitful opportunity. Some of the happiest times of evangelism I have ever known have been in homes when a group of friends or relations gathered over supper, and the chance came later in the evening to talk about the most wonderful person in the world and how one can meet him. It is all so natural, so relaxed, and you can go at the pace people can follow, handling difficulties and objections on the way.

A final thing to take away from these events at Caesarea is *the refusal to be prejudiced*. We are all prejudiced. Simon Peter was very prejudiced. He did not like Gentiles. And that prejudice had to be broken down if Peter was to be any use. It has to be broken in us, too. Many churches are prejudiced against the poor, amazing though it sounds. They are embarrassed if poor people come into the congregation, and the poor sense it. Many churches are prejudiced against people of another colour, against gay people, against prostitutes. In many Protestant circles there is a great prejudice against Roman Catholics, and vice versa. And it is utterly wrong. God must break prejudice down in us if ever we are to be able to move forward in bringing new people to faith. It could be that God wants to use you or your church for some major breakthrough in your area, but at present he cannot because of prejudice. How dare we call anything, anyone, 'common or unclean'? We are all a can of worms: the only difference between us and those we despise is that God has opened up the can of worms in our life and applied the disinfectant.

Antioch

Antioch is another church that is highly instructive (11:19ff). There is much that might be said about the outreach that brought it into being, and the outreach it gave rise to. But it will be sufficient here to look at four elements in its foundation. These principles may apply just as well to founding a Christian group at work, in a hospital or a school, as they do to establishing a new church. They are of universal validity in the advance of the kingdom of God.

First, it was a *lay initiative* which brought the church at Antioch into being. Those who had been scattered out of Jerusalem after Stephen's death and the subsequent persecution, simply could not keep quiet about Jesus. They went everywhere chattering the word (8:4). In the streets, the cafés, the laundries of the Phoenician coast, they found the conversation turning towards Jesus Christ, the discovery which had changed their lives. We are given only a tantalising glimpse of what they said. But we know they talked about the Lord Jesus (11:20). 'Lord' was a common term in those days. 'Come and dine at the table of the Lord Serapis', says one inscription of the time. 'There are Lords many . . .' said Paul (1 Cor. 8:5). Those early Christians would have said, 'And *we* have got a Lord to tell you about, one Jesus!' It is not difficult to imagine them getting a hearing. And of course the name Jesus, on which we are told they laid emphasis, means 'Yahweh saves'. They could be sure to make the most of that! When you have lay people motivated like that, the spread of the gospel is a foregone conclusion. Many Christians are discouraged at the level and quality of their church life, and how little seems to be initiated by the leadership. But that need not quench lay initiative. It is the privilege of all Christians without distinction to bear witness to their Jesus; they do not need to ask permission from their ministers. And it is salutary to remember that it was just this type of initiative which led to the church being founded in Antioch, one of the greatest cities in the Empire.

The second noteworthy thing about Antioch was their *transcultural fellowship* (13:11). Barnabas was from Cyprus, and he was a Levite and a farmer. Simeon the Swarthy was clearly a Nilotic; Lucius of Cyrene was another North African of lighter hue; Manaen came from the court circle round the Herods, and Saul from Tarsus in Turkey. A mixed cartel of leaders, with an astonishing variety of background. Cross-cultural fellowship is not easy. We naturally tend towards our own kind. But to mix with those from other nations, other cultural backgrounds, should be a particular characteristic and glory of the Christian church. God has, after all, chosen us from all our different backgrounds and put us together in one family. We need to demonstrate that family life. And it will be very attractive, in a world where real fellowship without judgmental attitudes is rare, and where loneliness is common. Christianity is not international: it is supranational. It is a family that is bigger and broader than any of the other solidarities to which we belong. I remember having that forcefully brought home to me by my colleague, David Prior, saying in a sermon, at the time when Britain had invaded the Falkland Islands, 'I have got far more in common with a brother Christian from Argentina than a non-Christian from England.' And he was right. There is nothing to touch the cross-cultural fellowship of Christians when they are Christians indeed. It comes forcibly up against the way of the world, for you just do not find it in normal society. That is what makes it stand out so boldly and so attractively.

The third striking thing about the Antioch church is its *shared leadership*. Most churches have a monolithic leadership. The church structures are pyramidal, and at the top of the pyramid is the paid minister. Below him are the assistants if there are any, then the elders of the church council, then the choir and organist, then the congregation itself. At Antioch you do not find a pyramid, but a ring; a circle of five very different men sharing the leadership of that church. There is a tremendous amount to be said for shared leadership. If one person is in sole leadership, he is sure to be very lonely. If one person is in sole leadership he is certain to be very good at something (or he would not be there) but is probably very weak at a number of other aspects of the job. Nobody can be good at everything. But if the leadership is shared, different aspects of the work of the church will be catered for.

A fourth thing about the Antioch church, which is a challenge to us, is *balance*, the way they held together their social concerns, their worship, and their missionary concerns. It is not often that you find a church which is strong in all three. When you do, look out! For such a church is going to be effective. We see in 11:28 how Agabus predicted a great famine in Jerusalem, and before it had even happened, the Christians in Antioch, hundreds of miles away, cared so much about these Jewish brethren they had never met, that they raised a lot of money for them. The Jerusalem church was very different from themselves. Their emphasis on circumcision and food laws must have seemed very strange to these more relaxed men of Antioch. Yet they cared enough to make a substantial collection for them. There could well have been suspicions in Antiochene minds of financial mismanagement in Jerusalem: we read nowhere else of the primitive communalism being repeated. The Antiochenes thought the sharing out of their capital was glorious, but mad! Yet they gave to support these brethren, all the same. Alongside that strong sense of social concern went a wonderful spirit of worship. Their prayer, their fasting, their openness to the Spirit, their 'liturgy' (for that is literally what 'worshipping' means in 13:2), their willingness to share their top leaders with others by sending them out, their sense of partnership with Barnabas and Saul – these things show a church where worship was exciting and highly committed. Praise and silence, Scripture and teaching, love and obedience flowed in the worship of that beautiful church.

And what a missionary spirit they fostered! It is no small thing to be open to giving your two best leaders to go on overseas mission. They could have argued that people needed them in Antioch, that they would be wasted in the backwoods, that they might never return. But they didn't argue thus: they fasted and prayed, to make sure that this was indeed God's will. They pledged their support by laying hands on them and commissioning them, and then they sent them off. I don't suppose the members of the Antioch church had been Christians themselves for more than a year or two, yet they were willing to back two of their leaders going off into the unknown with the gospel. That is very impressive.

When I was in Guatemala I came across the story of a witch doctor who was brought to Christ in a very surprising way. He went back to his village, and was responsible for the whole village coming to faith. The village then set out and evangelised another village, two days' journey away, with which previously they had been at enmity. They took their own food with them, and stayed for three months. They did not ask for hospitality, but cut down branches and fronds in the jungle to make night shelters. And by their joy and love, their worship and conversation, they led this whole village to the Lord whom they had only just come to acknowledge for themselves. When a church is born in mission like that, and maintains a strong missionary outlook, along with dynamic worship and deep social concern, that church will go places!

Thessalonica

The founding of the church in Thessalonica is no less instructive. Acts 17 tells of the coming of the gospel to this tough, north country city.

The first thing that strikes me is *the value of a short campaign*. It is apparent that conversions began to happen within three weeks (v 2), and it seems not to have been very long before Paul and Silas were thrown out of the city, after establishing a small church (v 10). Often we fail to attempt anything for God because we feel we shall not have the time to see it through. But the same God who gives spiritual life is well able to nourish it. I can think of a mere week's outreach in a city which was so effective that it led to the new believers launching out in evangelism on their own, further up the valley where they lived. I can think of a weekend visit with a team to one church which was so fruitful that it immediately began to send out 'missionary teams' of its own renewed members. We must not despise the value of the short campaign. As I write, I have just returned from one such enterprise, where a team of sixty of us spent a week in a small city and saw a truly remarkable impact. The churches were knit together in a new boldness: their unity was something beautiful to behold. Our own team members learned no end. We saw healings, prophetic pictures, and many conversions in all sectors of society. To be sure, one cannot continue at that intensity. But a concentrated, short-lived outreach can have great consequences. It did at Thessalonica.

Inevitably a campaign like this will court *opposition*. It certainly did at Thessalonica, and to judge from 1 Thessalonians 2:1-4 it was intense. I notice that it arose primarily from the most painful source – other people trying to honour God, people you would expect to be your allies. In this case it was the Jewish synagogue leaders. I notice, too, how Paul and Silas handled it. They did not draw back into their shells, or seek to reduce the offence of the gospel. They made sure their way of life was blameless. They were gentle and warm in their presentation. They sought no personal gain or credit from what they were doing, and they set out to please God, not men. They regarded it as such a privilege to have been entrusted by God with the gospel, that they were ready to share with the infant church not the gospel of God only but their very selves. It is rare for an evangelistic outreach to proceed without opposition. And the apostles have given us an admirable example of how to handle it.

A third lesson in church planting which can be gleaned from Thessalonica is *learning from your mistakes*! The Thessalonican Christians were charged with being troublemakers. The word used in 17:6, *anastatoo*, is sometimes translated as 'turned the world upside down', and as such is often used by preachers as a compliment to the first apostles. It was nothing of the kind. Its sense is pejorative, meaning 'to unsettle', 'disturb'. Similar complaints against Christians survive from other parts of the Empire. It would have been easy to accuse the Christian evangelists of sedition since they spoke of Jesus as 'king' (v 7): this could be viewed as a political threat to the Emperor. Moreover, there was clearly a strong eschatological tone to the preaching, as we see from I Thessalonians 1:9-10, and emperors feared those who foretold the end of their power! The whole thing would easily be represented as *maiestas*, sedition, a capital crime in Roman law. I think this rare example of referring to the 'kingship' of Jesus shows why, as they launched out into the Graeco-Roman world from their Jewish matrix, the apostles reinterpreted the 'kingdom of God' language of the Gospels into terms of allegiance to or faith in Jesus himself. The substance was the same. They simply adopted a form of expression which was devoid of unnecessary offence. I have no doubt that their painful experiences at Thessalonica enforced this lesson sharply upon the apostles: *fearlessly proclaim the gospel of Jesus, but do it in terms that are socially appropriate*. At Thessalonica they had failed to do this, and they paid the penalty. But they learnt by their mistake.

There are other things which I find significant about this church plant at Thessalonica. It is all too easy to think sociologically and demographically as we attempt to plant a new work for God. There is nothing wrong with that, but it is not nearly as important as *the painstaking work of care and prayer* which was lavished by Paul on his converts. We read of it in I Thessalonians 1:2-3 and 2:1-4, 17-20. Love flowed. Sacrifice abounded. Paul the tough apostle was both 'wet-nurse' to the babes in Christ who needed tender care (I Thess. 2:7), and 'father' to those who were a little older and needed discipline (2:11).

When I look at the Thessalonican church, I am impressed by the combination of the preaching, the power of the Holy Spirit, the conviction and sincerity of the preachers, and the impact of their example. These all jump out from the page in the first chapter of I Thessalonians. So do the notes of hard work, biblical Christianity, encouragement and a determination to live worthy of the Lord which are evident in the second chapter. All are crucial elements in church planting.

Ephesus

Ephesus was the New York of the province of Asia, not the capital but incontestably the greatest city. Its capture for the gospel meant an enormous advance for the Christian cause. Luke gives us glimpses, in Acts, chapters 18 and 19, of how it was done. One principle which stands out prominently is *the use of the home*. It is clear that the home of Aquila and Priscilla was an invaluable centre. It had been the hub of Christian church planting in Corinth. It had expanded to accommodate Paul and then Silas and Timothy. Now the couple moved to Ephesus and started it all over again. This time it was the gifted Alexandrian Jew Apollos whom they took into their home. They befriended him, taught him, and discipled him. And before long they had 'hatched' one of the most distinguished Christian teachers of the apostolic age. Could anything more clearly demonstrate the strategic importance of the home in church planting? There was of course a church in their house. And what a privilege the members must have found it. I was in such a home the other day, where an intrepid pair had just started church planting in an area of the country where no church existed. They asked me to come and speak on spiritual warfare – no pussyfooting over contentious issues, I reflected! I found some twenty adults and ten children crammed into this commodious house. There was love and laughter, food and friendship, new members (amazed by what they found), participation by the children, singing, teaching, question and answer, and friendships developing. That church plant will grow. It did at Ephesus – from the right home.

Another lesson I glean from Luke's account is the importance of *taking trouble with one group* (19:1-7). This was a difficult group, whose Christian status was in doubt. They could have been written off as heretical or hopelessly defective. Instead, this group of a dozen people was carefully loved and taught and brought into a full experience of the Christian life. No doubt they became pillars of the new work. It is, perhaps, a pertinent reminder to those who plant churches not to write off 'fellow travellers' who appear to be off-centre, but to get to know them, love them, and see if, in the light of fuller knowledge and deeper relationship, a valuable partnership does not develop.

We noted earlier the astonishing relationship of trust and friendship that Paul seems to have struck up with the Asiarchs (19:31), officials of the Imperial cult whose whole *raison d'être* was anathema to Paul but whose persons were dear to him. What an important lesson. It is wise, when founding a church in any town, to get to know the chief of police, the educational officials, the mayor and aldermen simply as human beings. Who knows, for one thing, whether they may not prove helpful one day in furthering the work of God, as the Asiarchs were to Paul? Who knows whether they may not themselves be brought to faith, as I saw in one chief civic official with whom relationships had been established? And the whole enterprise inevitably

takes the Christians out of the little ghetto into which they will be
tempted to retire, into the world of business, commerce and power
in the town where they are called to operate.

We have already noted the importance of what John Wimber would
call '*power evangelism*', the accompaniment of the preaching of the gospel with demonstrations of its power. This was very evident at Ephesus,
a city dedicated to occult powers which interpenetrated life at every
level. When conversions began in earnest, not only was there a major
confrontation with those involved in the occult, but new Christians
made a great bonfire of their occult charms and magic books. This was
a very costly act. Luke estimates their value at a day's wage for 50,000
men! No wonder that when this decisive break was made public, 'the
word of the Lord grew and prevailed mightily'. But this incident has
a deeper dimension. It draws attention to the spiritual warfare which
church planting is sure to have to face. Sometimes the church plant is
ineffective because the ruling spiritual forces of darkness in the area are
not discerned and, through prayer and fasting, cast down. Paul talks of
the importance of such ministry in passages like 2 Corinthians 10:1-6,
Ephesians 6:10-20. In recent years the experience of church planters in
different parts of the world from Samoa to Argentina has accentuated
the critical importance of winning these unseen battles against occult
powers if there is to be substantive advance for the gospel. Books like
Taking Our Cities for God by John Dawson or *Arming for Spiritual
Warfare* by George Mallone do not spring from the lunatic fringe. They
draw attention to a much neglected aspect of Christian advance.

There is another aspect of the Ephesian church which is worth
considering. It is *the role of the School of Tyrannus* in building the
church and spreading the gospel. As we have seen, it was here that
Paul 'argued' or 'dialogued' daily (19:9). This went on 'for two years',
we are told, 'so that all the residents of Asia, both Jews and Greeks,
heard the word of the Lord'. There are many interesting factors in this
brief note by Luke. First there is the obvious one, so rarely practised
in today's church, that secular venues are often much more effective
for communicating the Christian message than church buildings. On
a recent outreach we have found the most ready hearing for the gospel
in a swimming pool area, at a special children's funfair, and at a pig
roast. Often the town hall is the best place to hire, or a cinema,
or perhaps a pub. The impact of the truth of God is greatest when
it comes in an unexpected place.

But the School of Tyrannus is worthy of closer examination.
It clearly became Paul's headquarters for equipping leaders as well

as for debating with enquirers. I am indebted to my friend and colleague, Dr Sven Soderlund, for some of the following reflections on this remarkable institution, which has a great deal to say to our contemporary theological colleges and seminaries. For that is really what it was. It was not a one-man band. Aquila and Priscilla, Timothy and Titus will have shared in the work (see Acts 18:26, 1 Cor. 16:10, 19, Acts 19:22, 2 Cor. 2:13, 7:6). Shared leadership was exercised in the training. There was, if you like, a rudimentary Faculty in place.

And what of the students? Well, it is probable that Epaphras was brought to faith through this School (Col. 1:7, 4:12, Philem. 23), along with Aristarchus (Col. 4:10, Acts 19:29, 20:4) and possibly Tychicus and Trophimus (Acts 20:4, 21:29, 2 Tim. 4:20, Eph. 6:21, Col. 4:7, 2 Tim. 4:12 – note the Ephesus connection). Clearly the gospel spread out as powerfully from here in the first century as it did from Nottingham, England, in the nineteenth, and cities all around were brought within the sound of the gospel. This will have been the time when churches were planted in Colossae, Hierapolis and Laodicea; and it is not improbable that Erastus (19:22) and Gaius (19:29) and even Philemon heard the good news for the first time when on some business or shopping trip to the metropolis, Ephesus. This is conjecture, but it is far from improbable, and underlines the importance of a strategic ministry in a strategic secular building in a strategic city.

The School's curriculum is also worth reflecting on, especially in the light of the Letter to the Ephesians, where it is reasonable to suppose that Paul may have developed at great depth the themes he had already been teaching for two years and more in their midst. Theology, worship, and practical Christianity dominate the letter. Why should they not have dominated the curriculum of the School? All three are crucial parts of the development of Christian leaders, often neglected today in part or in whole. And throughout his efforts to equip the next generation of leaders in Ephesus, Paul was giving them practical, applied work. They would have accompanied him in the miraculous ministry of 19:11-12. They would have assisted in the exorcisms (19:13-14). They would have learned how to engage in spiritual warfare with dark forces (19:15-19) and they would have sallied forth in practical evangelism of the nearby cities, radiating out from the hub in Ephesus: we know that Epaphras did precisely that with his church plant in Colossae (Col. 1:6ff) – with all the agony and intense prayer which that involved (Col. 4:12). This is the way in which workers are trained by Roger Forster and Gerald Coates in the fast-growing house churches in Britain. It is high time that a similar approach

began to invade the seminary training conducted by the traditional
denominations if we are to have any hope of seeing first century
Christianity taking root again widely in twentieth century countries.

Corinth

A seventh church is Corinth. We read of it in chapter 18. Its founding reads like a fascinating, fast-moving novel. And there are a
number of things for us in the account.

First, *church planting often begins with one man*. It did in Corinth.
For all the value and importance of shared leadership, time and again
some great work of God begins with the vision, or simply the sheer
obedience of one man. Too often in a society dominated by ideas
of democracy we rely excessively on committees, and not enough
on the vision, leadership and initiative of an individual. The old
jibe that a camel is a horse designed by a committee is not far
from the mark. This one man, Paul, came restlessly to Corinth
after not having had a notably successful time in Athens. He was
tired, and probably discouraged. But he had a passion to spread the
gospel; and from this one man sprang, in due course, a very exciting
church. It is salutary to remember that one person plus God always
constitutes a majority. Many of the great works for God have been
achieved though the initiative of one man: think of Abraham, think
of William Carey, think of John Wesley.

Second, I see that Paul *sought out Christian fellowship*. Though he was
a pioneer, there was nothing of the prima donna about Paul. He knew
he needed partners, and he sought them in the most obvious place,
fellow countrymen who shared the same trade and the same faith. And
so he came to share the home of Aquila and his wife Priscilla. But
there were enormous differences between these three. Paul was the
commanding intellect; Aquila was a freedman from Pontus, up by the
Black Sea; and Priscilla seems to have belonged to the famous Roman
family of that name. In all likelihood Aquila had been an Oriental slave
in the Roman household, was brilliant at business, won his freedom,
and married the daughter of the house. This would not have gone
down well with her patrician family! Maybe that was a contributory
reason to their peripatetic lifestyle. But the main reason why they were
in Corinth in AD 49 is that the Emperor Claudius, irritated with Jewish
financial and business skills, had evicted all Jews from Rome in that
year. So this threesome, with their varied backgrounds, set up a shared
household. They worked together. They lived together. Where that is

congenial, it provides an attractive witness, halves the bills, and gives regular built-in fellowship. But whether or not accommodation is shared, we all need the encouragement and the mutual ministry of a small group for close fellowship.

Third, the church planting at Corinth produced the inevitable opposition, but it *reached a variety of types*. It reached religious people like Crispus, the ruler of the synagogue (18:8). It reached the irreligious – the scum of the harbour, including idolators, sexual perverts, thieves, drunkards and robbers (1 Cor. 6:9-10). It reached the city types, like Erastus, who is called the city treasurer of Corinth (Rom. 16:23). There is a delightful touch here. An inscription has been discovered which reads, 'Erastus, in consideration of his treasureship, laid this pavement at his own expense'. It is impossible to prove it, but in all probability that inscription brings us into direct contact with one of the city officials who was led to Christ by St Paul. The gospel reached all levels of society in that city. And so it does when it is faithfully proclaimed. One of the sad features in our own day is the homogeneous nature of most churches. Some will specialise in the inner city; most will specialise in suburbia, and instead of being light and yeast in the whole of a town, the Christian gospel is often restricted to one social or political grouping. But the gospel is the thing that brings people together. There is no greater need for a city than a widespread dissemination of this message of the father-hood of God, the brotherhood of believers, and the equality of all men and women within that family.

Finally, Corinth teaches us that this sort of evangelism needs *lots of encouragement*. And it is lovely to see that Paul got it. He was encouraged by friends (18:5). And the Lord has given friends to all of us. We often miss the encouragement they could be to us because we talk about trivialities like the weather when we meet, rather than what the Lord has done for us in recent days. Encourage one another! And Paul was encouraged not only by friends but by a vision (18:9). The Lord loves to encourage in this way. I was personally mightily encouraged by a very specific vision to leave Oxford and England, where I was working very happily, and relocate in Canada. I do not think I would have moved without that vision. A great many Christians receive these 'seeings' or 'pictures' but have never been told that they are valuable, and are embarrassed to share them. In this particular case at Corinth, there was a wonderful promise in the vision Paul received: 'I am with you.' And there was a wonderful plan: 'I have many people in this city.' That is how the gospel spread at Corinth, with divine encouragement to its chief exponent when he, like us, was in danger of losing heart and enthusiasm. The Lord says to us, as he did to Paul in that vision, 'You may be tired, and fearful, and uncertain. But do not be afraid. I am with you. So speak, and do not be silent. I have many people in this city.'

Lord, make us church planters!

9

What of Their Pastoral Care?

The nurture of those who came to faith was something which the early Christians took extremely seriously. The immediate aftercare of new believers on the day of Pentecost is, in its way, as impressive as their bold evangelism upon the streets. They had not done either before, and they were a group of unqualified people. Yet in all the excitement of that astounding day, they did not neglect the nurturing of these new converts. No doubt they remembered with deep gratitude the pains their Master had taken with them. And so, we read, those who received the word on that first day of Pentecost and were baptised, devoted themselves to the apostles' teaching and fellowship, to the breaking of bread and the prayers (2:42).

Nurture is as vital as birth, in the spiritual and natural world alike. Yet you would not think so, to judge from the practice of many evangelists. Evangelists themselves are not in abundant supply, nor are churches which make evangelism a priority, but among those which do there is a dangerous under-valuing of aftercare. When I hear people rejoicing in 'ten professions of faith tonight', I wonder, sadly, how many Christians there will be tomorrow. For it seems to satisfy some preachers if a person comes to the front or raises a hand or gives some other sign of response. However, people have all manner of reasons, some of them totally inadequate and even misleading, for making such a response, and unless there is careful nurture, very little is likely to come of it. Jesus took three years to get some understanding of discipleship into the Twelve. It is unlikely that a hand raised in a meeting will suffice.

I propose to look at seven ways in which the early Christians followed through with those they helped to faith. Those seven ways will have one very noticeable omission: prayer. I shall be writing separately about that.

They baptised new believers

The early Christians baptised new believers on the day of Pentecost; and it is clear, as we read the Acts, that baptism was administered as soon as possible after a person had made a profession of faith in Jesus. The Ethiopian treasurer in Acts 8:26ff. is a good example of this. He believes the preaching of Philip, and immediately he seeks, and receives, Christian baptism. It was the same with the Philippian jailer (16:31ff).

They had a wise instinct, these apostles. For there are three strands in becoming a Christian: the churchly strand of baptism, the personal response of repentance and faith, and the divine gift of the Spirit. We shall examine them more closely in the next chapter. These three are like different facets of the same precious diamond. They belong together. We should, accordingly, be very suspicious of those who in their dogmatic theology separate out and have a clear timetable for these aspects of the one Christian initiation.

The meaning of baptism
The meaning of Christian baptism is as complex and as profound as the Christian life itself, of which it is a sacrament. I have tried to write about it in my book *Baptism*. The imagery of dying and rising again is a most helpful insight into its meaning (Rom. 6:1ff). You go down in the waters which close over you and your past; and you rise from that watery tomb to a new life with Christ. How different from Jewish proselyte baptism, where you sat in the *tebilah*, the lustral bath, and washed yourself from your pagan impurities. You then emerged a Jew. In Christian baptism nobody ever washes himself. It is always done for you by another, so as to symbolise the vital truth that you are a recipient and not an agent in this matter of salvation. You cannot *contribute* to the grace of God which is held out to you in this sacrament. You can only *receive* it in total unworthiness and adoring gratitude. It is a poignant and very clear reminder that my salvation springs from the Lord, not from my decision.

And Christian baptism is so much more than a washing. It is a death. It is the end of the old life; farewell to all that. I am identified with Christ on his cross. He died there not just to save me but to take me with him. Down into death, and up into resurrection life. And so baptism is more than a once-for-all event in my past. It symbolises the whole of my Christian life. Until I meet my Lord in glory I will never be able to dispense with that daily dying to the old life and claiming his risen power for life and godliness. To be sure, I do not always live that way. I am Adam's child as well as Christ's, and often the old set of loyalties wins the inner struggle. But that does not invalidate the new connection. It calls me to repent, and then to implement those new commitments with renewed seriousness. Baptism is the standing mark, impressed upon our bodies, that we are not our own: we belong to Another, and we are called to progressively die to sin and rise to active goodness in the power of his Spirit.

Infant baptism?

Baptism is the mark of the Christian life. No wonder they administered it promptly to new believers. Why should they wait to have the uniform once they had joined the army? But we must ask, who are the proper recipients of Christian baptism? Adults? Or the children of believers as well? Christianity has been sadly divided over this issue, with the majority going for infant as well as adult baptism. It all depends on where you put your emphasis. Baptism is the mark of God's grace bringing me to new life as I respond to him in faith. His grace, however, long antedates my response. He has always loved me. Should baptism, then, be attached to the side of divine grace, in which case it cannot come too soon? Or should it rather mark human response, in which case it is appropriate only to those who know what they are doing? That is the fundamental theological issue. Baptism belongs both to grace and to faith. But which shall we attach it to? The Acts does not give us a definitive answer, but it gives what to me seem very strong indications of the way the wind blows.

In describing the gift of the new life on the day of Pentecost, Peter says that 'the promise is to you and to your children, and to all that are far off, as many as the Lord our God calls to him' (2:39). It is sometimes argued that 'your children' here means not your little people, but your descendants. That is possible. But it is not very likely, because we know that they baptised whole households in the Acts. One of the most interesting examples is that of the Philippian jailer. We are told only that *he* believed: yet his whole household was baptised with him (16:34). And anyone who knows much about the household system of the Roman world knows it is inconceivable that when the head of that household takes a decisive action over any matter, the rest of the household, children, wife, and slaves and freedmen, should fail to go along with it. They were not so addicted to our fragmented individualism! They acted as a *familia*, an extended household. And so you got people being baptised into the Christian church who had not yet come to personal faith. The believing came later; and sometimes, no doubt, it did not come at all. In which case the baptised had merely the husk of the Christian religion, not the wheat. The baptism of infants is not explicitly referred to until the end of the second century when it is firmly established in church practice, but it is frequently hinted at even in New Testament days: children are referred to as 'in the Lord', and that implies baptism. And of course it would have seemed very odd to Jewish people coming over to Christianity if the God who had commanded children to receive the mark of salvation under the old covenant (circumcision) refused under the new covenant to allow the mark of belonging (baptism) to the children of believers.

While therefore the matter can never be finally resolved because of the paucity of references in the New Testament and the almost total silence for the next eighty years, the probabilities are that the first Christians, along with their successors, without a word of disagreement for the next fifteen hundred years, did baptise the children of believers. The child then would have had the mark of God's call ever before its face, wooing it into faith.

Rebaptism

But what of rebaptism, a contentious modern problem? What guidance can the Acts offer on that? Quite a lot. There is no instance where anybody who has received *Christian* baptism is ever rebaptised. It is the once-for-all incorporation. It makes no more sense to rebaptise someone than it does to re-adopt them into your family, or to give them citizenship more than once!

Justification is once-for-all. Adoption is once-for-all. Baptism is once-for-all. It is, in fact, the sacrament of the once-for-allness of our salvation and of our commitment to him; just as the Holy Communion is the sacrament of our growing and ongoing life in him. As in a life, as in a marriage, there is both a 'once for all' and a 'continuing' element. God in his sacraments has given us a physical expression of each.

Nevertheless there is these days a very strong inducement to rebaptise. Some Christian churches demand adult believing baptism before they will accept you as a member, and exert pressure on the issue, claiming that what happened to you as an infant was a 'christening' and not a baptism, or that it was invalid because you had no faith. But the demand for rebaptism also often springs up spontaneously among your people who have come to vital faith. They want publicly to express their commitment, and baptism seems the obvious way. The wise pastor will, I think, refuse to give in to this pressure. No justification for rebaptising any who have been baptised in the name of the Trinity is to be found either in the Acts or in subsequent Christian history. You need to explain to the person concerned that baptism is the mark of the whole Christian life, and he has been marked by it – but hitherto it has meant nothing to him. Now it does. So what he needs to do is to stand up in the congregation and publicly speak of what Christ has done for him. All he lacked in his baptism as an infant was the personal faith and the public profession. Now is the time for him to make that good. You cannot sensibly rebaptise him, but you can give him the opportunity to tell the congregation what has happened in his life, and to renew his baptismal vows. Then gather round such a person, lay hands on him and pray that he may be filled to overflowing with the power and joy of the Holy Spirit. In this way you will preserve the uniqueness of baptism, and you will also give space for the very natural and proper desire in the new believer for a chance to take a public stand for Christ.

This was the first and foremost of the actions they took with new Christians. They gave them the comfort and assurance offered in baptism, this marvellous service of incorporation into Christ.

They provided warm fellowship

They took trouble about the new believer's need for fellowship and tried to meet it in a number of ways.

Personal attention

First, they gave *personal attention* to new Christians. Where, I wonder, would Saul of Tarsus have been were it not for Ananias, who started him off, and Barnabas, who helped him on? Spiritual babies need spiritual parents. Paul himself was able to say later on, 'Though you have countless guides in Christ, you do not have any fathers. For I became your father in Christ Jesus through the gospel' (1 Cor. 4:5). A very important point, that. If you led someone to Christ, you have a unique relationship with them. It is your responsibility to help him or her to grow: and if for some good reason you cannot do it yourself, you need to delegate it. I have found that one of the best ways of providing the fellowship new Christians need is to ensure that there is some older Christian who will take regular care of them, answer their

questions, read the Bible and pray with them from time to time, and
generally stay alongside, monitoring their growth. At the same time,
it is valuable to put them in a group with other new converts, so that
they can discover very early on the value of Christian fellowship, and
be thrilled to see that they are not mad or odd, but that this same
gospel has touched other lives. They cannot help noticing how others
in the group grow, and that has its own stimulus. So I place much
emphasis both on the personal attention and on the growth group
which, if competently led, guides the new Christians in the early days
of their discipleship, as they consider an important issue each week,
and see how the Scriptures speak to it.

Informal fellowship

Second, the early Christians provided *informal fellowship*. This is clear
in 2:42 – 'the apostles' fellowship'. Those early believers liked being
and sharing together, in their homes as much as in public worship.
We need to take a leaf out of their book, and make opportunities for
the new converts just to be around – a barbecue, a sporting occasion,
a picnic, perhaps a theatre visit. We need to give them opportunities
to eat together in someone's apartment. We need to see that there
are informal evenings for praising God with some simple musical
accompaniment; short modern Scripture verses set to a simple tune
can be a tremendous means of building them up. We need to teach
them how to pray. 'We are going to pray now, just one sentence
each. Nothing to be embarrassed about. You can talk to each other,
so you can talk to God. Let's begin.'

A very similar passage comes in 4:32ff, mentioning sharing testimony, practical generosity, and encouragement. These two summaris-
ing pictures which Luke gives of the first Christians have a lot to teach
us about the elements that go to make for good informal fellowship:
being together, sharing, eating, praising, praying, testifying, caring,
encouraging. These things are as applicable to the Inuit in the Canadian
Arctic as to the Zulu in the south of Africa. They are universal
principles of Christian fellowship, which will take on different colour
in different locations. And a beautiful taste of them can easily be gained
by a weekend away together as a group of Christians.

Lively church worship

So often our worship is not dynamic. But at Antioch it was. The
account of 13:1-3 is eloquent, both in what it says and what it
suggests. They had a shared leadership, consisting of five persons of

widely different backgrounds. There was trans-cultural fellowship. There must have been a deep use of silence as they waited on the Lord for his guidance. There was a pattern about their worship: we are told that literally 'they held liturgy to the Lord'. It would have had song and psalmody, readings, some teaching of Jesus, no doubt culminating in the eucharist. There was also a missionary dimension in their worship: they were prepared to send people out from their midst. There was a strong emphasis on prayer. There was a seriousness of resolve, marked by fasting. There was a prophetic element in their worship too. We know that Agabus provided one example of this at Antioch (11:28), but probably in this instance, too, the conviction that Saul and Barnabas should be released for overseas missionary work came through a prophetic utterance, which commended itself as truly from God to the whole congregation. There were prophets as well as teachers in the church at Antioch (13:1).

In these three verses we see so many different strands of vital worship. There is much to take to heart from these first Christians. If we did, nobody would complain of dull church services.

Temple worship
We notice that in the early days of the church (e.g. Acts 2 and 3) the disciples worshipped in the Temple. After that there was not much sign of it, apart from an occasion during Paul's return to Jerusalem with the collection when he engaged in a purification rite in the temple (21:36) – before being arrested! It was a gesture of solidarity with Jewish Christians which backfired, but there is every reason to suppose that Jewish Christians like James, and the many priests and Pharisees converted to the faith, continued to worship in the Temple as Jews who recognised Jesus as Messiah.

In Judaism there were four different dimensions of worship. On a Friday night, as sabbath began, there was the *haburah* in the home, a little gathering of family and friends to usher in the day of rest. It was candlelit, and comprised a meal and prayers. Second, there was synagogue worship, corresponding more to our church worship, when the congregation gathered on the sabbath for fellowship, the reading of the Scriptures, teaching, praise and prayer to God who had brought their nation into being. Third, there was Temple worship, where the morning and evening sacrifices were offered daily, where the cult of Judaism had its centre, its hierarchy and its headquarters. To worship there must have been a very impressive experience, reminding the worshipper that he belonged to something great, ancient, and much fuller and more embracing than the regular synagogue gathering he was used to. The fourth dimension of worship were the great festivals of the nation, massive celebrations at Pentecost, Tabernacles, the Dedication and so on. You approached the holy city in enormous processions singing psalms. It might take two or three days to get there, and you would camp out for a week or stay with friends in and around Jerusalem.

Are not these four elements of worship important for Christians too? We need the different emphases that can be provided in the home fellowship, the local church, the dignified liturgical pageantry of the denomination's formal gatherings, and finally, occasions when large numbers of Christians gather, perhaps on a city-wide basis, to share their joy in God together, to praise him for what he has done, to sense the largeness of the salvation he offers, and to show the sceptical world that Christians are alive and well and have something very special to rejoice in.

There does need to be the Christian equivalent of Temple worship, if we are to experience a rich quality of spiritual life, but it is nonetheless interesting that the Temple drops out of the picture so speedily. Perhaps it was because there was an early emancipation from the sacerdotal, hierarchical and nationalistic overtones that were associated with worship in the Temple. This is highly relevant to us today. Christian worship in some quarters corresponds to these overtones, and we need to be cautious of them. One is apartheid, only now being broken down in South Africa: the theory that God has ordained for black and white to live in separate compartments, with separate development. That corresponds almost precisely to the separate development so jealously guarded in antiquity between Jews, Samaritans and Gentiles. And the bastion of that Jewish apartheid system was the Temple. The Gentiles might not enter its main area on pain of death. There were strict regulations on where women might go and how far men might proceed. And in North America there is something familiar in the homogeneous unit principle, which is one of the more questionable aspects of the church growth movement. It is, of course, very attractive to be part of a homogeneous unit, because you are in with your own sort of people. But it can be a mildly Christianised form of the world's way of relating.

You find three people putting depth-charges underneath the Temple system in the earliest church. There is Stephen (6:13f) whose teaching of a universal fellowship, changed customs and so forth was rightly perceived as a threat to the Temple. There is Peter (chs 10, 11) who emerged from his inherited prejudice that salvation belonged to the

Jews, and accepted as brethren Godfearers such as Cornelius with whom he previously would never have had any dealings. This event was so important that two whole chapters are given to it, and there are repercussions stretching into chapter 15. And thirdly there is Paul (13:46ff), who after constant rejection by the Jews in many parts of the Empire bursts out, 'It was necessary for the word of God to be spoken first to you. Since you thrust it from you, and judge yourselves unworthy of eternal life, behold we turn to the Gentiles. For so the Lord has commanded us, saying, "I have set you to be a light for the Gentiles that you may bring salvation to the uttermost parts of the earth."' He was subsequently arraigned for bringing a Gentile into the temple, shattering the apartheid of the day (21:28).

So although there was Christian worship in the Temple early on, and doubtless it continued among many Jewish Christians, there is, in mainstream Christianity, an early and significant shift away from the Temple, its priesthood and sacrifices. These things were only a shadow (sometimes a very dangerous and misleading shadow) of the reality to be found in Christ. Believers had the reality: what use did the shadow serve any more? This was a line of reasoning which goes back to Jesus' Temple utterances, and finds its conclusion in the whole argument of the Epistle to the Hebrews that God has no further purpose for the Temple, the priesthood and the sacrifices of Judaism (John 2:19–22, Hebrews chs 5–10). Modern Christians would do well to value the strengths of the Temple tradition in comprehensiveness, liturgy and pageantry; but to avoid, as the early Christians avoided, the danger of assuming that God is more present in one place than another, and becoming entangled again in the ecclesiastical captivity of the church.

They gave regular instruction

The instruction given by the early Christians contained at least three elements.

The Scriptures
In Acts 20:32 we see Paul commending his leaders at Ephesus to God's gracious word which is able to build them up. That 'word' is, of course, the message of God, enshrined in the Old Testament and exemplified in the life and teaching of Jesus. New believers were pointed first and foremost to the teaching of the Scriptures and its fulfilment in the amazing events that Jesus had ushered in. We shall have more to say on this subject in a later chapter.

The teaching of Jesus

Second, they were schooled in the life and teaching of Jesus, the oral form of the material we now have in our Gospels. It gave those who had never met him in the flesh an understanding of who Jesus was, how he taught and healed and broke the forces of evil as he encountered them. It gave them too, we may conjecture, the material we have in what scholars call 'Q', the teaching tradition of Jesus as recorded both by Matthew and Luke, but absent from Mark. That would have been very necessary. When asked, 'What does your Jesus say about tribute paying, or divorce, or special foods?' the early Christians needed to have an answer. And that is precisely what 'Q' provided. Moreover the account of his deeds, as well as his words, provided the foundation for that *imitatio Christi* which was, and remains, such an important part of discipleship. Through the power of the Holy Spirit we are called to be, in a measure, like Christ. And how could that even be attempted without knowing what Jesus taught and did?

In this way the Gospels very early came alongside the sacred Scriptures of the Old Testament, and by the beginning of the second century we find them quoted in exactly the same way as the Old Testament was cited. As early as 1 Timothy 5:18 you find a composite quotation, combining a piece from the Old Testament with a saying of Jesus under the rubric, 'And the Scripture says'. It is not difficult to imagine the Twelve and their successors sitting down with new believers in small groups with a copy of the Old Testament Scriptures, and studying it together to see how it all came to a head in Jesus. It is easy to imagine the excitement of these men and women as the Scriptures sprang to life under their gaze. How important for us to follow in their footsteps. We need little groups for new Christians to belong to which will enable them to discover that the Bible is a talking book, and to learn how to read it profitably for themselves and apply it to their lives. It takes skill to lead such a group, giving members every scope for exploration, making mistakes, asking questions and finding treasure for their own spiritual lives.

A basic catechism

But in addition to the Old Testament Scriptures and the life and teaching of Jesus, it is clear that the early believers were schooled in what we might almost call a basic catechism. There is no doubt in the minds of most scholars that the early Christians had a 'form of teaching' in preparation for baptism and full membership of the church. Often baptism was deferred for a few months after initial profession of faith, to allow for this catechism. Sometimes, no doubt, it was post-baptismal teaching. In Romans 6:17 Paul thanks God that they have obeyed 'the form', or mould, of teaching to which they had been committed. The same idea is present in the Letters to Thessalonica, Ephesus, Timothy and Titus. What was this teaching?

In Colossians, there is a sequence of instruction that runs like this. 'Put off' the old nature. 'Put on' the new nature. 'Submit'. 'Watch and pray', and 'stand'. That might look like an arbitrary selection of imperatives out of Colossians, until you find an exactly similar pattern elsewhere. Ephesians has the very same themes with only one variation in order. 1 Peter begins with a strong emphasis on the new birth, and follows it with 'Put off' the old nature, 'Worship', 'Submit', 'Watch and pray', and 'Resist'. James, too, starts with the new birth, and follows it up with 'Put off', 'Be Subject', 'Resist', 'Pray'. This has been demonstrated with immense erudition and full documentation in Selwyn's *Commentary* on 1 Peter, Appendix A.

Now there is no slavish uniformity in these instructions, but there is clearly variation on a basic theme. These are the headings for their ethical instruction. And if you wanted to make your own Beginners Group, you might profitably have the first session on the new birth, and follow it by examining some of the things that belong to the old life which need to be put off through the power of the Spirit of God. Third, you might have a session on the image of God, and how it has got spoiled through the Fall, but is restored in Jesus, and is gradually imparted by his Spirit, who changes us from one degree of glory to another. Fourth, you might have an evening on the Christian call to submit. That was the Master's way. It befits the servant too. Our submission should be primarily to the Lord: but how will this work out in the family, at work, in the peer group, with the state and so forth? Fifth, the new believer needs to be taught to stand in the face of the assaults of the world, the flesh and the devil. He must learn to withstand the evil one, for temptation will increase once he has sided with Christ against the prince of this world. A sixth week could be devoted to the subject of watching and praying: the two come together, for unless he watches, he will not pray; and if he prays, he will watch to see what answer comes. Perhaps another evening could follow on love, and a further one on worship. It is clear that these themes were very important to the early Christians in their training of the new believers. I have written more fully on this subject in *Evangelism through the Local Church* where detailed notes for a course like this for new Christians are available.

Further instruction

Instruction did not stop with groups for beginners in the early church! There was teaching on false doctrine, and you see the heart of it in 2 Peter and Jude. There was a course on ethics, and you see the heart of it in Ephesians and Colossians. We, too, ought to be training people in these areas. We should also train folk for marriage, in a day when one out of two marriages in the West collapses, and when Christian divorce rates are not very much better than those of non-Christians. We need to train parents for family life and solidarity in a day when the family is falling apart. We need to train people for Christian lay leadership, equipping church members for evangelism and the leadership of house groups. Training is essential for worship leading, and for taking small teams out on weekends away for Christ. These things are important, and yet are so often neglected. The modern church seems to have forgotten its calling to train disciples. Not so the early Christians. When you find Paul spending a long time in Antioch, or Corinth, or Ephesus, it is to train up leaders. And remember that the training included visits to them, and letters to them. These showed continued love and care on the part of their mentor, even when physically removed from them. Who writes letters full of spiritual counsel and encouragement today? The art of Christian letter writing is almost dead. We need to revive it. We can learn from the example of E. J. H. Nash, who nurtured me. This amazing man would visit a town or a school simply in order to take one boy out for a meal, in the course of which he encouraged him, guided him, and helped him with any difficulties in his life. It made the boy feel tremendously cared for and important. I know: I was one! That man had a true pastor's heart. He made use of books, letters and visits to help us new believers to grow, and I pay him the honour that is his due. Would that others did as much.

They celebrated Holy Communion

It is interesting to observe that the Holy Communion seems to have been celebrated much more frequently among the early Christians than it is among most modern Protestants. It is probable that it was observed weekly among Christians on what they called 'the Lord's day', the day of resurrection (Rev. 1:10). Certainly by the early second century it was celebrated every Sunday. And as we have seen, Pliny, the governor of Bithynia, refers to Christians meeting on a fixed day of the week, early in the morning, 'singing a hymn to Christ as God, and partaking of food together, not however of a noxious kind!' This pagan governor had gained a remarkable half-insight into the heart of Christian worship.

The breaking of bread

It is curious that the Acts refers only to the 'breaking of bread'. It never speaks about the wine, and many scholars believe that this was quite deliberate. It is an intentional reserve about that which could so easily be misunderstood, the *disciplina arcani*. Had not Jesus linked his blood, the new covenant and the wine? And when you belonged to what must have appeared as a secret society which seemed to be a threat to the stability of the state, 'drinking the blood' of someone would seem extremely sinister. You knew that it would be wise to be discreet about what you said. By contrast, the breaking of the bread sounds innocent, and it was descriptive.

Communion in the church

The celebration of the Lord's Supper comes in two modes in the Acts. It takes place in church, and the classic instance of that is Acts 20, the time when Eutychus fell asleep owing to Paul's over-long sermon! The church celebrations took place in the big houses that a few Christians would have had, and these were not just what we think of as Communion services. They were real times of joyful celebration and feasting. Many of the Christians were poor, and went short on food, and this would have been the great occasion in the week to come together on the evening of the Saturday or Sunday for the 'love feast', the Agape. You get the flavour from 1 Corinthians 11 and Didache 9 and 14. There was a danger, of course, in these love feasts. They could lead to an intimacy which became immorality (see Jude 12 and 2 Peter 2:13), as well as to drunkenness and greed (1 Cor. 11:27-34). So before very long this love feast was discontinued, and the Eucharist was moved from the evening to the early morning. This was a great pity, because it curtailed the relaxed informality of an evening gathering. Many Christians today are reviving the Agape, and are combining a real meal and a time of fellowship, sharing and joy, with a celebration of the Eucharist. It is mind-blowing to those who have previously only seen this as a token meal.

We have in 1 Corinthians 11 a rich mine for our understanding of how the early Christians celebrated the Communion: 1 Corinthians was, on any showing, written before Acts, so we may be confident that it represents the common beliefs of the early church. Paul invites his readers to look back to the cross (11:25), where their love is rekindled as they reflect on what it cost Christ to die for them. They are to look up (10:16) to the fact that it is the Lord who nourishes them by his body in this sacrament. They are to look in (11:27) to ensure that there is no 'leaven', i.e. no unconfessed evil, in their lives: if there is, it must be dealt with before participating. They are to look round (11:18, 10:17) remembering that they are part of a fellowship, with whom they must live in peace and love: the Eucharist has a horizontal as well as a vertical dimension. And they are to look forward (11:26) until the Lord comes again, and his purposes for this planet have reached their consummation. Those five aspects of the Communion were rooted in the hearts and minds of the Christians from the earliest days. It was a very rich perspective.

Communion in the home

Not only was there a regular 'church' celebration of Communion. It often took place among small groups in homes. We read in 2:46 that they broke bread 'in homes' or 'from house to house': a very remarkable verse. If the 'breaking of the bread' is eucharistic, as most commentators believe, then two shattering consequences follow. First, it is said to be something that the converts did: it is a lay celebration. Second, it is done in the home. It is very significant that in the New Testament we are never told who presides at the Eucharist. There is never any suggestion that one particular category of Christians alone has the right to do so. There is no hint of a Christian parallel to the priesthood of Judaism. Jesus was seen as the eschatological priest, his death as the final sacrifice, his cross as the ultimate altar: the Epistle to the Hebrews makes that abundantly plain. What need, therefore, for human priests, additional sacrifice, or physical altar? It amazes me that alone among the great religions Christianity emerged at its very conception with this radical denial of the need for an intermediary caste of priests and all that goes with it. I have no doubt that one of the Twelve would celebrate, when present. I have no doubt that very soon a respected member of the little local church would assume leadership at the Communion. But that is very different from saying that nobody else has the right to do so; and that is the very point on which some of the major denominations of the world take their stand. Could it be that, like Cyprian who crystallised this trend in the third century, they are overly influenced by Old Testament and pagan parallels?

The use of Communion in the home is greatly to be commended, particularly to Protestant churches which, on the whole, tend not to give as full value to the sacraments as they do to the word. These 'home communions' can be one of the main ways of building up trust, love and fellowship in the house groups which constitute the living cells in the body of a healthy local church. A communion like that can be very real, relevant and informal. Nobody wears special clothes. The bread and the wine are very ordinary, perhaps served in a glass and a plate on the sitting-room table. There will be singing and confession; a word from Scripture expounding some passage from the New Testament for a few moments; and the prayer from a small group like this, as they lift up their hearts to God in their own words, is very moving. It involves everybody who wants to express some sentiment to God. Somebody present may have a verse from Scripture which is burning in their hearts: let there be space for such contributions. A picture may be impressing itself on somebody's mind: let them feel free to allow the group at large to judge whether or not it is from God. There may well be a 'kiss of peace' as members move round and greet one another in love. One Christian will administer to his or her neighbour the precious symbols of our redemption. Special needs for ministry may emerge at that time, and little groups may gather round to pray, perhaps to weep a little. The evening ends with expressions of praise from around the room, and maybe one or two songs of triumph, celebrating the exalted Jesus and trusting him for the week to come. A Communion like this, after an evening meal and a time of sharing news and concerns, can have a tremendous power in binding together any group of Christians. But whether at home or in church this is the way Jesus told us to remember him, and it should therefore be the main regular service for Christians. It was for the early disciples and their converts.

They cared for physical needs

The early Christians did not make the separation between the spiritual and the physical which has bedevilled much modern Christianity. They kept the two together, well aware, as Hebrews were, of the fundamental unity of the human being. Here are some of the ways in which their practical caring showed.

1. First, we cannot help being struck by their gift for *hospitality*. A good example is found in 21:4. Paul and his friends on the trip to Rome

arrived unannounced at Tyre, 'and having sought out the disciples, we stayed there for seven days'. It was the same in Caesarea: 'On the morrow we departed and came to Caesarea; and we entered the house of Philip the evangelist, who was one of the seven, and stayed with him. And he had four unmarried daughters who prophesied. While we were staying some days, a prophet named Agabus came down from Judaea' (21:8f). What an insight that gives into the warmth of their hospitality! Philip already has a houseful of at least six, and then cheerfully makes room, at the drop of a hat, for Paul and his party – and if that is not enough, he fits in Agabus as well. Amazing! I would love to have overheard the topics of conversation! Hospitality was clearly very characteristic of the early church, and was one of the means which facilitated extensive and cheap travel among the brethren. Of course it could be abused: it *was* abused. There is a delightful precaution in the *Didache*, warning that it was fine to order a meal when 'in the Spirit' – but that meal must be for someone else, not the one who ordered it! Again, you might well be one of the authentic travelling 'apostles' if you stayed three days; but if you stayed a week you were certainly a fraud. Very shrewd precautions: once bitten, twice shy! Our modern churches could learn a lot from the generous but shrewd hospitality of the first Christians.

2. Second, the famine collection (11:29), made by the Christians at Antioch for impoverished Christians at Jerusalem, is a strong reminder that they took *material need* very seriously as part of their Christian commitment. They were moved to help with the social needs of fellow Christians of a very different stripe, whom they had never seen, and never would. That is eloquent of Christian love in practical terms. Does that sort of generosity characterise most churches when the needs of the world are graphically and poignantly displayed upon our television screens, or do we close our minds and our hearts most of the time? A chilling statistic I gleaned in Canada is that, whereas the Revenue allows 20% of a personal salary to be offset against income tax for charitable purposes, over 90% take no advantage of it. That must include a great many Christians. Relieving famine is part of Christian care and Christian ministry. It is the way Jesus himself staked out for us.

3. Third, *shared accommodation* was another way in which the early Christians showed practical care for each other. It must have been an enormous mark of love and welcome for new Christians. The classic

passage on this is 4:34ff where the Jerusalem Christians minimised need by sharing houses and finances. You see it happening very naturally, too, in 18:3 where Paul sets up house with Aquila and Priscilla in Corinth. It is all very well for a group of students to do this: it is well understood. It is understandable, also, for singles. But our society is usually very surprised, so materialistic and jealous of our privacy have we become, when it finds two or even three *families* living together and sharing accommodation, finance and appliances. Sometimes most members of these extended households work so as to enable one or two of the others to engage in full-time Christian ministry. Sometimes a family will simply take on board a single person who has nowhere much of his or her own to go. It is both rare and attractive, for those who have the gift, to share in this way without getting stressed. If more of us did something of the sort, there would be less need and probably less crime in our society, and we should have displayed to a cynical world something of the cost and beauty of Christian love.

4. *Healing* is another way in which they cared about physical needs. Wherever you look in the Acts (e.g. 8:7, 14:8f, 5:15, 28:8-9) you find Christians really caring about the sick and praying with utter confidence to God to heal them. Where there is confident prayer to God to heal today, results often occur today, praise is given to God, and sceptics are intrigued despite themselves. It was like that in the early church.

5. *Protection* is another aspect of the practical care the Christians lavished upon those who joined them. A delightful example of this comes in 9:23ff. The Jews wanted to kill Paul. The gates were watched day and night; so the believers took him by night and lowered him over the town wall in a basket, and he got away. The sheer protection of others for the sake of Christ is powerful, and people notice it. When women like Corrie ten Boom risked their lives to smuggle Christians and Jews out from Nazi clutches into freedom during World War Two, that was something beautiful for God.

6. Another very obvious thing was *practical involvement*. When fires had to be made to warm the shipwrecked (28:2), Paul did not leave it to the natives and the sailors. He was there too, fully in-volved. Of course the incident is only mentioned because of the viper, but it reveals the practical caring which must have gone on all the time. Dorcas is another example of this lovely quality. She

spent her time making garments for needy widows. That too would not have been mentioned, were it not for her premature death which was reversed in response to the prayers of Peter (9:36-43). But these examples were typical. And churches which do take these practical steps to relieve need in their areas, churches whose pastors do get stuck into relief work rather than simply encouraging others to do so, are churches which grow, and which often trigger the conscience of secular society.

7. A seventh aspect of their concern for physical needs is seen in their *concern for the weak and defenceless*, particularly the widows (6:1ff). Widows had nobody to stand up for them in ancient society. Their chance of remarriage was slim. Their income was small or non-existent. There were no supporting social services. So the first Christians made it a priority to see that these poor members of their number were properly looked after. We see from 1 Timothy 5:3ff that there was a special list of 'widows' among the believers (1 Tim. 5:9). There was, as we see from that chapter, a good deal of care taken about who qualified for the list. If a widow had relatives, with children or grandchildren, the family should care for them. But widows who are 'widows indeed', with nobody else to rely on but God, should be the first to receive the loving care of the Christian community. And the same applied to small children and to 'virgins', who had dedicated themselves to the celibate life for the sake of Christ. These people were highly honoured in the ancient church, because what they did was so difficult, and showed a very deep dedication to the Lord. The church looked after the underprivileged. And so it must still.

If the church does not care for the unborn, who will hear their muted cry? If the church does not care for the retired people who have minuscule incomes, who will? Whenever the church has been at its best throughout the world and across the centuries, it has been marked by compassion to those who can never repay it, and whose usefulness to society may apparently be nil. But these people were made, the church realises, in the image of God, and deserve to have his fatherly compassion mediated to them through his servants.

Whichever way you look at it, these early Christians cared about the physical needs of their brothers and sisters in Christ, and we see both the church at large and individuals personally involving themselves in this ministry which was so close to the heart and example of Jesus.

They trained by discipling

The modern way of education is to sit people down to talk to them, or use blackboards, computers and videos. It is a clinical imparting of information with the minimum of personal involvement. That is not the best way to teach.

The best way to teach was well understood in the Middle Ages. They had apprentices who watched the experts at work, then worked with them, and finally were allowed to work under supervision until they became so adept that they could be trusted on their own, and were fit to train others. It is obvious that this is the method of making disciples which Jesus elected to use. Not for him the academic classroom, the essay, the examination. He went into the action with twelve close followers who learnt by being with him, watching him at work and gradually daring to follow in his footsteps until they became competent and were able, by the time of Acts, to train others in this very same way. And so we find Ananias disciples Paul, Barnabas disciples Paul (ch. 9), and together they model just this sort of training at Antioch (11:25f). Barnabas and Paul get hold of young John Mark; they think he would be a useful associate, and so they take him along on the first missionary journey (13:5). Young Timothy, a lad of mixed parentage, shows promise, so in 16:3 Paul takes him with him, and he is trained on the job. This was a thoroughly intentional procedure. It was not training by book learning, of which there was plenty both in the Roman and Jewish worlds, but by sharing the joys and hardships of actual ministry. Timothy and those like him were not students: they were apprentices. They became skilled as they learned the hard lessons which experience alone can give – but they had the blessing of having their experience interpreted by a senior colleague.

That has a lot to say to the modern church. Those who are leading churches, or nurses' Christian fellowships, or student ministry, might bear this principle in mind when next asked to speak away from home. Say 'No – unless I bring a team.' It may only be a team of one; but you train on the job – and you watch them grow! And pastors who want something solid to remain after their ministry is over would do well to take this principle of training with due seriousness. I know a man, now a household name in England, who, when he was an assistant in a parish, devoted himself to about a dozen young men. They became his living memorial, and most of them are currently involved in very significant Christian ministry.

If you pour yourself into a number of people in whom you discern rudimentary gifts, if you love them, spend recreational time with them, go to camp with them, allow them to minister with you in small ways at first, and then gradually more as you force yourself into the background – if you do that you will see lasting fruit and strong leadership in the church which you led for a short time, and then left to other hands, hands that have become uncannily capable.

The early Christians majored on discipling new Christians until some of them became leaders. This is an area where the contemporary church is weak.

They worked on pastors

One of the great goals of these early Christians was this: 'What you have heard from me before many witnesses, entrust to faithful men who will be able to teach others also' (2 Tim. 2:2). Paul wanted to leave trained men – pastors – behind him. It would be perverse to think that he was alone in this goal. Let us, therefore, look to Paul, who is better documented than any of the other apostles, and see what he has to say on this important topic of equipping pastors. The *locus classicus* is Acts 20:17ff.

Paul's understanding of pastors
1. It is plain from this passage that first and foremost Paul understood Christian oversight as a shared enterprise. It was the 'elders' of the church at Ephesus whom he called to meet him. There was no vicar, no senior minister, just elders. Paul understood the value of shared leadership, and we have seen the value of this pattern earlier in the book. Many churches, however, have not absorbed this most fundamental of all lessons about Christian leadership, but remain obstinately monolithic and autocratic. In the long run that spells disaster.

2. It is also worth noting that the men Paul called together were not lads straight from college. They were elders. You did not become an elder in Judaism until at least forty years of age. So these were men who had been trained in the battle school of experience, and over a number of years.

3. Moreover, it is clear from this passage that Paul saw them as the Lord's watchmen (20:26, 29). He saw himself in the same light. He

knew his Old Testament, and was well aware of that critical passage
in Ezekiel which was so important that it was repeated, in chapters 3
and 33. Ezekiel was called to be a watchman to the house of Israel.
If he gave them warning of impending destruction and they refused
to listen, their blood would be on their own heads. But if he ran
away and did not give warning, they would perish, but their blood
would be required of the watchman's hand. Paul saw himself in that
watchman role. He saw the elders at Ephesus as fulfilling precisely the
same role. It is part of the pastor's task to warn of impending danger,
and as v 29 suggests, to give warning about false teaching and corrosive
behaviour brought in by the 'wolves'.

4. Paul saw his elders also as 'overseers' (v 28a). This word indicates
those who take personal care of the flock, who guide and direct them.
It is the word from which we derive our 'bishop'. Those who are
elders have an abiding responsibility to take personal care of people
in the congregation. It will need to be shared out among them. But
it is important that church members can feel that someone is looking
after them and caring for them spiritually.

5. The last thing which Paul stresses about the nature of pastors in this
passage is that they should be undershepherds to Jesus in looking after
the flock (v 28b). It is a theme picked up by Peter in 1 Peter 5:2ff.
Leadership in Christian circles is to be marked by a deep sense of care
for those in the church, the very care which Jesus has for his people.

Paul's example to pastors
In chapter 11 we will look in detail at Paul's expectations of his
pastors. But what of his example? For without that, no exhortations
are likely to be very effective. Paul's example was very impressive, and
he mentions things about himself which none of them can deny.

1. There was his *consistent lifestyle*. It was see-through (v 18), trans-
lucent. It was consistent (v 18), humble (v 19), helpful to others (v 35),
generous (v 34), unselfish and non-materialistic (v 33). Those are
essential requirements in those who aspire to leadership.

2. There was his *uncompromising message* (v 21). Paul did not change the
essence of his message whether he was addressing Jews or Greeks. He
will have changed his approach, of course. But it always came down to
the basics: 'repentance towards God and faith in our Lord Jesus Christ'.

If modern ministers majored on these topics there would be a great deal more response to the Christian gospel than there is.

Nor did he water down his public teaching in his private conversations (v 20). He was insistent on repentance and faith, in all situations. If a pastor is known for maintaining the same message in private visitation as he does in public preaching, it is bound to have a great effect upon the hearers.

3. Then, Paul's *utter surrender to Jesus as Lord* could not but have affected those who were close to him (v 22-5). He did not 'count his life dear to himself'. He was determined to finish his course, cost what it might. He was a man to whom a life of sacrifice held no threats. He had already given up his home, his career prospects, perhaps his marriage, certainly his money. He was totally at the disposal of Jesus Christ. That is the sort of person God uses.

4. There was also Paul's *integrity and fearlessness* in making the counsel of God very clear to his hearers: 'I did not shrink from declaring to you anything that was profitable' (v 20), 'I did not shrink from declaring to you the whole counsel of God' (v 27), and 'I did not cease day and night to admonish every one of you with tears' (v 31). By contrast, in the modern church, there are whole areas of the Christian gospel which are soft-pedalled from the pulpit; notably holiness, sexual continence, judgment and hell. When do you ever hear any teaching on these subjects?

5. Another significant part of Paul's example is his *disinterest in money* (v 33). He must have come from a wealthy family. He was born a Roman citizen, he tells us (22:28). That means his father must have had a small fortune, in order to acquire the privileged position of being a *civis Romanus*. But Paul was prepared to work for his own living and for that of his friends (20:34). He was prepared to be a homeless refugee. He was willing to travel the length and breadth of the Empire *gratis* to bring others to the knowledge of the Jesus who meant so much to him.

6. A final stimulus to his friends at Ephesus who he wanted to succeed to leadership, was his *practical work and love for them*. 'I coveted no man's gold or silver or apparel. You yourselves know that these hands ministered to my necessities and to those who were

with me. In all things I have shown you . . . it is more blessed to give than to receive' (v 34f). One of the crucial secrets of successful Christian Ministry is the willingness to serve others and to love them, come wind come weather. That was the way of the Master. It must also be the way of the disciple.

A remarkable life! A shining example. And if we ask the secret of it, we do not have far to look. The secret lay in prayer. Public prayer (v 36) and private prayer (v 19). There is no ducking out of this most demanding of spiritual exercises. The modern church in the West has opted out of serious petitionary prayer, and it is paying a terrible price for its defection. Paul and the early church knew better. That is the secret of their power and of their growth.

The early church really worked on equipping pastors. They trained up the next generation of leaders, and they did it through apprenticeship. If they were called upon to give us four quick tips for developing pastors, the early Christians might well say:

* Take a Timothy with you on your next 'missionary journey'.
* Set the example to others in undertaking the rotten jobs.
* Give a John Mark a second chance when he fails you.
* Win the title 'Barnabas', the Encourager. That is the name of the Holy Spirit: it should be the name of every mature Christian as well.

10

What of Their Church Life?

No aspect of Luke's writing has roused more passions than rival interpretations of his teaching about the early church's life. Modern scholars are not exempt from the temptation of reading their own assumptions about the church back into the lifetime of the apostles. It is significant that every type of church government, from the Pope to the Brethren, looks to the New Testament in general and the Acts in particular for a validation of their claims! All of us run the danger of seeing in the life of the early church what we want, and omitting the elements which are uncongenial to us. Moreover, Luke does not set out to give any systematic interpretation of the church, its life and structures, its ministries and leadership, even of its growth and advance. He is an impressionist painter, not a detailed illustrator. Nevertheless what he does tell us can be very illuminating and instructive for our own situation, whatever particular aspect of the church we emphasise. It must never be forgotten that, as we have seen, Luke is at home in all the three major divisions of the church as we know it today. He can see the church as an extension of the Old Testament church, the Israel of God (2:38-40), just as the Catholic tradition does. He can see it as the fellowship of believers in Jesus (5:14, 10:45, 16:31), just as the Protestant tradition does. And he can see it as the community of the Spirit (10:47, 19:2) just as the Pentecostal tradition does. For Luke, though, these are not separate ropes up which competing brands of Christians may climb: they are separate strands in the one rope which God lets down for the salvation of sinners. With that caution in mind, let us examine some of the things which Luke does teach about the church, and see if it has anything to say to us today.

The vitality of the church

The first thing that strikes me about church life in Acts is its vitality. It seems to have been white-hot for many of them much of the time. We have already looked in some detail at the pictures of the church given at the end of Acts 2 and 4: their love overflowing in the sharing of possessions, their unity of purpose, their mutual encouragement, their practical care for any in need, their praise of God and fervent prayer, their sensitivity to the Holy Spirit, their concern for teaching and equipping.

Less well-known passages yield slight, almost unintentional sidelights on church life. Would anyone ever be able to describe the members of a modern church as 'walking in the fear of the Lord and in the comfort of the Holy Spirit' (9:13). We have forgotten what the fear of the Lord and the comfort of the Holy Spirit mean. Both of those descriptions tell me of a church which was vibrant with life. Not surprisingly, the church was multiplied.

I am struck by the spiritual sensitivity of these Christians. Take, for example, the members of the 'circumcision party' who criticised Peter for going to eat with a Gentile, Cornelius (11:3). When Peter had given a full and honest explanation of the way God had guided him, these critics turned right round. They glorified God for his new departure which they would never have dreamed of, but which they were delighted to see (11:18). I am struck by the fact that when Barnabas went down, at the request of the Jerusalem leadership, to see what was going on in the evangelism that had been reported at Antioch, 'he saw the grace of God and he was glad' (11:23). What a lovely touch – to rejoice at the establishment and growth of an 'unorthodox' new development which the church leadership had not authorised or envisaged! It speaks well for the vitality of these Christians.

On the journey from Miletus to Jerusalem, the little ship keeps stopping on the way, so Luke records the attitudes of some of the church groups they meet. We see this same vitality when, for instance, the little party left Tyre: 'they all with wives and children brought us on our way till we were outside the city; and kneeling down on the beach we prayed and bade one another farewell' (21:5). The fervour and the love of these first Christians puts us to shame. But it also points the way, the costly way, to renewal.

J. B. Phillips has some interesting comments to make about the vitality of the church. He was driven to reflect on it when he translated Acts into his own vivid prose:

The church began in power, moved in power, and moved just as long as she had power. When she no longer had power, she dug in for safety. But her blessings were like manna. When they tried to keep it overnight, it bred worms and stank. So we have had monasticism, scholasticism, institutionalism – all indicative of one thing: absence of spiritual power. In church history every return to the New Testament has been marked by a new advance somewhere, a fresh proclamation of the gospel and an upsurge of missionary zeal.

He went on to observe:

It is the church that is willing to die to worldly standards that will know the power of Christ's resurrection. It may be envied for its depth of loving relationships, or for its spontaneous joy. It may be hated and persecuted for its revolutionary lifestyle, exposing the hollow values and destructive selfishness of the society it seeks to serve: but it certainly cannot be ignored.

No, the first Christians were not ignored. Their vitality made that impossible.

The orientation of the church

The second notable thing about their church life was its orientation. They were not into maintenance but into mission. It is true that they had nothing to maintain in the earliest days: even by the end of the New Testament period they had no property to tie them down except the homes of their members. But one cannot avoid the impression, looking over the sweep of the Acts, that these people would never have settled for a maintenance mentality anyhow. It is impossible to miss the missionary thrust of this book and of this church. In 1:13 there are just eleven disciples, a few women and some of the family of Jesus. By 1:15 their number has increased to about 120, which is rather surprising. No doubt some who had trusted Jesus in the Jerusalem area and had encountered him after his resurrection, began to gather together. After Pentecost there were three thousand more (2:41) and the faith begins to spread rapidly in Jerusalem. Judaea and Samaria (8:1) are evangelised next, and a special manifestation of the Spirit overrides their natural hesitation at receiving Samaritans into the church (8:16). Indeed, it is significant that the church *at*

Jerusalem is now mentioned: a little earlier there was no other (5:11). Soon we read of a church (singular) throughout Judaea, Galilee, and Samaria (9:31). Next Cornelius, a God-fearing Gentile, is welcomed into the church (10:48), and this marked a notable step forward and the inevitable beginning of the break with Judaism. Wider still swings the gate as the Antioch church is founded, yet even here there is a mix of members from Jewish and from Gentile backgrounds (11:19f). Antioch, of course, becomes the missionary springboard of the early church, and by 13:46 we find Barnabas and Paul realising that their call is to the Gentiles. A chapter later we find that Gentile churches are constituted, with their own local eldership (14:23) and the direction of the church is set first to Europe and thence to Rome. The final word of the book is a defiant *akolutos*, 'without hindrance'. The shape of the work, envisaged in 1:8 is complete.

The whole attitude of the early Christians was one of confident discovery, and of braving every obstacle in order to reach out with the good news of Jesus to those who did not know him, whatever their background, religion or prejudices. The shape of the Acts, with the first half concentrating on Peter and the second half on Paul, must not blind us to the missionary outreach of the Hellenists, the unknown Christians who brought the gospel to Judaea and Galilee, and places like Troas and Tyre, Ptolemais and Patara. It was not the big names only who were passionately committed to outreach. Mission was the lifeblood of the church from the very beginning: they took seriously their commission to be witnesses.

It would, of course, be disastrous if all church members today were preachers. But it would be wonderful if all were witnesses, bearing joyful testimony to what Jesus had come to mean to them. That is how these people continued to maintain their outward orientation. The gospel spread most of all by the enthusiastic witness of nameless people who loved Jesus and could not keep quiet about him. It was a people movement, this early Christianity. That is why it succeeded. It did not depend on big names, but on little men who had a big God and were not afraid to put him to the test as they went out in his name. And if that is not a challenge and a rebuke to the modern church, I do not know what is. Shame on us for our vacillation, for our ignorance of the gospel, for our lack of motivation to spread it, for our indifference to need and our feeble syncretism. Once ordinary Christians get the good news in their hearts and on their lips, it will grow. Nothing can stop it. But so long as most of us remain so ignorant of our message, so unpersuaded of its truth, so fearful of mentioning it to anyone, the church will remain in eclipse.

The fellowship of the church

The third notable thing which it is impossible to doubt in the church life of the first Christians is the quality of their fellowship, and their sacrificial love for one another. It is hard for us to recognise the depth of that fellowship from our own perspective. We have no idea what it meant to embrace a slave owner and his slave in the same fellowship, yet that is what occasioned the Epistle to Philemon. We can hardly have any conception of the barriers of pride and prejudice which separated Greek and barbarian in the ancient world, yet both were to be found in the same family of Jesus. Paul explicitly says so (Col. 3:11). Because few of us share the background of centuries of hatred and bitterness we can hardly understand the breakthrough it was to have Samaritans and Jews in the same fellowship. And as for the Gentiles – they were beyond the pale to any right-thinking Jew; how staggering, then, to hear of Jews and Gentiles eating together as they shared table fellowship at Antioch. Jesus had given them a new window on the world. Mankind was united in its twin solidarities of alienation and of redemption. All men stood at the same level and were reached by the same grace. No human distinctions therefore must disfigure the beautiful unity Jesus had hammered out at the cost of his precious blood. That is why there was no sniff of racism in the early church. Romans and Samaritans, eunuchs and priests all come in on the same level. The gospel is good news for all simply and solely because all men stand in equal need of it. Black and white, slave and free, Jew and Greek, educated and barbarian – all the traditional *apartheids* of antiquity were smashed by this totally new thing, the gospel of Christ. You could not find it anywhere else. It was intensely beautiful, profoundly threatening, and utterly unique.

And the same love and unity which kept them in this astonishing racial and cultural mix also made them determined not to be defeated by the enormous differences between conservative Jerusalem Jews and way-out secularist Gentiles who had joined the church. Hence the vast significance of Acts 15 and its epoch-making conclusion. Nothing must be allowed to compromise the truth that Jesus Christ alone is the salvation of sinners. Nothing else could ever be required but what he, the God-man, had provided through his incarnation, atonement and resurrection. Therefore it was essential that circumcision not be demanded of Gentile Christians. On the other hand, the church must stay recognisably united. Therefore Gentile Christians must make their contribution to unity. They must be willing voluntarily to forego eating meat which had been offered to idols, meat from which the blood had not been drained, and immorality (or perhaps, marriage within the degrees prohibited in Judaism). The precise details of the Apostolic Decrees (15:19-21) are still hotly debated, but the underlying principle is clear. The Gentiles need to be willing to sacrifice something of their liberty in order to gain the higher good, the table fellowship and manifest mutual 'belonging' of Gentiles and Jews within the family of Christ.

Alas, modern Christians do not think that unity is particularly important. The speed with which new churches fragment and split for the most inadequate reasons, is proof of how little we will sacrifice to preserve unity. Yet it was this unity of Christians, which transcended all the divisions of a very divided ancient world, that proved such a powerful magnet to Jews and Gentiles alike. They forsook their mutual hostility, came to Christ, and so were incorporated in that *tertium genus* as they called it, that 'third race' of people who were defined neither as Jews nor Greeks but as brothers and sisters in a fellowship which transcended both. Unity like that makes a very powerful statement. The modern world has yet to see it in the church.

The ministries of the church

A fourth outstanding mark of church life in the first century was the wide variety of their ministries. They did not confine 'ministry' to what some official Christian leaders did. Ministry was service, and all Christians were called to it. Its shape was determined by the gifts which the Spirit gave to the individual. *Charisma* was given for *diakonia*, service. And the variety of ways in which they served was remarkable. Luke draws particular attention to it.

There is the ministry of *administration* (6:1ff). That is absolutely essential in any growing organisation, yet it is not something that they regarded as vital for the 'ordained' ministry. What we call the 'ordained ministry' exists to equip and enable all Christians for their work of ministry (Eph. 4:12). Administration should be done by someone in the congregation to whom the Spirit has given that particular charisma.

The ministry of *prophecy* was most obviously given to Agabus (11:28, 21:10f) but we read of prophets among the leadership at Antioch (13:1), Judas and Silas in Jerusalem (15:32), the unmarried daughters of Philip in Caesarea (21:8). The gift was widespread, and greatly valued. It persisted into the second century, and travelling prophets were regarded almost as highly as apostles – many of whom, to judge from Paul, also had the prophetic gift (see 2 Cor. 12:12). Prophecy did not always involve prediction, though it sometimes did. It was primarily a means of the Lord speaking directly to his people in a particular place for a particular purpose. It was not couched in mysterious speech, like tongues, but was clearly comprehensible. The medium of that message might be a picture or vision. It might be a dream. It might be a prophetic action, as in some of the Old Testament prophecies. Agabus provides a striking example of this when 'he took Paul's girdle and bound his own hands and feet and said, "Thus says the Holy Spirit. So shall the Jews at Jerusalem bind the man who owns this girdle and deliver him into the hands of the Gentiles"' (21:11ff). This was a particularly interesting prophecy. When it was uttered the church drew the wrong conclusion from it. They assumed that this warning indicated that Paul should not proceed with his desire to go up to Jerusalem with the collection from the Gentile churches (20:16). In point of fact, Paul was right in his conviction that he should indeed proceed, cost what it may. This shows what a difficult gift prophecy was to handle. The prediction was fulfilled to the letter, as it turned out: but when the prophecy was given, deeply committed Christians drew two contradictory interpretations from it. That difficulty, quite apart from the danger of false prophecy and self-aggrandisement, shows why the gift of prophecy fairly soon fell into comparative disuse, particularly after the Montanist *débâcle* at the end of the second century, when it was used for sectarian ends.

There were a host of other ministries actively pursued in the early church, and they were seen as such. There was the ministry of *leadership* (13:1ff). There was the ministry of *evangelism*: Philip was outstanding in this respect. He was what we would call a layman, with a home and job in Caesarea, but we always find him talking to somebody about Jesus. There was the ministry of *training*: we see Paul and Barnabas giving themselves to it for eighteen months at Antioch (11:25ff). There was the ministry of *healing and deliverance*. Then there was the ministry of *feeding the poor* from soup kitchens (6:1ff), the ministry of *providing clothes* and other needs for those who were destitute (9:36f), the ministry of *visiting* (9:10ff), the ministry of *letter writing* (Paul was pre-eminent here, as if he had nothing else to do, but not a mention of it appears in the Acts at all), the ministry of *intercessory prayer* (12:5ff), the ministries of *worship and of fasting* (13:1-3), *pioneer ministries* such as

Philip, Aquila, Prisca and Paul engaged in (see chs 8 and 17), and the ministry of *overseas mission* (13:4ff).

Those are just some of the ministries spread before us in the Acts. They are not highlighted. They are taken for granted. For Luke knows that all Christians are called to minister to the Lord, and that they do so in a multitude of different ways as the Spirit gives them the ability and the direction. It would be salutary for our modern churches simply to glance through these ministries which appear in Acts, and see which of them are taking place and being encouraged in their own congregation. Only in an encouraging atmosphere of love and tolerance and learning by experience can we expect the variety of ministries to appear which God longs to impart to his church.

The decision making of the church

Another interesting area where the early Christians seem to have differed rather sharply from ourselves is that of decision making.

How should decisions be made in the Christian church? In many churches, decisions are made by the minister alone, or by a group of elders. The assumption is that they know best; that they are appointed to lead, and that therefore the church would be wise to let them get on with it. However, this has led to some very bad decisions in many churches, so a strong reaction, coupled with cultural trends, has led to the opposite assumption: the church is a democracy and decisions should be made by arguing a case, by lobbying if need be, and then by voting. The fact that this leaves a dissatisfied and probably aggrieved minority is reckoned to be just too bad.

The trend in recent years, at all events in main line churches, has been to follow more closely the way of secular decision making with its politics, its synods and its powerful standing committees. The early church did not make decisions in that way. The overall principle which they adopted, as we shall see, was to seek the will of God together, and then resolve to follow it. There is no hint of voting, or of powerful groups behind the scenes influencing decisions. We see them proceeding in a number of ways.

1. The first decision in the Acts is reached by drawing lots! We have already glanced at the situation in a previous chapter. The Eleven, rightly or wrongly, felt that God was calling them (through the application of Psalm 69:25 and 109:8) to find a successor for Judas. The candidate needed to have been with them from the beginning

of the ministry of Jesus and to be a witness of the resurrection. Two
men were deemed suitable, so they cast lots after prayer. The lot fell
on Matthias, and he was enrolled with the Eleven.

Before we dismiss the whole procedure as crazy, let us notice several
things. First, they sought the guidance of the Scriptures. Second, they
recognised basic criteria that would be necessary in any candidate.
Third, they reflected on their membership and chose two good
names. Fourth, they committed the whole thing to prayer. And
finally they cast lots, and accepted the result. The procedure is not
so far removed from the way bishops are chosen in the Church
of England, when after scrutiny, much discussion and presumably
prayer, two names are submitted, both of which are acceptable to
the church; the Prime Minister selects one!

The apostles have been criticised for the way they went about
the selection of Matthias. Should they have waited until the Spirit
came? Should the twelfth place have been reserved for Paul? Were
they wrong in the man they went for, since he is never heard of
again, and they did not use this method again? We do not know
the answers to these questions. But the apostles may not have been
wrong at all. The Spirit had not yet been given, and therefore they
had recourse to the God-given way of seeking guidance in the Old
Testament through the lot (see Proverbs 16:33), a method used,
incidentally, by their contemporaries at Qumran (e.g. 1 QS 5:3). The
method is strange to us, but the principle is clear. These men felt
the matter was too important to push their own ideas. They wanted
nothing less than the Lord's will.

2. The second example is very different. It comes in chapter 6. There
is a row brewing in the church. Food is supposed to be shared among
needy people, and the widows were desperately poor. The newcomers
to Jerusalem from a Greek and provincial background were getting
neglected: that, at all events is how they saw it. Tempers were running
high. The Twelve knew they had more on their hands than they
could possibly cope with, and saw the importance of putting a board
of suitable men in charge of the rapidly deteriorating situation.

It is instructive to see how they handled it. First, they held a full
church meeting. The apostles did not come with any preconceived
answers. They came with the problem, with their own convictions
about their God-given calling to prioritise ministering the word of
God and prayer, and with the suggestion that the congregation should
pick 'seven men of good repute, full of the Spirit and wisdom whom

we may appoint to this duty'. What a conciliatory and wise approach! No wonder what they said pleased the whole multitude. It was the congregation, then, who chose the seven men (Luke never calls them 'deacons') for this important humanitarian, social and administrative task. All of them were Hellenistic Greeks, members of the group discriminated against! They were brought to the apostles, who prayed and laid their hands on them. And thus the decision was made.

Notice some very important principles. First, the 'ordained leadership' cannot carry responsibility for everything. They should make the ministry of the word and prayer top priorities, and not try to do everything else, but make sure that it is done by others suitably qualified. Second, when there is 'murmuring', it is particularly important to ensure that everything is done up front and that there is no suggestion of a preconceived plan which is being imposed by a minority in leadership. Third, when people feel discriminated against, see that they are fully represented in any solution to the problem.

How different from our tendency to pack the committee with 'safe men' who will vote the right way. Every one of these seven belonged to the Hellenists! What generosity. Fourth, allow maximum involvement in the decision making: allow the congregation to come up with names, but let the authorised leaders of the church, in this case the Twelve, lay hands upon them with prayer, and commission them for the task.

The decision making in this whole ticklish business was done with the maximum of integrity, compassion, involvement of the congregation, and responsible commissioning by the Twelve. There is no doubt that their supreme desire was to find the Lord's will for solving this difficult problem. I have no doubt that his will was shown them. It is notable that the supreme requirement for this administrative task was being full of the Spirit and wisdom and faith. If our administrators are selected in this way and with this aim, we shall do well.

3. A third mode of decision making is just as unfamiliar to us as the previous two. It is in response to what we would call spiritual gifts, dreams, visions and prophecies. That is how Ananias decided to go to visit Saul (9:10). That is how Peter decided to visit Cornelius (10:17). That is how Paul decided to go to Macedonia (16:9). Decision making in the light of a vision, or the sort of prediction which an Agabus might make, is profoundly uncongenial to contemporary intellectual Christians. Initially I believed God no longer guided people in this way. Then I reluctantly had to accept the extensive evidence which

came my way to show that he did, at all events to Christians in Third World countries. But then I had to humbly allow God to guide me and the church I served through visions and dreams. We learnt to prune our over-extended programme through a vision. We changed the whole thrust of our community house through a vision. We were provoked to entirely renovate the interior of the church, coffee house and bookstore, through a prophetic utterance which told us, among other things, not to worry about the money, which God would provide (he did: a million dollars!). God continues to guide in this way when we allow him to do so.

4. There is an entirely different way of decision making unfolded to us in the Acts, more of a debate than a vision. The situation is one we have already examined, the Council of Jerusalem, summoned to solve the most pressing of all the questions addressed by the infant church: what were the conditions of entry into the Christian life? The course of the discussion is fascinating.

First the 'liberal' delegation from Antioch is received with loving welcome, not suspicion, as well they might in the heart of conservative Jerusalem (15:4). If difficult debates in church life can be held in such an atmosphere it is a great start. The 'conservative' position is succinctly traced: 'It is necessary to circumcise them (i.e. the Gentiles) and to charge them to keep the law of Moses.' Then there was an open meeting for the whole church, and freedom for extended debate.

The crucial speech was made by Peter. He who had once been so conservative about the conditions of Gentile inclusion, now had the courage to make a complete volte-face in the light of what he had learnt through the Cornelius incident. He gives a speech which would have been highly appropriate in the mouth of Paul! His main point is that keeping the Law of Moses never was a means of salvation for anyone, Jews included: none of them was able to keep it, and the Old Testament had never designed it to be a way of salvation, but rather the response of a people God had himself rescued. Salvation comes through the unmerited grace of God to Jew and Gentile alike. It is received by faith. And this brings about the cleansing of the heart by means of the gift of the Holy Spirit. If both Jews and Gentiles are saved in this way, clearly the Law is an irrelevance for Gentiles. Many Jews who became Christians in Jerusalem did seek to keep the Law for other reasons, surrounded as they were by a Jewish culture. But they did not see this as the way of salvation.

This argument was powerful and seems to have silenced opposition.

It was followed by testimony, as Paul and Barnabas spoke of the supernatural work of the Holy Spirit, poured out among Gentiles through their ministry. James, who by this time seems to have achieved a presidential position in the Jerusalem church (probably because he was the half-brother of Jesus), enunciates the decision which has been growing in the minds of each member of the Council. That is a great gift in a chairman. When he had verbalised it, 'then it seemed good to the apostles and elders and the whole church'. The decision was based upon the argument of Peter, the testimony of Paul and Barnabas and the perceived relevance of Amos 9:11–12. James saw that this passage, which spoke of a new thing that God would do by incorporating Gentiles, had no mention of circumcision or law-keeping as any condition of acceptance. The result of the Council was therefore a clear recognition that response in faith to the saving grace of Christ was the way into the Christian fold, but that Gentiles should respect the sensitivities of the Jews and abstain from certain things that were repulsive to them in order to maintain the unity of the church. And, as we have seen, the decision was both written down and personally communicated – a wise way to win agreement over a difficult issue.

Though the method of decision making was so different on this occasion, the underlying principle was the same. These people were determined to find God's solution to this problem, not to impose their own. There was a loving atmosphere, open discussion, effective argument, personal testimony, openness to what the Spirit was actually doing, expounding of Scripture, good chairmanship, a conclusion that everyone recognised as coming from God, and wide circulation of that decision.

5. A final way in which we find the early Christians making decisions is as a result of a growing inner conviction. In 16:6–10 Luke tells us that 'the Holy Spirit' forbade the missionary team round Paul to preach the word in the province of Asia at that time; presumably the plan had been to visit through the coastal areas of the province of Asia towards Mysia at its north-west extremity. Equally, when they attempted to penetrate north-east to the Roman province of Bithynia, 'the Spirit of Jesus' did not allow them. That is a delightful description of the Holy Spirit, unique to Acts, 'the Spirit of Jesus'. It shows clearly that Jesus continues to guide his church, its growth and direction, through the Holy Spirit he has given to them.

We are not told in either case how the Spirit showed them that they were not to work in these areas, and speculation is unprofitable.

We are told about the vision of the man of Macedonia opening up the way to Europe, and about their response; but notice the comment in 16:10, 'concluding that God had called us to preach the gospel to them'. Luke was there on this occasion – notice how the narrative slips from 'they' to 'we' – and he records this conviction, this assurance that God had sent the vision and meant them to go to Greece. Decisions were made in the light of that firm inner conviction.

Those are five ways of decision making shown us in Acts: in response to the lot, to a discussion, to visions, to a council meeting and to a deep inner conviction. All of these varied ways of decision making have one thing in common: there was an utter dependence on God to guide them, and an overwhelming desire not that their personal preferences should prevail but that God's will should be done. Prayer, Scripture, testimony to the present working of the Lord were all part of the process that led to the decisions, and then it was put firmly in the hand of God for him to show his will. As a result there was growth and fruitfulness. And because it was done in this way, we do not find a minority of dissatisfied people angry with any of these decisions.

I believe that we have much to learn today from the decision making of the early church. I have been on many committees and councils where major decisions have been hammered out, and I have often missed the love and warmth I see in Acts, the prayer, the reverent wrestling with Scripture, the determination not to push one's own view but rather seek God's will. Certainly these things have sometimes been given verbal assent. There has been a prayer, maybe, before the room fills with smoke and the gloves come off. But my lasting impression over many years has been that very often our decisions are man-made. We seek to run God's church in our way and then ask his blessing on the result, or imagine that the Holy Spirit must be behind the majority. We ape the secular parliamentary procedures and wonder why the minorities are so resentful of what has been steam-rollered through by the majority. If we want to learn at all from the life and structures of the early church, we could do worse than allow ourselves to be influenced by their ways of making decisions.

II

What of Their Leadership?

Traditional questions about leadership

A good deal is written about the leadership of the early church as we meet it in Acts, and it must be confessed that it often rests on rather insecure foundations.

Apostles

We cannot be sure of the origin of the apostolic office. It derives from Jesus; clearly it is in some sense an echo of the twelve tribes of Israel; clearly apostles act as *shelichim*, authorised delegates of Jesus to continue his work after he has left them. They are the supreme authorities in the church: the church's doctrine and fellowship is called the apostles' doctrine and fellowship. Yet they appear very little in the Acts. They are shadowy figures, of whom only Peter and John are initially in evidence. We do not know what became of Matthias whom they appointed to join them after the suicide of Judas. We do not know if they called anyone else 'apostle' in addition to the eleven: Barnabas and Saul are only called 'apostles' in chapter 14 during the first missionary journey when they were 'sent out' (the root of the Greek word 'apostle') from the Antioch church. Apostolic authority clearly derived from their association with the incarnate Lord (1:22-3). Their function as guarantors of the continuity between the Jesus of history and the Christ of faith was by definition unrepeatable. They never contemplated a succession – when the *shaliach's* commission was completed it returned to the sender: he could not pass it on. So we never find them creating apostles after them. The apostles' primary task was to evangelise and plant churches, to safeguard the teaching of the church and to give themselves to ministering the

word of God and praying. We would love to know more. But Acts
does not satisfy our curiosity.

Presbyters

Presbyters (from which our English 'priest' is derived: it has nothing
to do with the Old Testament sacrificing priest) appear, without
introduction, in 11:30 as 'the elders' at Jerusalem. We do not know
for certain what their origin was, but in all probability the office
was taken over direct from the synagogue. There the 'elders' were
laymen who saw that the Law was observed, and handled the civil
and administrative duties of the synagogue. They had no liturgical
functions: these lay in the hands of the 'ruler of the synagogue' who
was not a priest of the Aaronic line, but a layman, like the elders,
and was elected for office. This was a very convenient model for the
first Christians to take over. We find Christian presbyters all over
the Mediterranean basin in the writings of the New Testament. In the
Acts itself we find them at Jerusalem, and at Ephesus, and we are told
that Barnabas and Saul returned to the churches they had founded
on their first missionary journey in order to appoint elders for them
in every church, with prayer and fasting (14:23). We may take it,
then, that presbyters or elders were the regular local leadership in the
churches of the New Testament. Their function was to be *episkopoi*
(20:28), a word from which we derive our 'bishop', and which means
'overseer'. In the context in Acts 20 it is explicitly stated that these
episkopoi of verse 28 are the 'elders' or 'presbyters' of verse 17. They
are identical. If you like, 'elder' is their title, and 'overseeing' is their
function. We are not told if they were ordained for this role by the
laying on of hands. In all probability they were: this was normal with
Jewish rabbis too. We know that elders were at least sometimes
appointed by the apostles (14:23). We learn more from other parts
of the New Testament, but not from Luke.

Deacons

If we look for 'deacons' in the Acts, we shall look in vain. Though in
Acts 6, poor relief is called 'deaconing tables', while preaching is called
'deaconing the word', the Seven are never called 'deacons': they were
a board of almoners set up to meet a particular need.

It is hard to avoid the conclusion that there is a highly undeveloped
view of ministry in the Acts. We shall not find the 'threefold ministry'
of bishops, priests and deacons. We shall not find much about the
apostles themselves. But we do find a fair amount about people

like Agabus, or the prophesying daughters of Philip; about James who sprang to prominence although not a member of the apostolic band; about Philip who proved himself such an able evangelist; about Stephen, who was such a charismatic leader, innovative thinker and courageous martyr; about Paul whom nobody but God ever ordained.

If, then, we persist in asking traditional questions of Acts about its pattern of ministry, we shall continue to receive unsatisfactory answers. There simply is not enough material to go on.

But what if we start asking a very different question, and enquire what Luke believed was important about Christian leadership? Then we get a very clear answer. And if we ask what characteristics he hoped to see in such leadership, the answer is both lucid and arresting, and will have a lot to say to the modern church.

Principles of Christian leadership

Let us begin with the first question, then. What does Luke tell us about the Christian leadership in which he clearly strongly believed?

Leadership is a gift of God. The first important thing about leadership is to realise that this is one of the gifts of God to his church. Leadership is not some office for which we can train. A leader is someone whom God raises up. That is how the Twelve came into leadership. Back in the early days of his ministry, Jesus took the initiative of calling them apart, so that they could be with him and that he could then share his work with them and continue it through them after he had gone. Their leadership was one of divine election. So was Paul's! That is exceedingly obvious. But it is also true that the leadership exercised by Stephen, Philip, Barnabas, Timothy, Silas and others did not spring from any role they played, or human authorisation they received. It was a God-given facility. It was the same with the Ephesian elders: it was the 'Holy Spirit who made you overseers'. While therefore there is no opposition between charisma and office in the Lucan writings, as there was later on in the church, it is plain that for Luke the divine charisma is the prerequisite for anyone exercising effective leadership. You did not receive the Holy Spirit for the task of 'deaconing' tables, for example, *after* the apostles had laid their hands upon you: you simply were not considered for the job unless you had *already* shown signs of being filled with the Holy Spirit (Acts 6:5-6). That is the opposite way round from our contemporary practice, where the act

of ordination is thought to provide the spiritual enabling. Alas, it
will not do so, as many powerless ministries demonstrate, unless the
divine enabling is there already.

Leadership is shared. The second important thing about leadership
in the Acts is, as we have seen, that leaders do not operate solo. They
work in teams. The elders are always plural in the Acts, as in the rest
of the New Testament. Peter and John worked together; so did Paul
and Barnabas, Barnabas and Mark, Paul and Silas, Paul and Timothy.
There is no single presbyter at Antioch (13:1) or at Ephesus (20:17).
They are a team. Shared leadership has obvious strengths. A team
demonstrates the fellowship of leadership. It is an example of the
small group of loving and praying friends which can so helpfully be
reproduced in a congregation. It preserves the church from imbalance
and from undue dependence on one individual leader. It preserves
the individual leader from megalomania and from burn out. It was
a very wise arrangement. But in many modern churches it simply
does not happen. There is usually one person who is the pastor,
and all too often the congregation's attitude is something like this:
'You are the expert. We have hired you. We expect you to get on
with it, with a little help from us.' And from that fundamental flaw
flows loneliness in ministry, polarisation between pastor and people,
exhaustion, blinkered vision, and an unsatisfactory situation where the
pastor is glad to have a stage to play on, and the people are glad to let
him, because they can then criticise him in peace, and can be spared
the inconvenience of undue commitment.

Leadership is diverse. The third interesting characteristic of leadership in the Acts is that it falls into clear categories. There is the
circulating, overseeing, church-planting ministry represented by the
apostles Barnabas, Silas, Paul, Philip and to some extent Agabus and
Apollos. And then there is the settled, local leadership which emerges,
or is appointed, in the local churches – the 'elders' at Jerusalem or
Ephesus, or the five men who lead the church at Antioch. We know
that this continued into the second century, when travelling teachers,
prophets and 'apostles' (in the sense of leaders sent out by some of
the churches to go round and minister) serviced the local leadership
of presbyters and their assistants, the deacons. The idea of the leaders
in the local church being respected *local* people is so obvious that
it is amazing how few of the main line churches have adopted it.
They have left it to the fast-growing house churches, which generally

recruit their leadership from within their own number. But it makes so much sense to appoint experienced local Christians who have shown their mettle over a number of years. They need to be equipped, of course; and that is where the mobile, circulating leadership comes in. We know of apostles, prophets and teachers circulating in this way during the first couple of centuries. All three would be able to provide an invaluable check and encouragement to the local leadership. The apostles could preserve catholicity and encourage mission; the prophets could equip in the area of spiritual gifts and warn and encourage; and the teachers add a depth of training which might well be beyond the local leadership.

Leadership is service. A fourth aspect of leadership which is stressed in the Acts is its servant nature. The leaders are not above the church, to dominate it: they are, if you like, beneath it to serve it. That is how Jesus served the church. And he told his followers in words which are important for Luke: 'The kings of the Gentiles exercise lordship over them, and those in authority over them are called "benefactors". But not so with you; rather let the greatest among you become as the youngest, and the leader as the one who serves' (Luke 22:25ff). That is the model of leadership we see being exercised by the apostles at Jerusalem, by the Seven to the widows, by Philip to the eunuch, by Saul and Silas to the jailer. It was a servant ministry, through and through. They gained respect not by demanding it, but by earning it. Theirs was the unanswerable authority of a leadership which gives and serves and loves. They saw leadership not as a status which deserved honour but as an opportunity to provide service; they operated as the representatives of Jesus the Servant.

Leadership is broadly based. A fifth fascinating characteristic seems to have been that those whom we would call 'charismatic' and 'non-charismatic' functioned in the same shared leadership teams. Antioch is the most obvious example. The shared leadership at Antioch consisted of five men drawn from widely different national and cultural backgrounds, some of whom were prophets, while others were teachers (13:1). On the whole, those two categories do not find it easy to get along together. The teacher finds the prophet unpredictable, wild, emotional and a little dangerous; the prophet finds the teacher over-prepared, bookish, predictable, and a little dull. And yet prophets and teachers were working as a team here in Antioch, as they were in Caesarea and Jerusalem. Does that not have something important to say to our modern church, which is often polarised over the charismatic issue, and tends as a result either to go short on good reliable teaching, or on the inspiration and immediacy of God's word to them through prophecy? We need both. Happy the church that is big enough in its sympathies to accommodate both.

Leadership is learned on the job. A sixth feature of early leadership, which Luke makes abundantly clear, is that they trained people on the job, not in any primitive attempt at a college. It is no good saying that there were no colleges available for them. They improvised many things, and could have improvised this if they thought it needful. Indeed, colleges were there in rabbinic Judaism, as much waiting to be taken over as the system of synagogue presbyters which, as we have seen, the Christians did take and adapt. But these apostles knew that you do not train people behind desks and with books. You train them in the heat of battle and with real encounters. You rarely get good ministers in churches if the only way that you train them is to take them away from their homes, send them to college where they prepare with *book* learning for an *oral* ministry, make them sit at a desk to listen to a professor lecturing, and require them to do very little in the cause of the gospel when they are there, apart, perhaps, from preaching one or two rather artificial sermons to fellow students. The church survived eighteen hundred years quite satisfactorily without having recourse to much in the way of theological colleges. I cannot believe that the way we train people today is realistic or effective. There is a real need for colleges to run short sandwich courses designed to equip those who have already shown some signs of leadership in particular areas which will be germane to their work. But to suppose that a young man or woman straight from university will be any good in a position of Christian leadership after spending three years at a seminary is certainly testing fortune. Sometimes, in the providence of God, it works. Often, predictably, it does not.

These six principles come out very clearly in the Acts account. They are fundamental to the quality of leadership which meets us in this exciting book, and which, sadly, is often missing among the leaders of our modern churches.

But can we go further? Can we ask, with any hope of an answer, what sort of questions went through the minds of early Christian leaders as they contemplated possible replacements and additions to their ranks? I believe we can. I believe that that is the main reason why Luke gives us such a detailed account as Acts 20, Paul's farewell to the Ephesian elders. He is showing us what Christian leadership was in Paul's own case, what he wanted to see in those elders at Ephesus, and what he hoped would characterise Christian leaders down the years until Jesus comes again.

Qualities in Christian leadership

Here, then, are some of the questions about the qualities to be sought in Christian leaders to which Acts 20 provides a clue.

Do they walk with God? Paul is able to describe his service to the Lord as willing 'slavery' (20:19 Greek) to speak of himself as 'serving the Lord'. Unless there is this fundamental dedication to the Lord, all Christian leadership is a sham. But it is all too possible to be in leadership in the modern church without a passionate commitment to the Lord. There can be the desire to serve him without first allowing him to serve us. There can be a humanitarian concern for needy people. There can even be some form of spiritual pride and paternalism. People go into Christian leadership for all manner of reasons. But there is only one reason that will bear the weight put upon it. And that is a call from the Lord, a deep love for him, and a passionate determination to serve others for his sake.

Do they believe in shared ministry? There is no room today for the 'one man band'. Nor was there in the first century. As we have already seen, presbyters were always plural. In our situation, we place enormous pressures on people by expecting them to exercise a one-person ministry, or at best, ministry with one assistant. This is fundamentally unbiblical and misguided. I would want to ask any applicants for Christian leadership today whether or not they believe in shared ministry. And this includes the shared ministry of men and women. To be sure, we do not find women presbyters in the New Testament. But we do find that Jesus' attitude to women was staggeringly accepting. We do find women being the first witnesses of the resurrection. We do find women deacons. We do find the statement that in Christ there is neither male nor female (Gal. 3:28). We do find that women received the Spirit as well as men (2:17). We do find them owning and using Christian homes for the cause of the gospel (12:12). Paul's first convert in Europe was a distinguished businesswoman, Lydia (16:14). Priscilla, who often in the New Testament is mentioned before her husband Aquila, joined him in

instructing Apollos in the faith, and their homes in Rome, Corinth
and Ephesus were centres of Christian worship and teaching. We find
women like Mary, Tryphaena and Tryphosa engaging in Christian
leadership, 'labouring in the Lord' (Rom. 16:6, 12). We find women
associating with Paul in spreading the gospel (Phil. 4:3, Acts 18:1ff).
We find a woman like Phoebe not only being the deacon of the
Corinthian church (Rom. 16:1), but being *patrona*, a prestigious social
position which would inevitably have involved her in leadership. We
can go further. Women both prayed publicly in church and uttered
prophetic messages (1 Cor. 11:5, Acts 21:9). They were 'joint heirs
of the grace of life' (1 Pet. 3:7).

The question is insistent: does the candidate for leadership believe
in shared leadership? It may be right for the male to take the lead. It
may not always be so. But it *is* imperative to recognise that women,
no less than men, have a place in Christian leadership. Our Christian
forebears were enormously courageous in contending against the male
chauvinism of their day. We need to follow their example.

Can they inspire others? The function of leadership is *proistasthai*, 'to
go out in front'. It may mean going out on a limb. It certainly means to
inspire and challenge. Leaders need to lead. And if that is not your gift,
do not aspire to leadership. Nobody can doubt the leadership gifts of
a Peter, a Paul, a James, a Stephen, a Philip, a John.

They had the gift of leading others, of inspiring them. But many
of those who are nurtured in our seminaries have no proven gift
of leadership. Nobody knows if they can inspire others. They have
never tried. They have never been observed. It is a solemn thought
that we are ordaining a great many people each year who may have
no gift whatever of Christian leadership. And there is nothing more
frustrating to members of a congregation than to have a minister,
supposed to be a leader, who is in fact somewhat unsure of the faith,
unskilled in training others, unwilling to engage in evangelism, and
incompetent to teach within the congregation. A P. D. James novel,
which I read recently, observed that the most that could be hoped
for from a sermon was to survive it. That is not the principle on
which the first Christians operated!

Do they pray? The prayer life of Paul is phenomenal. It shines
through this passage. He had prayed for years for his young leaders
(20:31). He prayed corporately with them on the beach before leaving
Miletus (20:36). How many Christian leaders do that? The first

paragraph of most of his letters shows what a top priority prayer was for the apostle. Without prayer we are powerless. Without prayer we cannot lead others. One of the first questions I would want to ask about anyone who was being considered for leadership is this: is this person steeped in prayer? If not, as the heat and pressures of the ministry take their inexorable toll, the supposed leader will wilt. If there is any lesson that needs to be imprinted on church leadership today, it is the vital importance of prayer.

Are they humble? Humility is not a matter of self-denigration. It is not pretending that one has no gifts. It is recognising that whatever gifts we have come from God, and can be exercised effectively in his strength alone. Accordingly, a tremendous leader like Moses can be accounted the meekest person on earth, simply because he did not take the credit for his giftedness, but ascribed that credit where it was due, to the Lord. We insult the Holy Spirit who gives gifts to men and women if we claim that we have no gifts. We most certainly have. The important thing is to identify them and to recognise their source. Then we will be able to exercise them without pride, or false humility. Real humility does not say, 'I am useless and have no gifts.' It says, 'Without the Lord I would be nothing. With him I can be something.' And Paul, that highly gifted man, served the Lord 'with all humility of mind' (20:19). He knew full well that he had no power of his own to do anything in the Christian enterprise. All his enabling came from the Lord. That humility of mind is a priceless asset in any who offer themselves for leadership in the church today.

Are they enablers? Paul gave wise advice to his young colleague Timothy: 'What you have heard from me before many witnesses, entrust to faithful men who will be able to teach others also' (2 Tim. 2:2). The essence of all New Testament leadership is to be an enabler of others. And that is precisely what Paul, with his three years at Ephesus (19:10), had done with his Ephesian elders. He had poured himself into them. He had loved them, encouraged them, taught them, trusted them. In a word, he had enabled them. And now that he was moving on, he had no doubt that they would carry the torch into the next stage of the race. Paul, for all his brilliance, was an enabler of others. 'I have shown you' he said (20:35), and it rang true.

That is not a notable characteristic of today's leadership. There are too many stars around, and not nearly enough equippers. But how crucial that role is. However brilliant the star, that star will set. And then there will be darkness, unless he has equipped others to follow him into leadership. We need enablers. We need petrol pump attendants, who will equip other cars for the race, rather than rushing ahead personally. The supreme privilege for anyone in leadership is to equip others to make their offering of ministry to the Lord and his church.

Do they care about people? Paul had a passionate concern about people, even though he was such an intrepid church planter, and brilliant intellectual. He loved them so much that he taught them house to house as well as publicly (20:20). He told them all they needed to know, keeping nothing back (20:27). He toiled to support the weak (20:35). He reckoned he was clear of the blood of all men, not having shrunk from making plain to all of them the whole counsel of God (20:27). Paul had that marvellous mixture of deep commitment in prayer, profound wrestling with doctrinal issues, but also the love for people which led to them weeping and kissing him on the beach when it was time to go from Miletus towards the dangerous city of Jerusalem.

The modern pastor must love people. If not, he or she will comprehensively fail. Christian leadership involves the application of the grace of God to real people. And if you do not love them, that is something you cannot do with any credibility.

Are they examples? It is impossible to exaggerate the importance of example in leadership. You cannot ask people to do and be things you are not prepared to do and be yourself. Paul is not embarrassed about the example he has shown these young followers of his. His life has been open to inspection at every point, and over a period of years (20:19, 31). It had been consistent (v 18), dedicated (v 19), humble (v 19), persistent in the face of pressures internal and external (v 19), hardworking (v 34) and bold (v 22). He had not *told* them to support the weak: he had *shown* them (v 35). The quality of his example was such that these people would do anything for him. He was a man of warmth and prayer (v 36), of generosity and practical labour (v 34), a man full of the Spirit and devoted to the gospel of the grace of God (v 23-4). One could go on. This whole passage is eloquent about the example of this great Christian leader, who was about to pass on the torch to the next generation. They were anxious to pick it up primarily because of what they had seen in him.

It is very sad when a work of God shrivels away because of the poor example of the appointed leaders. Only this morning I have heard how discouraged and even cynical a promising congregation has become for just that very reason. What we are does in fact speak louder than what we say. There is nothing a church needs more than the holiness and example of its leaders.

What do they believe? That it is another crucial question to bear in mind when considering suitability for Christian leadership. Does the candidate genuinely believe the faith of the New Testament? Paul is very explicit about what he believes. He is supremely concerned to testify to the free unmerited favour of God to sinners, 'grace', as he calls it (v 24), and to urge upon his hearers the appropriate response: repentance and faith (v 21). It is never easy to preach repentance, but Paul has not been selective in his preaching to the Ephesians. He has told them the whole counsel of God as he understands it from the Old Testament Scriptures and from the life and teaching of Jesus. It is very easy to fail in leadership at this point. If we proclaim the whole truth apart from whatever flies in the face of contemporary errors and prejudices, then we are not preaching the gospel of Christ, however orthodox what we do say. It is characteristic of much modern preaching to avoid ruffling feathers and taking on contentious and painful issues. Real leadership is not afraid to do just that.

Do they make Scripture their guide? When Paul bade the Ephesians farewell he commended them to God; that is natural enough (v 32). We might do the same. But if you were to add one more thing to 'God' in your commendation, what would it be? For Paul it was 'God and the word'. By this he means, of course, God's self-revelation in the Old Testament Scriptures and their fulfilment in the life and death, the teaching and resurrection of Jesus of Nazareth. That is God's word, his supreme and final self-disclosure. And simply because it is *God's* word, it has every claim to be taken with the utmost seriousness by Christian leaders. We are not at liberty to change it. We need to study it so that we can open it up for ourselves and others. Scripture does not contain man's ideas about God, but God's ideas about man and his salvation; does the proposed leader believe that? It will make an enormous difference, one way or another, to his leadership, if he is a person who is determined to allow Scripture to be normative in all his teaching about the faith. It will be unfashionable, but it will be effective. Look at what Paul is confident that this 'word' can do. It can build up believers, as milk and meat build up a physical body. The spiritual life needs nourishment, and the word is one of the most nutritious foods in the world. And it can also 'give' people their inheritance among the people of God. By this he means that the careful study of Scripture will open the eyes of Christians to the spiritual wealth which God has in store for them. Just as a cheque 'gives' us the written title to someone's wealth, so the 'word' gives us the written title to the good things that God has waiting for those who love him. It is critical, therefore, to see that this word is prominent in personal devotion, group study and public preaching. We need leaders who bring this about.

Can they teach? Paul is concerned about this. In the lists of qualities requisite in Christian leaders which he gives in Titus chapter 1 and 1 Timothy chapter 3 there is one, and only one, that is not a moral quality. The candidate must be *didaktikos*, 'apt to teach'. If not, he or she will suffer much frustration in the ministry of the church, and so, for that matter, will the congregation! Paul mentions three ways of teaching in Acts 20. One is teaching by example (v 35). The leader needs to be a real worker, deeply concerned for the needs of the less fortunate members of the church, and deeply imbued with the generous spirit of Jesus which gives and goes on giving, aware that 'it is happier to give than to get'. When that sort of teaching is given by the example of a church leader, it tends to catch on very quickly in a congregation.

The second type of teaching Paul mentions is public teaching (v 20). He had done that, and he expected those who followed him to engage in public teaching of the faith and its implications for daily living. This would involve study. It would involve taking pains to make the teaching memorable and applied to the contemporary situation. It would involve taking pains to see not simply that he taught acceptably but that the congregation actually learnt – a very different matter.

The third type of instruction to which Paul refers is 'house to house'. This involves visiting. Unless a pastor really knows the life and home situation of his congregation it is impossible for him to teach them appropriately. It will all be in generalities, ill applied. The importance of this home visitation can scarcely be over-estimated. But it is widely neglected today. Visiting has fallen into disuse, and we are the poorer for it in our church life. Moreover, the vast majority of people who do not go to church are also the poorer. They do not know that anyone cares. Ignorant as they are of Christ, they remain ignorant because nobody cares enough to visit them. Sadly, it is often the Mormons or the Jehovah's Witnesses who visit them, but not the Christians.

There is actually another way of translating the Greek *kat'oikous* in this verse. It may mean 'in houses'. If so, it suggests house meetings for teaching the faith. This was certainly much used in the apostolic period, and has been throughout the history of the church. We have already said something about it in a previous chapter. But it is an important skill for a leader to acquire: to provide home meetings where groups of Christians can learn together without necessarily being taught by any one 'qualified' leader. It can be learning by group discussion of a passage of Scripture or a prepared topic, followed by prayer and action. Preparing material for such groups and being willing to stand off and let them operate on their own, requires of the leader different skills from those he uses in public teaching of the faith in church. But these skills are increasingly important in an age in which people are allergic to dogmatic utterances from whatever quarter, and much prefer to work things out for themselves. Leaders need to be 'apt to teach' in this variety of ways.

What is their attitude to money? Paul left a considerable fortune when he became a Christian minister. As such he had no regular income apart from what he earned in tent making. He might well have been tempted to avarice. But if he was, he overcame that temptation conclusively. His own industriousness provided enough not only for his own necessities (not luxuries) but for those who accompanied him and who presumably did not have skills which could be put to use in almost any location, like tent making (20:34).

There is a terrible danger of being in Christian leadership for money. Covetousness still accounts for the downfall of many in the ministry. There is a dangerous tendency in some quarters to require payment for preaching a sermon. Ministers are anxious to be as well paid as other middle-class executives. Paul was so reliable and so unselfish over money matters that he could amass a very considerable collection of money from the Gentile churches to bring up to Jerusalem, without being suspected of malpractice. Happy the church leadership which can do likewise. Integrity in this area is imperative if any leadership is to retain credibility.

Dare they face unpopularity? We all love to be loved. But some-times, if we are faithful, we have to confront. Paul was willing to do this, and to risk ensuing unpopularity. We have seen it in the way he did not shrink from telling them any part of the gospel that they needed to know, however unwelcome it might be. Now he warns them very directly (20:28). They must take heed to themselves above all, if they are to qualify for Christian leadership. They must take heed to the flock entrusted to them. They must take heed to the wolves, with false teaching and false ethics, who would be sure to invade after Paul's departure (vv 29-30). Leaders do not always take kindly to warnings about their personal lives, about the handling of their church work, or about their responsibility to speak out against a false teaching and practice. It is not popular, but it sometimes needs to be done. And the person who is not prepared to do it should not be in a major position of Christian leadership. For leadership requires courage, the courage to do the unpopular thing if necessary. We need leaders like that, in an age when the tendency is to appease rather than confront, to tell what people like to hear rather than what they need to hear.

Can they endure hard times and suffering? The story of Paul's ministry is the story of his sufferings. He has been opposed, vilified, beaten, shipwrecked, attacked, and at times left for dead as he has gone blazing the trail of Christ across the Middle East. 'And now behold I am going to Jerusalem, bound in the Spirit, not knowing the things that shall befall me there; except that the Holy Spirit testifies to me in every city that imprisonment and afflictions await me. But I do not account my life of any value, nor as precious to myself, if only I may finish my course and the ministry which I have received from the Lord Jesus, to testify to the grace of God' (20:22ff). Here was a man whom no hardships, no suffering or prospect of suffering, could deter from what he believed the Lord was calling him to. That is the sort of leader whom people will follow through hell and high water.

Are they wholehearted? If someone undertakes Christian leadership for the financial rewards, or the prestige, or the popularity, or simply as a suitable job, the result will be disastrous. Nothing less than wholeheartedness will suffice. For leadership is hard. Disappointments abound. There will be many reverses. The temptation to give up will sometimes be strong. It is going to require someone who is prepared to work hard: 'these hands have ministered to my necessities and to those who were with me' (20:34). It is going to require sleepless nights: 'remember, that for three years I did not cease night or day to admonish every one of you with tears' (v 31). It is going to require deeply caring 'for the church of God which he obtained with the blood of his only Son' (v 28). It is going to necessitate a firm and unshakable resolve 'not to account my life of any value nor as precious to myself', and 'to finish my course and the ministry which I received from the Lord Jesus' (v 24).

We need to relax and to have fun, of course, or we shall become both dull and overwrought. But there needs to burn within us that deep commitment to accomplish the task committed to us. We need a leadership which is not there for the money or for a job, but for the Lord, and counts it the most privileged employment on earth.

Are they able to receive ministry from others? If as leaders we are going to be of real help to hurting people, we cannot appear to be above the pressures and pains which engulf them. We often give the impression of invulnerability: if you do not believe me, go and listen to a group of ministers meeting together and talking about their work. You very rarely hear them admitting failure and need. They have the feeling that if they open up, they will have come off their pedestal, and it will lie shattered. But that is precisely what is needed. People in our congregations will relate far more honestly and gladly to a leader who is 'touched with the feeling of their infirmities'. To admit our own pressures and failings will not mitigate the respect given to us; it will increase it. And it will mean that people are able to get close enough to us to love and encourage us. It will mean that they are more compassionate towards us as a result. It will further encourage honesty and integrity in the congregation. Leaders need never be ashamed of being seen as the wounded healers. After all, that is what their Master was. Paul, too, was willing and able to receive ministry from his peers and his juniors in the Christian life. 'They all wept and embraced Paul and kissed him, sorrowing most of all because of the word he had spoken, that they should see his face no more. And they brought him to the ship' (20:38). Happy the leader who, like Paul, can gracefully accept the ministry that those in his congregation delight to bring.

Are they truly open to the Holy Spirit? That is the vital ingredient in all great leadership. We need to be full of the Holy Spirit of God, so that it is not so much our leadership, as the leadership of the Spirit through us. This has been much emphasised throughout the Acts, but it is not often emphasised today, so it is well to close this chapter with it. Paul allows himself to be bound in the Spirit (20:22). He is sensitively listening for the quiet voice of the Spirit, even if that voice tells him things he would rather not hear, that imprisonment and afflictions await him (v 23). He is not only full of the Spirit, sensitive to the Spirit, but determined to obey the Spirit. And that is something he longs to see in his young assistants as they take over the leadership in Ephesus. It is the Holy Spirit who has made them overseers. If they are to lead, they must do so in the wisdom, the love, the courage and the power that he supplies. There is no substitute for Christian leaders who are full of the Holy Spirit.

These are some of the leadership qualities set before us in this wonderful chapter. They may serve to remind us that, contrary to the claims of some commentators, the requirements for leadership in the primitive church were not crude and rudimentary: they were very demanding. If we asked these kinds of questions when considering men and women for the ordained ministry of the Christian churches, we might find ourselves with fewer disasters, and a great deal more effectiveness, in ministerial ranks.

12

What of Their Hardships?

There was once a man called F. R. Maltby, and he used to say that Jesus promised his disciples three things. They would be absurdly happy, completely fearless, and in constant trouble. That seems to be a pretty fair summary of the first Christians. Joy and sorrow were interwoven in their lives, as in the life of their Master. The tenderness of the Last Supper was the prelude to betrayal, injustice, suffering and death. The dazzling glimpse of eternity on the mount of transfiguration was followed down in the plain by unbelief and battles with the demonic. The two are woven together, it would seem, inextricably.

The disciples found the same. The joy and mighty power of Pentecost, resulting in conversions, healings and wonderful signs of divine might, were followed by imprisonment, injustice and suffering. The extraordinary multiplication of the church in Acts 6, where we read that a large number of priests became believers (6:7), was the prelude to the martyrdom of Stephen and the wave of persecution against the church which made Jerusalem too hot to hold most of them (chs 7, 8). Throughout the rest of the New Testament, Christians are warned to expect no less. 'Beloved, do not be surprised at the fiery ordeal which comes upon you to test you,' wrote Peter, who had seen it all in his own experience, 'as though it was some strange thing that was happening, but rejoice insofar as you share in Christ's sufferings.' He continues, 'If you are reproached for the name of Christ, blessed are you, because the Spirit of glory and of God rests upon you' (1 Peter 4:12-14). Hard times are bound to come to human beings in a world like ours; how much more to Christians in a world which turns its back on Christ and his values.

The Book of Acts depicts hardship and pressure coming to the believers from at least five major sources: the circumstances of life, the secular society in which they have to live, the failures and weaknesses within the church, direct Satanic opposition, and the constant inner battle with the self. We should expect the same.

Hard times – through circumstances

Disasters
There is no denying that some of the hardships we face as Christians today simply come from the way life is. That was true also for Paul. The man who is in touch with God gets exposed to the shattering experience of a shipwreck: he is not exempt from the trials and tribulations of life (27:43f). But he is the man with poise, confident that nothing can possibly separate him from the Father's love. For if he dies, he goes into the nearer presence of his Lord.

It is also noteworthy how Paul, in this crisis, assumes control. He is supposed to be the prisoner, but it is he who summons, instructs and organises the doomed ship's crew. Not only so, but Paul's practical helpfulness stands out. He is not the sort of preacher who tells others what to do without getting involved himself. He is out gathering wood like everyone else (28:3), to restore warmth into chilled bones and dry soaked clothes.

Christians win great credit for their Lord when they respond to unforeseen disasters, like this shipwreck, with poise, prayerful initiative, and practical helpfulness to others enmeshed in the same situation.

Disease
Disasters are not the only unpleasant circumstances that come our way. Disease is another. Publius, a key man in the island of Malta, and one who had shown great kindness to the shipwrecked crew, fell ill with a fever and dysentery (28:8). Their future might have been at risk, had this friendly supporter died. Disease had struck as suddenly as shipwreck. So what does Paul do? He goes in and prays for the man, laying his hands upon him.

I did the same thing yesterday in an underground garage, early in the morning, because someone was ill. We ought to pray to the Lord with expectancy in the face of disease. Sometimes the answer is what we hoped for; sometimes not. It is a great mystery. But one thing I know: Christians who pray in faith and lay hands upon the sick see a great many more of them healed than those who lack expectant faith. When my wife was in Fiji recently she wrote to me. 'We are seeing lots of healings and deliverances from evil spirits here. In fact, experiencing healing is one of the main avenues to conversion among the Hindus.' It is one of the main things the church of Christ should be actively and prayerfully concerned about.

Constraining circumstances

Constraining circumstances often form part of the hardship we undergo: they did in the early church, too. In chapter 28 Paul is under house arrest. He would face more rigorous confinement later, but this was a sufficient drag on the liberty of this fiery, active evangelist. Did he let it get him down? Not at all. 'He lived there two whole years, at his own expense, and welcomed all who came to him, preaching the kingdom of God, and teaching about the Lord Jesus Christ quite openly and unhindered' (28:30-1). Is that not delightful? He did not want to be there, but he turned disaster into an opportunity. Interestingly enough, we learn from Philippians, how effective he was as a prisoner among the constantly changing guard of soldiers, chosen from the imperial élite, the praetorian guard, as was sometimes the case with important detainees. 'What has happened to me has really served to advance the gospel. It has become known throughout the whole praetorian guard, and to all the others, that my imprisonment is for Christ' (Phil. 1:12f). You could not guard Saul of Tarsus without hearing about his Saviour! What a way to react to confining circumstances, by making the best of what they offered. And as a result there were 'saints in Caesar's household' (Phil. 4:22).

Many Christian women experience a sudden and great constriction when children are born. With two children under the age of three, they feel in chains. They cannot get out any more. Yes, but what a draw they have in those children. Others can, and will, come in to them. Young mums will get together while the children play. And if positively handled, this contraction of her world can become a marvellous liberating experience as she seeks to share Christ with her neighbours and friends. Like Paul, she may feel imprisoned, but will discover that 'the word of God is not bound' (2 Tim. 2:9).

Hard times – from secular society

Another element in the hardship we undergo comes from living as a Christian in the midst of a worldly society. We shall find the tide flowing against us.

Outright opposition

One form of this opposition will be outright. There will be no politeness disguising it. Thus at Philippi Paul and Silas faced naked, merciless opposition on a fabricated charge. They had delivered a girl from a demonic spirit. Her owners saw that she would be no good for spiritism any more, and were furious. They dragged Paul and Silas to the magistrates, complaining unjustly that these disciples were teaching customs which, as Romans, they could not accept or practise. What a trumped up charge! Only a minority in Philippi were Romans, and Paul and Silas were teaching nothing illegal.

As the chapter progresses, you will find not only this mis-representation, but a miscarriage of justice, then a beating of innocent people, then an imprisonment, and finally a low form of deceit and face-saving: when the earthquake has taken place and the jailer has been converted, 'the magistrates sent the police saying, "Let these men go"' (16:35). Notice Paul's response. 'They have beaten us publicly, uncondemned, men who are Roman citizens, and have thrown us into prison: and do they now cast us out secretly? No, let them come themselves, and take us out!' (16:37f). Paul was no pushover. He had not hitherto made any claims for personal justice. He had not mentioned that he was a Roman citizen; but he wanted to set the record straight in the face of malicious opposition and fictitious charges. We are not called to be doormats. There are times when, in the face of injustice, it is right to say, 'May I set the record straight?' There needs to be a toughness in the Christian response to opposition, as well as the meekness and gentleness of Christ.

Another striking example of outright opposition and its sequel comes in the remarkable story of Peter's imprisonment, recorded in chapter 12. Herod had killed James the brother of John with the sword; that went down well with the religious establishment so he determined to do the same thing with Peter. How did the church respond to that? It drove them to prayer: 'Peter was kept in prison, *but* earnest prayer was made to God for him by the church' (12:5). That is one of the great 'buts' of Scripture. It was specific prayer, earnest prayer, God-centred prayer, corporate prayer, repeated prayer. Prayer is not about moving the hand that moves the world. Prayer is about submitting to the hand that rules the world. It is co-operating with God in his purposes. We all have to die some time, and that was the time for James to die, in the providence of God. But it was not yet time for Peter's death. God still had work for him to do, and prayer was the instrument God used to get this man out of prison.

We do not know why it was God's purpose for James to die, and for Peter to be released for a time of further ministry. God does not disclose these things to us. But we can trust him: he has proved himself trustworthy. Prayer is submitting to that reliability. That is what we find in the Jerusalem church while Peter hung between life and death in those terrible days. That is what we should find in our own churches today, whenever we face danger or opposition.

Political pressure

In addition to outright opposition, there is often political opposition. In the brief account of the evangelisation of Iconium (14:1ff), you find a number of very unpleasant features: malice, division, riot and pogrom. In the face of all this, the disciples carry on as long as they can, and then leave. And yet in verse 21 we see that Paul and his friends have bounced back into Iconium, to revisit the saints.

There is a fine sense of godly realism in all this. Do not court death by staying on in a situation where you are clearly not of any use. Go where you can be of some use. Be realistic in knowing when to cede and to step back. Do not feel that is the end of it all. In due course the political climate may change: there may be an election or a coup, and the scene will be entirely different. When opportunity occurs to return to a place from which you have been ejected, grasp it with both hands.

Political opposition can be a devastating experience. When such things happen, and you are hassled by the political power, be it the matron of your hospital, the police of your town, or the headmaster of your school, you maintain your stand as long as you can, and then you need a time of recovery. In 14:28 there is a delightful reminder that the needs of the first Christians were precisely the same. Battered and shell-shocked, they got back to Antioch, told the church all the news, and 'remained no little time with the disciples'. It is a fitting end to the first missionary journey. We need such times. Do not be surprised at opposition; but get away, if you can, some time during the year, for much needed refreshment.

There is another notable example of political opposition in 19:23ff. Here we find the riot about 'Great is Diana of the Ephesians' taking place in the theatre at Ephesus. When you analyse this opposition, you find commerce, establishment religion, and political expediency joining hands to put the Christians down. That is a very powerful coalition. If it happens to you, be very cautious, as Paul was. At such times, it will help if you have friends in high places. We have already looked at the astonishing relationship between Paul and the Asiarchs, although they were totally opposed to all that he believed. You will sometimes get help from the most unexpected quarters, if you have built links with the leaders of the community. Christians need to make a determined effort to escape from the ghetto, and the round of endless church meetings. They need to get out among unchurched people and make friends with them. Who knows where this may lead in the future? I am sure Paul did not know, when he built relationships with the Asiarchs!

Syncretism

A third way in which hardship arises from secular society is through syncretism. This is very common, and on the increase in modern society. It is acceptable to revere Jesus so long as you equally revere Krishna, the Buddha, Mohammed and so on. All roads lead to the top of the same mountain: that is the prevalent view today among people who do not think deeply about the subject.

We are to have nothing to do with syncretism. The first Christians were insistent on this score. Indeed, it was no new problem for them: it was present in the eighth century BC with the seductive alternatives to Yahweh worship provided by Caananite worship. It is what the prophets like Hosea were always inveighing against. Yahweh is not one in a supermarket of gods. He is the Almighty, the One, and he brooks no rival.

It was the same with Jesus in Acts. People would have been very happy to include him among highly respected teachers, but once his ultimate claims came to be recognised, the opposition was fierce. And so it was in the Acts. You do not have to go beyond chapter 4 to find it. 'This is the stone rejected by you builders, which has become the head of the corner. And there is salvation in no one else, for there is no other name under heaven given among men by which we must be saved (4:11-12). 'Greek has two different words for 'other'. Both are used in this verse. There is no *additional way*. There is no *alternative way*. Christ is *the* way to salvation.

This looks very narrow-minded. Why should there be no other way? Because nobody else brought God into our world in human form. Because nobody else took personal responsibility for the evil of which the whole world was guilty. And because nobody else ever rose to new life from the cold depths of a tomb, three days after interment. That is why. The disciples did not go round casting aspersions on other expressions of religious faith. They did, however, point to Jesus as the only way in which God has fully come to man, and the only way by which man can fully come to God and know him as Father. It may well be, and they would not deny it (any more than their second century followers denied it) that God would save many people who had never heard of Jesus. After all, that is what happened with the patriarchs. But they would maintain, and did maintain even to their dying breath, that any such are saved because of Jesus, his incarnation, his death and his resurrection. There was a radical particularity about them which did not make them popular in religious circles. And so it is still. There is nothing which makes religious people more angry than ultimate claims for the supremacy of Jesus Christ. Yet that is what we must do if we are his followers. There is no possibility of compromise on the matter. And therefore religious opposition is always likely to befall those who, in whatever country or circumstance, maintain the deity and all-sufficient atonement of the Messiah Jesus.

Cynicism

Like the first Christians, we are sure to encounter cynicism. And cynicism from intellectuals brings its own type of hardship. It did to Paul at Athens. He was distressed by the idolatry of the place, so he began arguing about Jesus both in the synagogue and in the market place, only to be met by the cold water of cynicism. 'What would this babbler say?' is the derisory enquiry of the philosophers of the day (17:18). 'He seems to be a preacher of foreign deities' – these of course were utterly beneath the contempt of the Athenians! Their approach was riddled with arrogance and cynicism, and that is painful to endure. Cynicism plays the game intellectually, but never gets involved. Paul's way of handling this corrosive attitude was highly original: 'The times of your ignorance (a wounding touch to Athenians!) God overlooked, but now he commands all men everywhere to repent, because he has fixed a day on which he will judge the world in righteousness by a man whom he has appointed, and of this he has given assurance to all men by raising him from the dead' (17:30). God does not suggest repentance; he commands it. It is essential for everyone, not everyone except philosophers. What an aggressive approach! But that is often the only way to pierce through cynicism. Paul told these cynical intellectuals that they were culpable, that they would be judged and condemned unless they changed their attitude and put their trust in Jesus. No doubt they laughed him to scorn. So he continued, in effect (v 31), 'Very well, you do not believe me? God has given you evidence to back his command to repent. And that evidence is "a man". That man is different from all others. For God has raised him from the dead. That is how you may be sure that judgment awaits you, unless you repent and claim his proffered mercy.' What Paul is doing is to argue from one highly improbable event in the past to another in the future. They do not see the need of repentance. They do not believe the reality of judgment. But it is as certain as the resurrection. The 'man' whom God raised from the dead will be the judge of all men and all actions at the end of time. A very powerful way to break through the walls of apathy, cynicism and intellectual pride, and one which is as effective today as it was then in that self-centred intellectual capital of the world. A direct frontal assault is often best.

Ask the cynics what good they have done, what change of direction has been fuelled by their attitude, what benefit to others, what relief of social conditions and hunger. Such a challenge may take the breath away, but it cuts through the intellectual cobwebs of those who love to play with ideas but do little or nothing for anyone else. It is often an effective approach. It was partially successful at Athens.

Anger
A sixth thing which will be sure to come our way, as it did the first Christians, is the anger of others. And that produces its own pressures. Saul of Tarsus, a leading anti-Christian, has become a believer (ch 9). Such a thing always causes wrath. My predecessor at St Aldate's Church in Oxford ministered during the heyday of humanism in the university. And he regularly led the president of the Humanist Society to Christ! It happened year after year. The fury in the ranks of the humanists was intense. So it was among the Jews when Saul was converted. 'When many days had passed the Jews plotted to kill him' (v 23). Expect such a reaction. It is very natural. And be sure to protect the new believer who will be the main target of their anger, as the disciples did Saul. They cared for him, and secured his escape down the town wall in a basket. Saul needed that security, that care and then that time of quiet preparation before his ministry exploded. He would not have had the success he did if the Damascus Christians had not reacted so wisely to the fury which his conversion produced among his erstwhile companions.

Provocation
Sudden provocation is also something which is likely to produce painful consequences. There is a sombre example of this in 23:1ff. Paul is facing the sanhedrin: 'Brethren, I have lived before God in all good

conscience until this day,' he claims. The sanhedrin might be excused for regarding that as a highly tendentious description of Paul's activities! And the high priest, Ananias, not surprisingly, 'commanded those who stood by to strike him on the mouth'. He lost his cool. And Paul lost his: 'God shall strike you, you whitewashed wall! Are you sitting to judge me according to the law and yet, contrary to the law, you order me to be struck?' Those who stood by said, 'Would you revile God's high priest?' and Paul, quick to attack, is also quick to retract his insult. 'I did not know, brethren, that he was the high priest.' Ananias was, in fact, a very unworthy holder of the office. Appointed in AD 47, he was a hot tempered character, according to Josephus, and it so happens that he died a very violent death, as Paul predicted. But that does not exonerate Paul for his loss of temper. He was sorely provoked, but he did not handle it well, and it led to an ugly scene in which there was some possibility of his being killed by the mob (v 10).

So often these things catch us on the raw when we are not walking closely with God. I suspect Paul was not in close touch that day. We can sense his contrition before God for a day that had not gone well and where he had suffered hardship largely because of his own wrong behaviour: 'The following night the Lord stood by him and said, "Take courage, for as you have testified about me at Jerusalem, so you must bear witness also in Rome"' (v 11).

Sustained opposition

Sustained opposition is something which we may well have to face. The believers at Damascus certainly had to put up with that from Saul of Tarsus (9:1). He was still breathing threats and murder against the disciples. It was a settled passion in his heart: he must kill these heretics. It led him to arms. It led him to the high priest for an order to arrest the Christians. It was a deep-seated hatred, and the infant church both felt and feared its force.

It is salutary to remember that this sustained opposition collapsed like a pack of cards when Saul was converted. It is often the case that those who appear most opposed to the gospel are actually very much nearer than we or they might suppose. The very vehemence of their opposition may well spring, as it did with Saul, from a bad conscience. He knew that the Christians were right about Jesus. He had known it since he held the clothes of Stephen's killers and had seen the glory in the martyr's face as he died and surrendered his spirit to the Lord Jesus. He knew – but he was not going to admit it to himself, or to anyone else. The very intensity of his opposition sprang from the battle royal that was going on inside him. When a person is under conviction of sin, he often hits out fiercely against anything that reminds him of God. And then, suddenly, he gives in, as Saul did, and everyone marvels at the change. This should encourage us to expect the conversion of our biggest opponents. It is often the way.

Hard times – from the church

Hard times from circumstances and from worldly society are to be expected, but hard times coming from churchpeople are a different matter. It is tough to bear. But it often has to be borne. It hits the first disciples in a number of ways.

Defection
In Acts 1 the church was hit by the defection of Judas, and they set about prayerfully seeking to replace him. It was a stunning blow. Nobody knows for sure what motivated Judas to defect. It could have been self will. It could have been financial greed. It could have been disappointment in Jesus who had not turned out to be the political Messiah he had hoped. At all events he fell away. It is always a very painful shock to the church when this happens. But when it does, it is important to be sure that it has not happened because of failure on the church's part. If that is the case, a humble and handsome apology is needed. If it is for some other reason, then prayerfully get up and go on, as the Twelve did.

Deceit
Hardship in the church sometimes comes from deceit. It came early to the disciples, with the terrible case of Ananias and Sapphira in chapter 5. There was no reason why this couple should have given up their money: the communalism of the early Christians was totally voluntary. But they wanted to be thought of as spiritual front runners, and deep in their hearts they were not. They deliberately tried to deceive their fellow believers by claiming they had shared all their belongings when they had done nothing of the sort. When this happens among prominent members of the church, and it does, Acts 5 gives us a clear prescription of what must be done. It must be exposed and cut out. Far too often the church limps along powerless because corruption and wrongdoing is rife in the administration or leadership of the church. God cannot and will not bless a church which is tolerating unconfessed sin.

Jealousy

Jealousy is a hardship you will have to face if God entrusts you with any measure of success. Peter found that the high priest and his colleagues were filled with jealousy (5:17). Sometimes it comes from among one's own fellow workers. It is an ugly phenomenon. If yours is the most lively church in town, do not expect to be popular among the other churches. Act with humility, gentleness and co-operation, and these things may minimise the jealousy. But it is very hard to root out (because it is so rarely confessed) and is very hard to bear. The way to avoid it is explained by Paul in 1 Corinthians 12: we Christians are to see ourselves as limbs in Christ's body, the church. It is his Spirit who distributes appropriate gifts to each member, so we have no reason to be proud of our gifts, or jealous of those given to others. Our task is to act responsibly with the gifts we have. Indeed, we can be thankful that we do not have more, for then we would be the more accountable! Both pride and jealousy are stupid, but in fallen human nature they occur!

Stress

Fourth, hardship often comes to a church through internal stress. It can be utterly crippling. There was stress in the Jerusalem church. It seemed that the Hebrew widows were being looked after, and the Hellenist widows, who spoke Greek and lived in a less overtly Jewish manner, were being neglected (6:1-7). That sort of thing speedily leads to division in a church. There was wonderful sharing, but inequitable distribution. 'What are these people from Cyrene doing here, taking bread out of our widows' mouths?' That is always the cry of the home community in the face of immigration. 'We have our own needs. We can't provide for these foreigners.' You hear it today when there is a suggestion in the church meeting to give more money to missions. But that is not the way the kingdom of God operates, and it is marvellous to see what the apostles did. They were utterly fair. They organised a group of seven to oversee the matter, all of whom had Greek names! How about that for generosity? Moreover, they handled it promptly. It is a telling example to us of the need to meet internal stress and the hard feelings it engenders with generosity and prompt action.

Conservatism

Excessive conservatism is another hard thing which may afflict the church. In Acts 6:11-15 we read that the Hellenists, and their leader Stephen, were suspect because they believed in a God who was on the

move, a Temple which was not a building but the body of Christ, and
a Jesus who was not merely a Jewish Messiah but the risen, reigning
Son of man with world dominion (just as Daniel 7:14 had foretold).

Today, too, there are a great many Christians who are addicted to
a particular building, a particular way of doing things, or a pattern of
worship laid down long ago in a book. In opposing every new advance,
they do nothing but bog a church down in protracted debate (warfare,
even) over secondary matters, while the primary purpose of worship
and love and partnership in the gospel is allowed to slide.

When faced with a mindless conservatism on secondary issues we
should explain that God is on the move, that he is (not was) the
God of Abraham, Isaac and Jacob. Stay wise, like Stephen (6:10).
Stay shining, like Stephen (6:15). Stay full of Spirit, like Stephen
(7:55). And stay forgiving, like Stephen (7:60). You may well fail,
as Stephen failed. But such a failure will be glorious, and may well
win over your opponents.

Legalism

A sixth pressure point on the church from within is legalism. If you
have never had this in your church you are fortunate indeed. We have
a prime example in chapter 15. All the parties involved are keen on
Christianity. That is not at issue. But the believers whose origins had
been in the Pharisee party said, 'It is necessary to circumcise them (i.e.
the Gentiles) and to charge them to keep the law of Moses' (15:5). If
these Gentiles were to be accepted Christ would not suffice: it must
be Christ *plus*. In their case it was Christ plus a lot brought over from
Judaism. In our case it is Christ plus the laying on of hands, Christ plus
speaking in tongues, Christ plus rebaptism, and so on. We multiply
our legalisms and call them orthodoxy. There is no flexibility about
us. We mistakenly believe we are being faithful. So did these first
Christians who came from the Pharisee party. But they were not
being faithful. They were being legalistic.

Once again, the apostles were given tremendous wisdom, from
which we can still profit. First, they allowed free and open debate.
Second, they stood firm on essentials. Third, they compromised on
inessentials. Fourth, they were happy to have variety in practice
among Gentile and Jewish Christians. Fifth, they were anxious for
love to reign and for fellowship not to be broken. What a brilliant
handling of legalism among the first Christians! And notice those
wonderful words commending Paul and Barnabas, who were major
negotiators in this crucial Council of Jerusalem: 'They are men who

have hazarded their lives for the Lord Jesus.' When people have a real credibility about their life, it makes an enormous difference to their effectiveness as negotiators in a situation like that.

One final tip from this passage. Get the agreement written down, minuted, and circulated, so that nobody can go away with a variety of interpretations of what happened!

False teaching

Another internal pressure on the church comes from false teaching. It is inevitable, and very unpleasant. Paul warns the Ephesian elders, 'I know that after my departure fierce wolves will come in among you, not sparing the flock; and from among your own selves will arise men speaking perverse things, to draw away the disciples after them' (20:29).

There are usually two main categories of false teaching. One comes from outside, from the 'wolves' who come in to tear the flock apart. The other comes from inside, as 'from your own selves men arise to draw away the disciples after them'. And there are often two characteristics among the endless variety of false emphases that continually arise. One is a schismatic tendency – 'to draw away disciples'. The other is a self-glorifying tendency 'after themselves'. Nearly always you find an egocentric personality at the heart of every new cult or wrongful emphasis, and often he or she becomes rich on it. Two good questions can be asked of those hawking a dubious position around the church. Is it schismatic? Is it linked with the prominence and the fame of some particular person? Glory should belong to the Lord, not to any man.

Paul warned his fellow leaders at Ephesus that they needed constantly to be alert about these things: they must 'take heed' (v 31). Never was that vigilance more constantly needed than today. Pernicious cults masquerade under a multiplicity of names in order to hide their true identity and to penetrate places where they would never be able to gain access if they flew under their own colours. We are certainly not called on to be heresy hunters, neurotic about the minutiae of false teaching. The Christian body can absorb and eject a good deal of poison, just as the human body can. But when self-improvement movements, covert Hinduism, modern forms of Gnosticism and pantheism assail the church – and they do – vigilance is the price of healthy growth.

Misunderstanding

An eighth pressure point within the church is misunderstanding. Paul

was wilfully misunderstood as defiling the temple by bringing Gentiles
into its holy courts (21:27f). He was actually expressing solidarity with
some Jewish Christians who were fulfilling a Nazirite vow which
culminated in making costly offerings in the Temple (vv 21-4). Paul
purified himself along with them and financed them, and nearly
got lynched for his trouble. It is ironic that he should have been
accused of defiling the Temple at a time when he was deliberately
undergoing ritual purification so that he would *not* defile the Temple!
And if we feel that this is an uncharacteristic thing for Paul to do,
remember I Corinthians 9:20. 'To the Jews I became a Jew that
I might win the Jews.' He had a deep consistency to the Lord
which often produced an apparent external inconsistency. And he
was dangerously misunderstood by those with smaller minds. What
he does, in this situation, is to explain what has been happening. He
does not get angry or argumentative in the face of misunderstanding,
multiple though that misunderstanding was. He was nearly killed
in the riot; then, rescued by the Roman tribune, he was wrongly
thought to be on the Roman 'Wanted' list (v 38). When he had cleared
up that matter of identity, he gained the opportunity to speak to
the crowd, and did so in their own language (v 40) making superb
use of Jewish history in his apologia. Unfortunately, he could not
resist telling them what was true, but neither necessary nor helpful
– that God had commissioned him to go to the Gentiles (22:21). It
was hardly the most tactful thing to say when arraigned for bringing
Gentiles into the Temple, but very characteristic of the fiery apostle!
Where the hardships of misunderstanding are strong, explain carefully,
but do not provoke gratuitously.

Unresolved tensions

Another way in which hard times assail a church is by age-long
tensions which have not been resolved. That was the situation with
the Samaritans in chapter 8, which we have already looked at. The way
in which that centuries-old apartheid was resolved is instructive. Jewish
Christians, who thought themselves in the strong position, took the
first step: they came to Samaria and laid hands upon those Samaritans
who had professed faith in Christ. They touched them, something
that neither nationality would tolerate outside of the reconciliation
they had experienced in Christ. They expressed a unity which wiped
out the hurts of the past and mirrored the free acceptance with which
God welcomed both parties. It was beautiful to see. It had marvellous
healing results. But it was very hard to do. It must have been just as hard

for Jewish Christians in chapter 15 to accept on equal terms Gentiles who had come to Jesus, without insisting on the supreme badge of Jewish particularity, circumcision. It was unbelievably magnanimous of them to do that, but they did. They did not allow these long-standing differences to lie buried; they brought them to the surface, like some wartime unexploded mine from long ago, and defused them.

So many churches suffer from these buried, unexploded mines. Bring them to the surface! It is a beautiful action, when you are being defamed by a couple in the church, to invite them to dinner with you. In the course of that meal a lot of the hassles can emerge and be dealt with – rather than coming out in cantankerous phone calls and polemical letters.

Hard times – from Satan

There is another major aspect to opposition which Acts reveals: direct assault from Satan. In Acts this generally comes through involvement in some form of the occult, but not exclusively so. It is plain from the way Luke records the hazards of the journey to Rome and the shipwreck, that he sees their arrival in the central city of the Empire as a triumph (notwithstanding their chains) which all the forces of nature and all the attacks of Satan could not prevent. But main instances of Satanic opposition come in chapter 8, where Simon amazed the Samaritans with his magic; chapter 13, where the magician Elymas gets more than he bargained for; chapter 16, where the Philippian slave girl was set free from a spirit which could predict the future; and chapter 19, where the sons of Sceva attempted an exorcism without being in touch with Christ, and unleashed a hornet's nest.

This element of the Christian battle is either down played almost to nothing by much of the contemporary church, or else exaggerated out of all proportion. We should never be surprised to find dark forces manifesting themselves, particularly in those who have deliberately pledged allegiance to Satan. If the local church does not believe it, the local police will be well aware of such people. We should never be surprised, but we should never go seeking to root out the occult. God will bring us face to face with what he wants dealt with at the right time. Then, like our exemplars in the Acts, we need to act firmly: 'resist the devil and he will flee from you' (James 4:7). It may need more than one session. It will be sure to involve a small team ministering together and another in the background praying. It may be a long battle. But he will leave. Satan is a defeated foe, and he cannot withstand the person and the cross of Jesus.

It is important not to allow this type of ministry to consume too much time. The way Paul handled the affair in chapter 16 shows that he simply wanted to get it out of the way so as to be free to proclaim the kingdom of God. He did not propose to set up in business as an exorcist. And we would be wise to follow his example. I know of few things that can be so consuming as preoccupation with a ministry of deliverance. Nevertheless, there will be occasional encounters with the demonic. Never look for it: but never fear when it comes your way, because in the name of Christ you will be victorious.

When the victory comes, it is important to clear up any association of the demonic infestation. In Acts we read that 'many who practised magic arts brought their books together and burned them in the sight of all: and they counted the value of them and found that it came to fifty thousand pieces of silver' (19:18f). Costly though it was, this clear break with the past was essential. Without it there would have been a return of the dark forces. I have often been involved in the clear-up of a house after evil spirits had been banished, or in destroying idols, rings and images used in satanic worship once the person concerned has been set free.

Some time ago a close colleague and I led a team in a town mission and came across a woman in one of the meetings who was deeply involved in every imaginable form of the occult. She was in a terrible state, gashing her private parts with razor blades and on the brink of suicide. She had round her neck a talisman that had been there for thirty-two years. It was plain, as we tried to help her, that the talisman was crucial to her being set free. It was some three hours before she was willing to let it go, and to entrust her life to Christ. In the middle of the night we broke it from her neck and threw it into the river. The change in the woman was immediate and wonderful. Next morning we went to clear up the occult paraphernalia in the house where she lived. We found her parents in the sitting-room, so utterly amazed by what they had seen of change in their daughter that both of them knelt and entrusted themselves to this mighty Lord Jesus who has such mighty power to transform crippled lives. That was a very first-century situation!

Hard times – from ourselves

There is one final area from which hard times come: yourself. You and I are the biggest obstacles to our growth in spiritual stature. Like the golfer who was asked his handicap, our reply must be 'Myself'. In 20:28 Paul urges his friends at Ephesus, 'Take heed to yourselves.' *Prosechete*, cries Paul. Take heed, beware! It is a vital theme. We are encouraged to take heed of the Scriptures (2 Pet. 1:19). We must take heed to our discipline (1 Tim. 3:8), and take heed that there is no occult material in our lives (1 Tim. 4:1). Plenty of people in Christian ministry are indisciplined in the areas of food and sex, drink, sleep and exercise. Plenty have ceased to read and personally apply the Scriptures, and some are involved with negative spiritual forces. It is all too easy to drift into these things unless we take heed.

Take heed, says Scripture, to your public teaching (1 Tim. 4:13f): many preachers do not work at it – hence the decline of preaching in our day. We are warned to take heed that we do not simply have externals in religion (Matt. 6:1). Take heed, says Jesus, that you are authentic, not a sheep on the outside and a ravenous wolf within (Matt. 7:15). Take heed that there is no double life in you (Luke 12:1), and that you do not lead others astray by what you allow yourself (Luke 17:3). Take heed that you are not among the status seekers, looking for recognition and promotion, like the Pharisees (Luke 20:46). Take heed that worldliness and loss of zeal do not find you eating and drinking and living a careless life on the day when Jesus comes again (Luke 21:34). Take heed to the way you judge other people (Acts 5:35). These many practical warnings should help us to avoid the pitfalls to which our fallen nature makes us prone, and to grow in the likeness of our Lord. It is with ourselves that we shall have the longest and bitterest battle. We must watch ourselves like hawks.

A remarkable outcome

Hard times will come. But before we leave this study of opposition in Acts, it is worth glancing at the sequel. What came out of hard times to which the Christians were subject? There were at least three important results.

First, they were able to preach in the sanhedrin to the council of seventy-one elders of their nation. They would not have got in otherwise, nor could they expect sanhedrin members to attend their meetings. But through this uncomfortable experience they were privileged to address the whole leadership of the nation. It often happens that, through hardship, God brings us into a position of opportunity we would never have dreamed possible.

Secondly, they won popular sympathy (4:21). Many became Christians (4:4) – the numbers had swollen to five thousand very speedily. There was popular support, and lasting fruit. This has often been the case in the history of the church. Hardship has brought a surge of feeling for the oppressed believers, and this in turn has led to people being so impressed that they have joined the family of God. As Tertullian observed long ago, 'the blood of the martyrs is seed: and the more you mow us down, the more we grow'. If we take the hard knocks with love, gentleness and humour, then we will find a degree of popular support, and some of that will crystallise into new believers.

A third result from that opening bout of persecution was that the whole church was purified and strengthened. There was a new boldness, a new depth of fellowship, a new impetus to prayer, a new experience of the Holy Spirit, and newly refined characters. All this is plain from chapter 4. They were purged of materialistic tendencies. They bore testimony to Jesus with great power, and there was a lot of mutual encouragement. If you talk with Christians from Eastern Europe, where there has been systematic persecution of Christians for decades, you will not find that they want to change places with us in the West and acquire our material benefits. They have been refined by their hardships to a quality of spirituality of which we know little, but which must bring them close to the suffering Saviour's heart.

These three results often come in the wake of opposition. Good reason, then, to 'count it all joy when you meet various trials, for you know that the testing of your faith produces steadfastness. And let that steadfastness have its full effect, that you may be perfect and complete, lacking nothing' (James 1:2).

We are called to be disciples. And for us, as for our Master, it will mean a mixture of joy and pain, endurance and delight. It cannot possibly be easy. Jesus is looking for disciples who can face and overcome hard times, from whatever source they come. There is a famous saying of Jim Elliott, who was martyred as a missionary to the Auca Indians in 1956. He said, as he reflected on the cost as well as on the glory of the Christian life. 'He is no fool who gives what he cannot keep, to gain what he cannot lose.'

13

What of the Holy Spirit?

The significance of the Holy Spirit

Let us begin at the beginning. And in the very beginning, the Spirit of God brooded over the face of the emerging cosmos (Gen. 1:2). That same Spirit progressively began to make himself known to man. The Hebrews had a perfectly good word for the human spirit, *nephesh*, but they did not use that word for God's Holy Spirit. Instead they used a very strong word, *ruach*. It denotes the breath, the wind, the Spirit of God.

Centuries before Christ, God began to reveal himself by his Spirit to the prophets. There is a strong link in the Old Testament between the word of the Lord and the Spirit of the Lord (e.g. 2 Sam. 23:2). The Spirit is not only God's creative power, but his self-disclosing word, which breaks in on particular people in Old Testament times, particularly on prophets, on kings, and on special men anointed for a particular mission. Think of the Spirit of the Lord coming upon Samson, for example, and making him unbelievably strong; or on Bezaleel, and making him a marvellous craftsman; or on a king like Saul or a prophet like Samuel.

But if you look carefully at the Old Testament teaching on the Spirit you will find three characteristics. The first is that the Spirit of the Lord was limited to certain people. The king might have the Spirit, but his maidservant would not. The great prophet might have the Spirit, but not an ordinary person like you and me.

The second is that in Old Testament days the Spirit of the Lord was fitful in his manifestation. He could be withdrawn. He *was* withdrawn from Samson and from Saul, when they gave themselves over to disobedience.

The third is that in the Old Testament the Holy Spirit was disclosed as sub-personal power. There was little to suggest that this power was personal.

Those were three disadvantages to the Spirit in the Old Testament: he was restricted to special people, he was fitful, and he was perceived as sub-personal. And by the end of the Old Testament period there was an even greater disadvantage. He was seen as past history. After the last of the prophets, the Holy Spirit was not in evidence in Israel. The Temple had been rebuilt, but there was no *shekinah* glory residing in it, as there was in the first Temple of Solomon. Similarly, the Spirit of God appeared to have retired from human affairs, and you had to make do with the *bath qol*, the 'daughter of the voice', a second-hand substitute for the Spirit of God.

However, the prophets, notably Joel, Ezekiel and Jeremiah, were clear that in the end-time the Spirit of the Lord would come again, and would be widely disseminated. In Jesus Christ it happened. And Luke is at pains to bring this out. He does so in various ways, particularly by mentioning the Holy Spirit a great deal. It is very noticeable in the beginning of his Gospel: the Spirit in Simeon, in Anna, in Mary and Elizabeth, surrounds the coming of Jesus, because Jesus is the man 'full of the Spirit' (Luke 4:1). That Spirit which surrounded his birth and early days was concentrated upon him at his baptism. John picks up the image from Isaiah 11:2 about the Spirit resting on the Servant, and makes it plain that this took place precisely at the baptism of Jesus (1:32). There is nothing fitful here: the Spirit made his home in the incarnate Christ. And instead of the second Temple where there was no *shekinah* glory, John maintains that Jesus 'templed' among us, and in him we beheld God's glory (John 1:14). There is an important link between these three concepts: the new temple consisting of Jesus' body, the Spirit of the Lord, and God's glory.

Thus the Spirit, widely diffused in the Old Testament, was concentrated in the person of Jesus while he was on earth. He was the man full of the Spirit. He was the ultimate king, the ultimate prophet, the ultimate servant of Yahweh – all three roles that had been marked by the Spirit in the Old Covenant. All were concentrated in Jesus – that is why we hear so little of the Spirit while Jesus was on earth.

What, then, happened at Pentecost? Simply this. The three restrictions of Old Testament days were wonderfully removed. The Spirit became available to one and all. He was now recognised as personal; he was not naked power, but marked with the lineaments of Jesus of Nazareth (Acts 16:7). And he would never be withdrawn:

he would remain with God's people both individually and corporately until the end of the age (15:8).

That is not only a wonderful fulfilment of Old Testament indications. It is also an important corrective to some current misconceptions about the Spirit. For it reminds us that the Spirit is always the Spirit of Jesus. He is the touchstone of what can properly be understood of the Holy Spirit.

Jesus is the touchstone of the Spirit in *religion*. The task of the Spirit is to bear witness to Jesus. We should not regard anything as the teaching of the Spirit if it does not relate credibly to the life and teaching of Jesus, the man full of the Spirit.

Jesus is the touchstone of the Spirit in *doctrine*. You will often find doctrines ascribed to the Spirit which by no stretch of the imagination could hold good of Jesus. The Mormons are a case in point. They go with quite a lot of Christian teaching, though Jesus sometimes gets short shrift; but they claim that a further revelation by the Spirit was made on gold tablets to Joseph Smith many centuries later. That cannot match up with the touchstone of Jesus. It is important, not least in these days when interest in the Spirit is high, never to believe anything that is claimed of the Spirit which cannot equally be claimed for Jesus. The Holy Spirit does not 'speak of himself', Jesus said. He glorifies Jesus (John 15:26, 16:13f).

Furthermore, Jesus must be the touchstone of the Spirit in *behaviour*. We are prohibited, as Christians, from regarding any form of behaviour as normative which cannot be demonstrated as part of the lifestyle of Jesus.

We could take all this much further. I have tried to do so in my book *I Believe in the Holy Spirit*. The Spirit assured Jesus of his Sonship, commissioned him for servanthood, and equipped him for witness. All those strands are evident in his baptism as recorded both in Matthew and Luke. And when you have made due allowance for the fact that we are not Christ, those same three roles await the Christians. The Spirit assures us of sonship: he enables us to cry 'Abba, Father' (Gal. 4:4). The Spirit commissions us for costly servanthood. The Spirit gives us power for witness, just as he did to Jesus. All this began with Jesus, and spread to his followers. And Luke picks that up. Acts 4:14 stresses that the ministry of Jesus was exercised in the power of the Spirit, while Acts 1:2, 5, 8 indicates that this is precisely the calling of the church. The Gospel of Luke shows what God began to do through his servant and anointed witness, Jesus, equipped with the power of the Holy Spirit. The Acts shows what God continued to do through his servants, his anointed witnesses, equipped with the power of that same Spirit. Such is the major significance of God's Holy Spirit.

The Birthday of the church

Why Pentecost?

At one level the church began with Abraham. He was the father of the faithful. At another, it began with Jesus, who called the first disciples to come, follow him. But it is no less true to see the birthday of the church as the day of Pentecost, when God's Spirit fell on the disciples to equip them for their world mission.

But why should the Spirit have fallen on that particular day? Here are five reasons.

First, Pentecost was the first great feast of the Jews after Passover. Jesus had died at Passover time. More than a million Jews would converge on Jerusalem for the great feasts. If, in the strategy of God, a new thing needed to be, the feasts were the time to do it. Leviticus 13:15 tells us that Pentecost is fifty days after Passover. It was one of the two Jewish harvest festivals a year. Therefore it was a highly appropriate day to mark the first 'harvest' of people into the kingdom of God. Perhaps this is part of what Jesus had in mind when, in John 4:35, after bringing the Samaritan woman to faith, Jesus speaks of the harvest waiting for reaping. And now, through his spirit, Jesus brings 3000 people on one day into the family of God. Pentecost is the beginning, the first fruits, of the harvest.

Second, at Pentecost the Jews celebrated the giving of the Law to Moses by God on Mount Sinai. They deduced this from Exodus 19:1. One of the rabbis put it like this: 'The feast of weeks (i.e. Pentecost) is when the Torah was given.' That is very significant. The trouble about the Law is that it was external to us. But Jeremiah had looked forward to the day when it would be interiorised. God would put his law within their hearts (Jer. 31:33). How appropriate, then that the coming of the Spirit should fall on the day when they celebrated the coming of the Torah! Here is no external Law given by Moses, but an internal power and motivation given by God within the heart of the believer. That is something Paul revels in in 2 Corinthians 3:3f.

Third, the giving of the Spirit at Pentecost may have been particularly appropriate because of the ascension theme. Moses had ascended Mount Sinai in order to receive the Torah. Jesus had ascended on high in order to receive and distribute to longing hearts the gift of the Spirit (2:33, cf Eph. 4:7ff). The ascended Christ had poured out what the participants on the day of Pentecost could see and hear.

There is a fourth reason. The rabbis had an illuminating myth that Moses proclaimed the Torah in the seventy languages which were believed to belong to the entire world, as if to say 'This is God's universal will for mankind.' How fitting, therefore, that on the day when the Spirit is given you find representatives gathered together from all over the known world amongst whom the Jews were dispersed. It is as if God is saying, 'Here is something for everybody.'

Finally, only Jews received the Torah. But the Spirit is for all, as Joel had foretold (see Acts 2:17). What better day, then, for God to send his Spirit than the day when the Jews celebrated the gift of the Torah? This fits in precisely with the missionary purpose of Acts.

There are no certain ways of discerning why God sent his Spirit at Pentecost: it lay within his own purpose and discretion. But these are five reasons why Pentecost might have commended itself as the most appropriate time.

Tongues at Pentecost?

The traditional understanding of the tongues given to the disciples at Pentecost is that they were miraculously enabled to speak in many different languages which they had never learnt. If this is so, and it may be, the gift could mark the first stage in the progressive launching of the new movement. For there are three, possibly four, places in Acts where tongues are mentioned in outreach situations. The first is in Jerusalem. The second is in Caesarea with Cornelius (10:46f). The third is in Ephesus, the centre of Greek culture (19:1ff). The same may well have happened in Samaria: this is hinted but not stated (8:16f). Jews, Samaritans, Godfearers, Greeks: a possible progression. If so, we have a very interesting thing. Tongues are mentioned (or implied) at four critical places, and four only, in the unfolding story of the Acts: when Christianity was launched among the Jews, then in Samaria, then among the adherents on the edge of the synagogue, then among those living in the heart of Greek culture. It would be possible to argue, if you believe that these 'tongues' are human languages, that God equipped the early Christians at those four points with a signal mark of his blessing and his presence. It could be seen as the curse of Babel lifted once and for all. Mankind had tried to reach up to God by building a great ziggurat or tower in early Old Testament days. God demolished this instrument of human arrogance, and a babel of voices ensued. The peoples of the earth were unable to co-operate because of the discrete languages of the world; but with the coming of the Spirit in tongues at Pentecost, Babel is reversed. Instead of man trying to reach up to God, God's Spirit comes down to man.

However, there is no hint of tongues being a human language in the incidents involving Cornelius, the Samaritans or the folk at Ephesus. A foreign language was not even necessary: all of them could speak Greek. When Peter 'standing with the eleven lifted up his voice' and addressed the mixed multitude at Pentecost (2:14f) he set out to explain the apparently drunken-sounding utterance of his companions. He would have had no difficulty in making himself understood if he used Greek or Aramaic: they would all have been able to speak Greek, the common language of antiquity, and most of them, being Jews, could speak Aramaic.

It seems to me most probable therefore, that Peter gave his sermon in Greek, and that the tongues-speaking was *glossalalia*: the praising of God in a language given by the Spirit but not normally understood by the person speaking, unless God adds a further gift, that of interpretation. If so, it is not surprising that people thought them drunk. I recall the first time I heard people praising God in tongues; I felt it was very weird! And if it was indeed *glossalalia* into which the Twelve were plunged on the day of Pentecost, it would not be intended for communicating with the crowd (which Peter would do in Greek) but for expressing a love and gratitude to God beyond the level which ordinary language could carry. There was nothing unique to the early church about this outpouring of glossalalia: it happens widely throughout the world church today.

What, then, was the miracle at Pentecost, apart from the wonderful outpouring itself? Surely the gift of interpretation which God gave to the crowd. 'We hear, each of us in his own native language . . . we hear them telling in our own tongues the mighty works of God' (2:8, 11). It was a miracle of *hearing*, of interpretation. The apostles celebrated (in vocabulary they could not understand but which was inspired by the Spirit) the mighty works of God, supremely no doubt the coming, the death and the resurrection of Jesus, along with the glorious power of the Spirit which was being shed upon them.

The rabbis used to say of the original gift of the Law on Sinai, 'The law was given with a single sound, yet all received it in their own languages' (*Tanchuma* 26c). That is just what, I believe, was happening at Pentecost. The Twelve praised God in tongues, and the multitude understood, each in his own language, what this signified. They knew these strange people were praising God for his mighty works. The giving of the Spirit came to these first Christians as the Law came to Moses; and it has universal significance in the new covenant just as the Law did in the old. The gift of tongues at Pentecost is a mark of the universality of the gospel.

The Spirit: God's strategy

In his lifetime, Jesus had foreseen three things that would happen before the end of the age (Mark 13:9-13). First he predicts tough times: there will be trials, betrayals and ecological devastation. Second, it will be the time for mission: the gospel will be preached to all the nations. And third, it will be the time of the Spirit: he will inspire and carry home the witness given by the Christians. These three strands are interwoven.

In John 15:26-16:2 something very similar emerges. The Spirit will come and bear witness. The disciples too will bear witness: such is the call of the church. And there will be tough days ahead: believers will get thrown out of the synagogue, and even martyred. Hardship, witness, the Spirit – the same three strands are interwoven.

We find the same in Acts 1:6-9: witness-bearing as the primary task of the church, the Spirit as the enabling gift, and (as the story unfolds in the rest of the Acts), constant hard times.

So the time between Jesus' first coming and his return is not empty. It is full of the Holy Spirit and mission. They belong together. And the context in which they happen is one of opposition and hardship. Through the Spirit and mission the kingdom is demonstrated to the world before the return of the King. The Spirit and the church belong together, but it is noteworthy in Acts that the Spirit always takes the lead. The church can only live by evangelising, and by following the paths that the Spirit indicates. It was not the church leaders who decided on an evangelistic campaign. It was an ex-Pharisee, converted through opposing them, who was the main agent in that outreach under the prompting and the power of the sovereign Spirit of God. Hardship was inevitable; the Acts and his own letters give us a glimpse of the tremendous cost.

Such is the divine strategy. And as we look at the ineffectiveness of many churches today, I wonder if we have not reneged on each of those intertwined strands. We do not expect leading from the Spirit and do not trust it when it happens. We are very reluctant to bear any sort of witness to Jesus. And we are most unwilling to bear any kind of obloquy and hardship, criticism and abuse for the name of Jesus. If

we implicitly deny the three power lines God has intertwined, can
we be surprised when little progress is made?

Baptism in the Holy Spirit

In chapter 9 we looked in detail at the whole area of Christian
initiation, and how the Holy Spirit plays a part in it. We saw that
there are three elements to Christian initiation – baptism, repentance
and faith, and the giving of the Spirit. Different Christian traditions
have tried to separate out or over-emphasise what Luke insists is a
threefold rope that binds us to Christ. But here I want to tackle
another controversial subject which has been much to the fore in
recent years, the baptism 'in' or 'with' the Holy Spirit. What does
it mean? Is it always accompanied by tongues? Is it a second experience after baptism in water?

There are seven New Testament references, and seven only, to
baptism in the Holy Spirit. Four of them are the Gospel accounts of
the prediction of John the Baptist, that whereas he baptised in water,
the coming one would baptise in the Holy Spirit (Mark 1:8, Luke
3:16, Matt. 3:11, John 1:33). The preposition uniformly used is *en*,
a little word that can mean 'in', 'with', or 'by' in Hellenistic Greek.
Those therefore who affect to discover some difference between being
baptised in the Holy Spirit and being baptised by him simply display
their ignorance of Greek usage!

In addition to these four references to the forthcoming baptism
in the Spirit at the hands of Jesus, there are three more. One of
them comes in Acts 1:5 where Jesus quotes the Baptist's prophecy,
and applies it unambiguously to Pentecost. The disciples will soon
discover what it means to be baptised with the Spirit, 'before many
days'. The sixth instance comes in Acts 11:16. Once again the very
same prediction is to the fore: 'John baptised with water but you shall
be baptised with the Holy Spirit.' Peter is speaking, and explaining his
astonishing time with Cornelius. 'And as I began speaking,' he said,
'the Holy Spirit fell on them, just as on us at the beginning.' The
sixth reference is also, therefore, related to an initiatory experience.
Cornelius and his household entered the realm of the Spirit just as the
disciples had done at Pentecost, and precisely as John had predicted.

The last reference is in 1 Corinthians 12:13. 'By one Spirit we were
all baptised into one body,' writes the apostle; Jews or Greeks, slave
or free, it made no difference. This was the indispensable beginning
of Christianity for one and all. Does this seventh reference teach

something different from the combined testimony of the other six? The answer must be that it does not. There is no suggestion here that this was a second, high-octane experience into which some Corinthians had entered and others had not. Quite the reverse. The Corinthians had written to Paul about spiritual gifts (12:1). The 'charismatics' among them were only too keen that Paul should accede to their own high view of themselves and their spiritual giftedness, and their superiority to the ordinary Christians at Corinth. But Paul does nothing of the kind. Instead, he maintains fiercely that *all* the Corinthians had been baptised by the Spirit into the one body of Christ. Not several communities: one body. Not several levels: one baptism. It must have been hard for the 'gifted' Corinthians to accept that they were on precisely the same level as everyone else. It must have been very encouraging to those who had felt put down. After all, the ground is level at Calvary; none of us has anything to boast about. We are accepted into the family – or baptised into the body – simply and solely on the ground of what Jesus Christ has done for us.

There is therefore no possible justification, among those who take the New Testament as their guide, in claiming biblical support for a doctrine of 'second blessing', a mandatory further experience after conversion called the baptism in the Holy Spirit. In each of the seven references, the phrase 'baptism with the Spirit' is unambiguously used of an initial plunging into Christ. It is not talking of the higher reaches of Christian experience, but about the basics of being a Christian. It is not always that we can be so sure about a controversial issue: but in this case the language used of baptism with the Spirit admits of no other conclusion.

But having established that according to the New Testament it is incorrect to speak of any second Christian experience as 'baptism in the Holy Spirit', we still have not settled the matter. For the Pentecostals and their charismatic cousins (among whom I would humbly count myself) may be wrong in their nomenclature, but right in what they are expecting to see in Christian experience. A great many Christians *do* have a notable second milestone in their lives, when they experience the reality of Jesus, the power and love of his Spirit, and receive one or more spiritual gifts in an entirely new way.

It is often so real and so exuberant that it makes any previous Christian experience seem grey or positively unreal. It is this sudden turning on of the lights in a twilight room which has encouraged some to regard 'baptism in the Spirit' as a second stage of Christian initiation. And that is very understandable. It does not help in the least if those who have no such passion for Christ seek to pour cold water on the Pentecostals' biblical exegesis; we need to hear the Pentecostals when they expect to see radical change in Christian lives, passionate courage in spreading the word, burning love and self sacrifice, and faith that God will act naturally and supernaturally as his people venture out in evangelism, deliverance ministry and healing.

Normal Christian birth does embrace the baptism in water, the repentance and faith, and the powerful and discernible presence of the gift of the Spirit. But it is true, is it not, that our faith is often so dim, our expectancy so low, our ignorance about the Spirit so great, our fear of committing ourselves to anything challenging so strong, that many of us have had a *subnormal* Christian birth, and an anaemic Christian experience? And it may be that what we need is a major injection of the Holy Spirit into those bloodless lives of ours. I believe that with all my heart. This breaking out of the Spirit in our life, this irrigation of our dry desert with his water is a paramount necessity in many parts of the church. But let us not make the mistake of allowing the change from subnormal to normal Christian living to create a necessary doctrine of initiation in two stages. Sometimes it comes in two stages. But such need not be the case. When I lead someone to Christ these days I lay my hands on his or her head and pray that the Spirit of God will deeply and fully baptise the new believer into Christ. We need Christians like that today, full-blooded Christians, not ecclesiastical ghosts. Baptism in the Spirit is the common lot of all Christians. Nowhere in the New Testament are *Christians* told to wait for it, or to seek it, or to receive it. In his booklet *The Baptism and Fullness of the Holy Spirit* John Stott expressed it judiciously: 'The gift or baptism of the Holy Spirit, one of the distinctive blessings of the new covenant, is a universal blessing for members of the covenant, because it is an initial blessing . . . Further, baptism in water is the sign and seal of baptism in the Spirit, as much as it is of the forgiveness of sins.'

The fullness of the Holy Spirit

If baptism is the initial experience, fullness should be the continual state of Christians, though all too often it is not. Those who are real Christians are never told to be baptised in the Spirit. That has already happened. But they *are* told to be filled with the Spirit. On the day of Pentecost the disciples were both baptised and filled with the Spirit. The baptism was complete, unrepeatable and inalienable. But the filling could be both lost and regained. That distinction is very important. You and I can resist the Spirit of God (Acts 7:51). We can grieve the Spirit (Eph. 4:30). But when we return, in repentance, trust and obedience, we can be filled afresh with the Holy Spirit. I have been filled hundreds of times, and hundreds of times I have run dry. This is not a once-and-for-all experience, but a constant offer from a generous, renewing God. It is very like the two sacraments Christ left us. Baptism is unrepeatable and marks the once-and-for-all aspect of our salvation: Communion is to be constantly repeated and marks the ongoing side of the Christian life. We need not only the once-and-for-all baptism with the Spirit, but the continuous being filled with him.

Thus it is made very clear in the Acts that Christians should be filled with the Spirit, as Jesus was (Luke 4:1). The disciples were all filled at Pentecost (2:1ff). Subsequently Peter was filled afresh with the Spirit (4:8) although he had recently been filled with that self-same Spirit on the day of Pentecost. He needed another filling for taking on the sanhedrin – so would you! Stephen, equally (6:5) was a man who is described as full of the Spirit, and he needed to be in view of what he was going to have to face. Saul of Tarsus (9:17) was filled with the Spirit for the ministry which God called him to. The seven, often known as deacons, were chosen because they were men full of the Spirit (6:3). On occasion we are told that the whole church was filled with the Spirit (13:52).

But what are the characteristics of those who are filled with the Spirit? When Peter needs divine courage to go and speak before the sanhedrin he is said to be filled with the Spirit (4:8). When Christians are engaged in really united prayer (4:31) they are said to be filled with the Spirit. Administrators in humble social work can be filled with the Spirit (6:3). When Christians are encouraged and built up to lead a holy life, they, too, are said to be filled with the Holy Spirit (9:31). When a good man rejoices with single-hearted delight to see God at work in others, as Barnabas did (11:24), that is a sign that he is full of the Spirit of God. And when disciples under difficult social conditions are filled with exultation, then that too is an expression of being filled with the Spirit (13:52). But equally, when you are calling God to act in judgment against an evil man like Elymas you need to be filled with the Spirit or else the whole thing could grievously backfire (13:9).

Being filled with the Spirit, then, is neither the monopoly of the 'charismatics' nor the 'non-charismatics'. Nobody has a monopoly in this area. Luke, with his glorious balance, will give joy under persecution as a mark of being filled with the Spirit: equally the

supernatural judgment wrought on Elymas through Paul was a mark
of being filled with the Spirit. One was 'charismatic', the other not.
We are limbs on one body, and we need each other.

So we should beware of dividing Christians into the ordinary
run-of-the-mill sort, and those who are 'Spirit-filled'. That is not
New Testament language, nor is it real. However often we may be
filled, we soon need filling again. We evaporate. We leak. We need
refilling. And what is more, we Christians are often filled with spirits
and attitudes which are very far from the Spirit of God, however
greatly we may have been used beforehand. Being filled with the Spirit
is not a state we can claim as a permanent possession: it is a standing
call to us to come again and again to the Source and be filled afresh.

The Holy Spirit and tongues

Should all Christians speak in tongues? The answer of the Acts is,
I am convinced, an unambiguous 'No'. The suggestion that we
should is based on three verses alone: 2:4 when the first Christians did speak in tongues on the day of Pentecost, 10:46 when
Cornelius and his friends did, and 19:6 when the 'Ephesian dozen'
did.

Tongues is a gift from the good Lord to some people. He has
given it to me, and I am grateful for it. But as we have seen,
there is no suggestion in any of the initiation teaching of the New
Testament that it is the invariable mark of the presence of the Spirit.
Glossalalia accompanied the preaching of salvation in those three
instances, and perhaps others, including in Samaria. We have no
way of knowing how widespread it was. Indeed you could argue,
if you were so disposed, that all three of those references have little
to say to our condition. Acts 2:4 is not relevant, because we have
not journeyed with the Jesus of history and had to await the coming
of the Spirit. 10:46 is not apt for our situation because here the
point is that the Spirit was given to Gentiles as well as to Jews,
and the need for that lesson is past. And 19:6 does not speak to us
because these were Jews who believed under the old dispensation,
and were now receiving the benefits of the new age. That is an
unrepeatable situation. So from Acts one certainly cannot demonstrate
that all should speak in tongues.

But equally from Acts one *can* say that this is a real gift of the
Holy Spirit which he pours out on some of the Christian family,
just as he lavishes other gifts on different members. It is valuable

for starting us in prayer when we feel little appetite for it. It is valuable for lifting our hearts in praise and adoration. It is very helpful in spiritual warfare, especially when we are in the presence of dark spirits brought in by the occult. But let us not unchurch those who are given other gifts by the same Spirit. 'He distributes to all people severally as he wills' (1 Cor. 12:11). 'Are all apostles? Do all work miracles? Do all possess healing gifts? Do all speak with tongues?' asks the apostle (1 Cor. 12:29). The answer to these rhetorical questions is in each case a resounding 'No'!

The Holy Spirit in the church

There is a striking contrast between the Acts of the Apostles and the writings of Paul. In Paul the emphasis about the Spirit is more interior: it is for building up the believer in holiness and Christ-likeness. We are changed by the Spirit from one degree of glory (or Christ-reflectingness) to another (2 Cor. 3:18). In the Acts the Spirit is more concerned with the corporate life of the church. It is more external in its impact. It is more gift-centred. It is more concerned with the growth and expansion of the church than with the holiness of individuals within the church.

There was a great missionary to China many years ago, Hudson Taylor. His biography is in two volumes, *The Growth of a Soul* and *The Growth of a Work for God*. One could almost say that Paul's understanding of the Spirit is 'The Growth of a Soul', while Luke's is 'The Growth of a Work for God'. Neither is exclusive, but such are the major emphases in Paul and Luke.

When we look at how the Spirit operates in the Acts, it is exciting to see the effect upon believers.

First it is obvious that they were *thrilled to belong* (2:15–16). They were confident and joyful in this new experience of God that had opened up to them.

Then they were *keen to pray* (2:42, cf 4:31). Disciples and new converts alike were anxious to pray, once they experienced the coming of the Spirit. He is the great enabler of prayer when our own enthusiasm is low. He is, after all, given to us in order to enable us to pray (Rom. 8:26).

They were *bold to speak*. They had been the very reverse, but not when the Spirit came upon them. Now they were bold to preach in the streets (2:14), to preach to a beggar (3:1ff), and to preach before the town council (4:8ff). I wonder when one of us

last spoke in such situations! They were bold to speak in homes
and synagogues, as the Acts goes on to record, and the mixture of
conviction, boldness, and love had powerful effects and drew many
to Christ.

Fourth, they were *hungry to learn* (2:42). The converts devoted
themselves to the apostles' teaching. That always happens when the
Holy Spirit grips someone. There is a hunger to go deeper and to
learn more of the Lord and his ways.

They were *willing to give* (2:45). They even started capital tithing.
They found their purses opening up as wide as their hearts. This
was the work of the generous, free Spirit of God who had come
upon them and thawed their selfish instincts. As a result, they had
few financial problems, for these were shouldered by the whole
community, not just by a small generous minority in the church.
In many a church it is true that, despite appearances, there are no
financial problems: only spiritual problems!

They were also *longing to share* their hospitality (v 46), to share in
the Holy Communion, especially in homes (vv 42, 46). They shared
their goods (v 45). This loving to be together, this open hospitality is
a tremendously attractive mark of the Spirit's presence. I was speaking
once in Canada about the needs of international work carried on by the
church I then served. One of the people present, although she had no
funds that she could give, was so moved by this that she went out and
bought a salmon, cut it up small and barbecued it in a delightful,
relaxed supper party, made a profit on it, and then came along happily
the next morning with thirty dollars! That seems to me very much
the spirit of the early church, and it is something very beautiful for
God. It is a mark of the Spirit flooding a life.

Those are some of the qualities we find early in Acts when the
Spirit comes. There were tongues and healing and deliverance too,
but I have not mentioned them yet, for they are gifts of the Spirit
which may or may not be entrusted to us. But these qualities of joy,
boldness, prayer, generosity, hunger to learn, are universal indicators
of the presence of the Lord the Spirit. They are indispensable in
any church which seeks to grow.

Spiritual gifts

Whether you look at the Jewish mission led by Peter, the Hellenistic
mission led by Stephen, or the Gentile mission led by Paul, the Spirit
is active throughout the Acts, shedding his spiritual gifts widely among

the workers. It is instructive to examine the extent, purpose and conditions of these spiritual gifts.

The range of spiritual gifts

It is important not to construe the range of spiritual gifts too narrowly. Often one hears that there are nine gifts of the Spirit, no more and no less, and that they are all to be found in 1 Corinthians 12:7-11. The implication, further, is that unless you have one of these gifts you are an impoverished Christian. That is not the teaching of the New Testament. At Pentecost, as we see, there were tongues, boldness, prophetic insight – particularly insight into the meaning of the Scriptures (2:16ff), praise, prayer, fruit in conversions, unity, love, generosity, hunger for teaching, and more. There is no distinction made between gifts of the Spirit which would today be termed 'charismatic', such as tongues and prophecy, and the others. All came from the same Spirit. This distinction between 'charismatic' and 'non-charismatic' gifts (with the accolade going to the former) is quite unbiblical, and very damaging. Indeed, the word 'charismatic' is a misnomer, if applied to only some Christians. You cannot be a Christian at all without entering into God's *charisma*, which means his gracious gift. And nowhere is that more clearly stressed than in a famous verse, Romans 6:23, where we are told that the wages of sin is death, but that the *charisma*, the gracious gift of God, is eternal life. That is the heritage of every child of God. We need to be careful about misusing great biblical words like 'charismatic'. If we shrink them, we are guilty of excluding those whom God has included.

The purpose of spiritual gifts

The Acts gives us at least five explanations of why God lavishes spiritual gifts upon his children. I am sure that these five are not exhaustive, but they are certainly illuminating.

1. One reason for these gifts is *to confirm*: they are given to underline the spoken proclamation of Christians. In Iconium, Paul and Barnabas. 'they remained for a long time, speaking boldly for the Lord, who bore witness to the word of his grace, granting signs and wonders to be done by their hands', (14:3). The Elymas incident is another such occasion where a manifest miracle, given by God, confirmed the stand the apostles were taking (13:10-15). We read that 'the proconsul

believed when he saw what had occurred, for he was astonished at the teaching of the Lord'. He was not converted by the *miracle* of Elymas' blindness, but by the *teaching* of the Lord backed up by God's power at work. The miracle confirmed its message. These spiritual gifts in confirmation of the word could either be in judgment, as it was on Elymas, or in healing, as it was with the cripple of Lystra (14:8).

2. Spiritual gifts may be given *to evangelise*, and classically you see that in the case of Saul of Tarsus. First comes the direct divine intervention, as the Jesus he has been struggling so hard to avoid catches up with him and brings him to his knees on the Damascus Road. Second, there was Saul's blindness; when he got up, he could not see. Third came the dream, which drew a very reluctant Ananias to visit this erstwhile scourge of the church. Fourth was the restoration of Saul's vision. And fifth was the new birth and filling with the Holy Spirit (9:1-19). This last supreme gift of the Spirit transformed his whole life in the most graphic way. But these are five different spiritual gifts which were used in a very important evangelistic situation. And I have to say that I have seen more spiritual gifts in operation when I have been on missions and outreach campaigns than at any time in the normal run of the church's life. God seems particularly to send them when his followers seek to fulfil the Great Commission.

3. Sometimes these gifts are given to *demonstrate God's compassion*. That, I take it, explains the occasion when Paul was able to raise up from death through a terrible fall a young man called Eutychus who had fallen asleep in the apostle's lengthy sermon (20:9-11)! There is no suggestion that any deep theological reason lay behind that resuscitation: it was simply a lovely humanitarian act which prevented a pall of gloom and mourning ruining Paul's last night with his friends at Troas. Or think of Publius healed through Paul's agency of mercy and care (28:8-9). It was a spiritual gift exercised for a humanitarian cause.

4. Another purpose for these gifts was *to declare*. As in the Gospels, sometimes these miracles took place in order to demonstrate Jesus' Lordship over the power of the devil. We see this in a number of instances. Why is so much space given to account of Saul's shipwreck (27:27f)? Surely because Luke wants us to know that not all the forces of chaos (and the Hebrews certainly saw the sea in that light) can prevent God's purpose in bringing his foremost representative

to the heart of the Roman Empire, there to stand trial and bear witness before Nero. The devil himself cannot prevent the God-given shift of the Christian mission from the back streets of Jerusalem to the heart of the known world.

It is much the same with the liberation of demonised people (e.g. 16:18, 19:13-20). They are set free by the gift of the Spirit, and this is not only for their own benefit, though it includes that: it is to demonstrate the Lordship of Jesus over Satan.

I mentioned in a previous chapter the current movement from Hinduism to Christ in Fiji; it is being induced largely through the ministry of deliverance and healing, which declare the Lordship of Jesus.

5. A further purpose of these spiritual gifts was *to direct*. We have noticed how, in chapter 10, God made use of a double vision to lead the church in a new direction, towards the Gentile mission. The Lord also guided the community quite clearly by means of dreams. Paul is frustrated in various attempts to preach the gospel in areas where, for some undisclosed reason, opportunities did not open up (16:6-10). He and his friends were 'forbidden by the Holy Spirit to speak the word in Asia'. And then, one night, God guided Paul and his colleagues into a vital new direction through the dream of the man of Macedonia, calling for help. The entire European orientation of the gospel sprang from that incident, and it was launched by the spiritual gift of a vision in the night, directing the course of events. Again, in chapter 8, we find Philip is directed by a gift of knowledge or discernment (8:29). The Spirit nudges him to draw alongside this strange man, who stands reading the Scriptures in his chariot as it moved along the desert road. Highly improbable, but it was the right thing to do and it led to the founding of a church in Ethiopia. It only happened because Philip was obedient to the prompting, the inner whisper of the Spirit, which he could so easily have set aside as a meaningless hunch.

The Spirit uses promptings like this, and he does it to lead us in a direction we might not otherwise travel. We need to learn to listen for those whispers. God wants to guide us through them.

These are five purposes for which God gives us spiritual gifts. Happy the church that is open to receiving and profiting by them.

The conditions for spiritual gifts

Three things need to be said on the conditions for receiving these gifts. First, there is no suggestion in the Acts that they were restricted to the apostles or to a privileged minority of Christians. On the contrary, these gifts broke out from the day of Pentecost among the converts as much as among the Twelve. They were widely disseminated among Stephen, Agabus, the Hellenists, Paul, Ananias, Philip, Silas and Barnabas. But you did not need to be a famous Christian to have spiritual gifts: you might be one of the prophesying daughters of Philip, or one of the people converted from the streets in Corinth.

Second, it is important to remember that the distribution of spiritual gifts was not manipulated by man, but was in God's hands alone. He was the supreme arbiter of where and when particular gifts should be disseminated. People were not always delivered from prison. Some were. Some people were delivered from diseases of long standing, like the cripples of Jerusalem in chapter 3 and of Lystra in chapter 14; but Trophimus was left at Miletus sick, although Paul, if anyone, had gifts of healing. Some Christians had remarkable deliverances from death in the Acts but Stephen, James and many others were martyred. Humbling and perplexing though it is for rationalist human beings, we do not know the mind of God, nor are we clear why one is spared for a few further years of life and usefulness and another is not. We do, however, need to remember that Jesus is Lord; and if so, we must trust him through thick and thin, whether we can understand him or not. He may decide to give one of the spiritual gifts which will bring release in a particular situation; or he may, in his infinite wisdom, know that the gift is better withheld. He is the Lord of the gifts. We cannot and must not question his wisdom, but rather pray, trust and co-operate with whatever he does.

But, thirdly, there is something we can do to dig the ground for spiritual gifts to grow. The whole climate in the Acts was facilitated by prayer (4:30ff), awe (5:11-12), courageous outreach (8:6), hardship (think of the imprisonments, the stonings, the absence of medication) and expectant faith (3:1ff). When these things were present in men and women full of the Spirit, spiritual gifts were no exception: they were part of the normal run of Christian life. There are parts of the world where those conditions are fulfilled, and the same results are to be seen today. Why should it not happen with us?

Spiritual maturity

Acts makes it very plain that the mature Christian does not concentrate on gifts, but on the Giver. Transformation into the likeness of Jesus is God's supreme goal for us. To be full of the Spirit is to be Christlike. Love, generosity, courage, humility, joy, unity, radiance – these are the qualities which Luke highlights. And nowhere is this more clearly portrayed than in the death of Stephen who radiates these qualities as he dies, because he is full of the Holy Spirit (6:15ff): 'His face was like the face of an angel.'

We are bidden, therefore, not to develop a mindset of the Christian press button, designed to acquire gifts; but of the Christian walk, which is designed to produce holiness. That is the supreme aim of the coming of the Holy Spirit. The way of the church, the way of the Spirit, the way of evangelism, involves the costly following of a crucified Saviour.

This means that, like Jesus, we must learn obedience through suffering (Heb. 5:8). There will be an element of trial and error in all this, as is manifest from Acts 16:6ff. Our faculties, as Hebrews 5:14 reminds us, must be trained by experience to distinguish good from evil, genuine from bogus. The purpose of the Spirit's coming to the people of Jesus is not primarily to give gifts, though he does that, but to produce in us Christlikeness of character, a people like their Lord. He wants to make us mature in our Christian discipleship. By his presence, his power, and his gifts, he offers us the resources for that supreme vocation for Christian disciples this side of heaven.

14

What of Their Priorities?

Any selection of the priorities of the early Christians must be somewhat arbitrary and subjective, but it would be hard to deny that any of the following topics should be omitted from the list of their priorities. Here are six things which they clearly valued very highly for their life and mission. I believe we can learn from them.

The priority of prayer

Prayer, not activism, is what they relied on. There is a tremendous amount about prayer in Acts, and that is not surprising in the light of two great influences on the author. Luke came, as we have seen, from a very prayerful church, that in Antioch. And he clearly learnt from them. If our churches make prayer a priority, there is every reason to hope that it will rub off on a number of the members, and become a governing factor in their lives, as it did with Luke. If, on the other hand, our church is virtually prayerless, that too will rub off on the members.

If his home church was one major influence on Luke's appreciation of prayer, the prayer life of Jesus was the other. No other evangelist stresses the prayerfulness of Jesus as Luke does. It made an enormous impression on him. He tells us how Jesus prayed before starting his ministry (Luke 3:21), before his healings (5:15), before choosing the Twelve (6:12) and before the transfiguration (9:28). His example prompted his disciples to ask, 'Lord, teach us to pray' (11:1f). His teaching on the importunate friend, the unjust judge, the Pharisee and the publican all stress different sides of prayer. Jesus dies, as Stephen dies, with a prayer on his lips (23:46).

In Acts, prayer is central. In 1:14 we find the disciples praying before the coming of the Spirit. In 1:24 we find them praying about choosing a successor to Judas. We find them gathered together, doubtless in prayer, as Pentecost dawns (2:1), and as that day ends they are drawing the new believers to share in their prayers (2:42). In 3:1 we find them going up to the Temple to pray, and so on throughout the book. When people pray, the Spirit comes, the place where they pray is shaken, prison doors break open, and people dare to die with radiance. It will be worth paying some attention to the book's teaching on this important subject.

1. It is plain, first of all, that for Luke *prayer was the convincing mark of spiritual life*. In 9:11 the only indication Ananias has of Saul's change of heart is that he is praying. Ananias does not know he is praying: he has only the vision to rely on. *He is praying!* In those few words lie the key to the whole future life of Saul of Tarsus. He had been a religious man for years. He had been a Pharisee. He had said prayers many times a day. He was the most orthodox type of Jew. But he had not begun to pray! He had all the framework of prayer, but he lacked the heart of it. He did not know the Lord. He was not able to look into his face and cry, 'Abba, my Father.' But from the day of that encounter with Jesus on the Damascus Road he was able to do just that. It really is astonishing. As a Pharisee he would have prayed seven times a day: but like the Pharisee in Luke's Gospel he prayed 'with himself'. He did not get through. There was a great barrier of unforgiven sin in the way, and he was ignorant of the risen Lord. But now he had the new life of the Spirit coursing through his veins. He was praying. And prayer is a mark of spiritual life. Children talk, do they not? The heavenly Father has no dumb children.

2. Second, *prayer was a way of life* (1:14). There they are, the eleven disciples, the women and the family of Jesus, devoting themselves to prayer. They have a world mission to accomplish. They need to get moving. And all they do is to pray! Prayer was a way of life for them, and I notice several things about their prayers. First, there was privacy. They got alone with God in the privacy of that upper room. There was unity in their prayers: they got together with the family of Jesus who, in the days of his flesh, thought that Jesus was mad. There was expectancy in their prayers. They were waiting on tiptoe for the breaking in of the kingdom of God and the arrival of the Spirit. There was also openness, openness to whatever God led them into with regard to a successor for Judas, and openness to the

timing and the mode of the coming of the promised Holy Spirit.

At the other end of Acts (20:36) we find Paul kneeling down and praying with them all, embracing and kissing them, because he thought he would never see them again. That is how Christians say goodbye: in prayer. I recall doing something similar in Durban airport. A dozen of us were gathered together in the concourse praying, and they had to page us because the last call for the flight had gone out and we were blissfully unaware of it! Let us not be ashamed of being seen praying with one another. It is intended to be a way of life.

3. Moreover, *prayer was a top priority* for the Christians we meet in Acts. That is very evident from 4:24ff. It is a remarkable passage. The disciples have been released from the first of many imprisonments. The authorities did not know how to act, so they let them go. And they went straight to their friends, and to prayer. It was a top priority. They gave the news, briefly. You need that, if you are to pray intelligently. They were in a wonderful state of unity with one another, for 'with one accord they lifted up their voice'. There was real adoration here: they did not come to God with a list of their needs, but rather gloried in his sovereignty. Their prayer was informed by Scripture, and in this way they knew that they were praying according to the will of God. There was little petition about it – they preferred to leave things in the hands of the God who neither slumbers nor sleeps. But there were two things that they asked for (v 29): 'Lord, look' and 'Lord, grant'. They asked the Lord to keep a close eye on the threatenings of the Jewish authorities. And they asked God not to grant them an escape from this difficult situation, not an easy ride, but boldness to face it unafraid. That is the attitude of men and women for whom prayer had become not merely a mark of life and a way of life, but a top priority.

4. As we see from 4:31, *prayer was the gateway to spiritual power*. Power to witness. Power to share. Power to be gracious as well as bold. Power to give. Power to encourage, like Barnabas. That is what the end of chapter 4 introduces us to: life-changing power. And it only happened because these men and women put prayer at the top of their priorities.

5. Indeed *prayer was one of the foundations of Christianity*. Right at the start of the Christian movement the converts devoted themselves to the apostles' doctrine and fellowship, the breaking of bread and the prayers. What a superb balance for all Christians anywhere. They

need to be rooted in the apostles' teaching, which they find in the New Testament. They need the apostles' fellowship: fellowship in all its varieties from the big inter-church rally to the small meeting in a private home. They need the breaking of bread, be it in church or in an informal gathering. And they need the prayers, or, as it may be translated, 'the prayer meetings'. It is not good enough to claim 'I can't pray in public': if you can talk to one another you can talk to the Lord. And there is really no excuse for not doing so. Short prayers, from the heart: why can we not do that? Prayer is one of the basic pillars of the new life, and the Acts makes it plain that it is the doorway to signs and wonders and evangelism.

6. Often, too, *prayer opened the door to vision*. So many of our churches have little vision: and without vision the people perish. A vision is brought very clearly before Peter, that leader of the early church, as he prays (10:9f). It is a vision which breaks the barriers of apartheid. It is a vision which enables the gospel to spread to those who are not Jews. And it has to be inaugurated by God, because man would never have thought of it. And so you have both Peter and Cornelius being taught by God in a vision, when each of them was at prayer. The vision which revolutionised the early church and broke it out from its Jewish cocoon, was born in prayer. If you want vision for your church, why not have a night of prayer?

7. *Prayer changed things*. We find a marvellous cameo of effective intercession in 12:4-17. Herod had killed James, and had imprisoned Peter with a view to executing him too. 'So Peter was kept in prison, but earnest prayer was made to God by the church for him' (12:4). Peter was in prison, with no hope of release. Yet he got out, as prayer was made. Notice some factors in their prayer for Peter. It was corporate: offered by the church, as they gathered together for prayer, night after night. It was specific: made for Peter. It was not a vague prayer for blessing in God's church; it was prayer for Peter and his release. It was directed to God, not prayed for the benefit of those who were present; far too many prayers in a prayer meeting are horizontal, not vertical. What is more, it was regular. That comes out clearly in the Greek of 12:5. They went on praying for Peter's release, just as the Anglican Church worldwide recently prayed daily for the release of the Archbishop of Canterbury's envoy, Terry Waite, and other hostages who had been incarcerated by Arab terrorists. Regular prayer has great power. Then their prayer was earnest. That again is

very apparent in the Greek *entenos*. The word denotes involvement, commitment, strain even. These people really cared. They got into the action, and they prayed fervently for Peter's release. They battled in prayer over this matter. Ironically, the one thing that their prayer was not was expectant, for when the answer to their prayer came and knocked on the door they wanted to send it away!

8. *Prayer was a many-sided thing.* It embraces adoration (4:24ff), petition (12:4ff), penitence (8:22), fasting (13:3, 14:23), praise (16:25, 2:47). If our prayer times were lit up more with praise, we should be lifted into the presence of God. When adoring prayer is unleashed, vision is given, and fasting seems natural. Chapter 13:1ff is an interesting scenario in this respect. There is sharing among the leadership, then worship in which they wait on God for his direction. It is accompanied by fasting, then surrendering these two prized leaders, Barnabas and Saul, then going out in mission. And it all springs from prayer. In many parts of the world, there is a marked lack of leadership in the church and of impact on the unchurched, because we Christians do not pray. We do not make it a top priority as the early Christians did, and we reap the consequences of our neglect. A statistic released some time ago found that the average Christian in North America prayed for one minute a day, and the average minister for two minutes! If we are to turn the tide of apathy and scepticism in our generation, it will not happen without fervent prayer. Contrast that with the following excerpt from a Ghanaian student's report after returning from an evangelistic mission in which a number of us had been engaged:

Just before the service ended, the pastor called me back into the pulpit and asked me to share my experience as an evangelist in Ghana. Often I am hesitant to do so because I feel people in North America are not ready for such experiences, and also being a woman I do not know how they would respond. However, I shared briefly with them what we do in Ghana, and indeed in all of Africa. Person to person evangelism is a daily practice. Prayer meetings, with fasting, take more than half of our preparation time for evangelistic outreaches. I mentioned that we engage in what we call spiritual warfare, and when the battle is won in the spiritual realm and the bondages are broken, the physical battle is much easier than we think, and people are ready to come to the Lord. I also shared with them that every Friday the whole nation is covered with prayer from 10 p.m.

to 4 a.m. We call it 'all-night prayer' – and so it is, except for some minutes' coffee break to keep intercessors awake. Almost all evangelical churches in Ghana have it on their program.

The priority of the word

It is apparent from the repeated sermons scattered through the Acts how deeply versed these early Christians were in the Old Testament Scriptures and their fulfilment in Jesus. They were not narrow fundamentalists. Their citation of Old Testament texts were often approximate rather than precise, but there is no mistaking the reverence they gave these oracles of God, the direction they derived from them and the confidence they placed in them. It is Paul who tells us that the Spirit's sword is the word of God (Eph. 6:7).

'The word' is a major theme in Acts. It occurs more than thirty times, and it means God's self-disclosure through the ancient Scriptures of Israel and its recent fulfilment in Jesus of Nazareth. That is the message to which they are committed. That is the message through which the church grows. As we read what the word accomplishes in the record of Acts, it is almost impossible to exaggerate its influence.

When Hellenistic Christians are thrown out of Jerusalem, homeless and penniless, they cannot keep quiet about this word, wherever they go (8:4). When 'the word of God increased' in Jerusalem itself, to our amazement we find that many of the Jewish priesthood joined this new movement (6:7). No doubt they were aware of how strong was the note of expectation in the Old Testament, and how it might possibly have received its fulfilment in Jesus. Even so, it was an astounding step for them to take, under the impact of the word. When Paul was somewhat discouraged and spiritually run down at Corinth after a rather unfruitful time in Athens, we read that 'he was gripped by the word', as Silas and Timothy joined him in the reading of it (18:5 Greek), and a whole new dimension to the ministry in Corinth began.

It was much the same in public speaking in which Paul engaged for two years in the school of Tyrannus at Ephesus. He would never have been able to sustain such a demanding daily ministry if he was not deeply rooted in the Scriptures. They informed everything he had to say, and because his well was so deep, he never ran dry, and people from all over the province of Asia came and 'heard the word of the Lord' through his mouth (19:10). It was the word of God that broke down the centuries age-old prejudices of the Samaritans and brought them to the feet of Jesus (8:14). The word in the mouth of Philip, with the Scriptures confidently expounded, brought the treasurer of Ethiopia to Christ (8:35).

You sometimes hear it said that scriptural preaching puts people off. Well, it did not seem to bore anyone to tears at Pisidian Antioch. After a brilliant overview of Israelite history and a powerful application, Paul and his party were invited to preach again next week. When they did, 'almost the whole city was gathered together to hear the word of God' (13:44). If people are spiritually hungry, there is nothing in the world that satisfies them except the word of God. And if they are deeply entangled in the occult, there is nothing in the world that can bring liberation and new life like the word. It was in Ephesus that startling progress was made among those trading in magic (19:20): 'the word of God grew and prevailed mightily.'

No wonder the apostles gave themselves to the ministry of the word and prayer (6:4). They knew what a powerful instrument it was, and they wanted to study it without distraction, so as to be able to minister it to others. The social work, which they delegated, was vital: but not more vital than the ministry of the word. When you study it you know you are being built up. When you expound it you know you are feeding those who hear. God's word is food; it is light; it is a sword; it is a fire. It is the supreme instrument of Christian growth. That is why the disciples made it such a priority.

No wonder, equally, that Paul commended his young lieutenants to read this book. When the Ephesian elders bade farewell to Paul, they were left in the hands of God, and with this book which would build them up and show them more and more of the inheritance they possessed in Christ (20:32). It is the most precious book this world affords, for it contains the title deeds not only to this world but to the next. And when people give themselves to it and get gripped by it, the impact is enormous. Think of a writer like C. S. Lewis, a translator like J. B. Phillips, a theologian like C. H. Dodd, or a preacher like John Stott.

It is not surprising, then, that sometimes when Luke means that the church grows he simply says that 'the word' grows and prevails (e.g. 6:7, 12:24). We need to take that to heart. We are not at liberty to change 'the faith once for all delivered to the saints' (Jude 3). We must interpret it, relate it to the contemporary culture, apply it, of course: but we have no right to change its content. Yet that is what is happening these days in a great many churches. Teachings are given which are not only absent from the Bible but are at total variance with it, while the central affirmations of the faith are rarely heard. Scriptures are never unleashed in all their fullness to the congregation, which is

accordingly half-starved. No wonder such churches do not grow. An
eviscerated Christianity has no power to change the world. Only a
full-blooded, biblical Christianity can transform. And it is interesting to
notice that this is precisely what is happening in developing countries.
Christians with almost no education, but a deep trust in the Spirit
and the word are making enormous headway in the face of daunting
odds. In the West, it is often the very conservative churches which
are making real headway. This is not because they are right in all they
maintain: far from it. Often they are narrow and legalistic. But they
have an attitude of reverence towards God's revelation. And God can
use churches like that, and he does. I believe such churches should
be seen as a real challenge to sophisticated Christians in our society.
Instead of despising and writing off as uninformed the fundamentalists
and the Pentecostals, Christians who have had the benefit of a good
education should be willing to learn from the zeal and faith displayed
by those who have not had their advantages, while at the same time
seeking to avoid their mistakes and excesses.

   If we are to profit from the priorities of these early Christians
there are few areas to which we need to pay closer heed than to
the word they preached. We need to study it sympathetically, to
know our way around it, to use it to help others individually and
in public preaching. We need to train others in its effective use.
We need to have confidence in it.

   The Bible is not a book about men in search of God. It is the record
of God in search of men. It is revelation, and we need therefore to
come to grips with it at every level, for it contains the message of
what God requires of us and what he has done for us. The only
Christianity which will go on to be effective in the twenty-first
century is a Christianity which has been pruned to its biblical core.

The priority of outreach

The first Christians were totally committed to outreach. It is impossible
to exaggerate this characteristic. Whether you look at the day of
Pentecost at the beginning of the book, or at the captive apostle at
the end of the book 'who welcomed all who came to him, preaching
the kingdom of God and teaching about the Lord Jesus Christ quite
openly and unhindered', the emphasis is identical. These are men with
a message. They have something of passionate importance to declare. It
may be in the comparatively familiar haunts of the synagogue; it may
be in front of sorcerers or Roman officers; it may be in the Jerusalem

they knew so well, or it may be in the wilds of Galatia or the sophisticated streets of Athens. Always the direction was outwards. What accounts for their tireless activity? I do not know that I can range their motives in any order, but I am clear that the following factors all weighed with them.

1. There was *the plain command of their Master*. He had told them to wait in Jerusalem for the promised Holy Spirit, and then to fan out worldwide as Christ's witnesses, in the power of the Spirit (1:8). The coming of the Spirit on the day of Pentecost, and the enormously fruitful preaching on that occasion confirmed this calling, and the plan of the rest of the Acts shows that they systematically set out to fulfil the Master's bidding.

2. Another factor in their enthusiasm was *the loving sacrifice of Jesus*. He loved them. He died for them. How could they withhold the proclamation of such a God from a world crying out in hurt and need? A little phrase in 20:28 illustrates this passion which must have burnt deeply in apostolic hearts. The church was God's purchase, so to speak, of men and women at enormous cost – 'the blood of his Only One'. That is one rendering of the Greek: the other is even more daring, 'with his very own blood'. However we take it, the cross is the supreme demonstration of the love of God. It is the length to which he was willing to go in order to win us rebels back into fellowship with himself. They knew that there was a divine compulsion in all this, springing from the loving heart of God: 'Christ must suffer, and by being the first to rise from the dead, he would proclaim light both to the people and to the Gentiles' (26:23).

3. *The sheer need of men and women* moved them greatly. If you believe, as they believed, that 'there is salvation in no one else, for there is no other name under heaven given among men by which we must be saved' (4:12) then you would be heartless indeed to keep silent. They saw men and women trapped in idolatry (14:15) and superstition (17:16ff). They heard them crying out under the power of demonic forces (16:16f), under the burden of physical handicap (3:1ff) or in terror about their future (16:30); and they had compassion. They told them where rescue, love and healing – salvation – was to be had. When we allow our hearts to be moved by the plight of our fellow men many of them without God and without hope in the world, how can we withhold from them the good news of Jesus?

4. *A strong sense of the rightness of what they were doing* underlies the evangelism of these first Christians. Imagine them, unlettered peasants, arraigned before the highest court in their land. After the case has been heard, they are given the undreamed-of good news that they are going to be released on bail – so long as they keep silent. They must not 'speak or teach at all in the name of Jesus' (4:17). But this solemn warning fails to silence them. They have a deep sense of obligation to God which overrides all other constraints. Peter and John answer the court: 'Whether it is right in the sight of God to listen to you rather than to God, you must judge. For we cannot but speak of what we have seen and heard' (4:19f). It is very difficult to dissuade people who have that sense of conviction!

5. There is no doubt that *a sense of privilege* dominated the minds of the early Christians and sustained them during epic hardships. They were God's ambassadors. They were Christ's spokesmen. It is plain from the speech of Stephen before his accusers and of Paul before Agrippa that the Christians saw themselves as the heirs of Abraham, the true children of Israel. It was an enormous privilege to bear the word of the Lord to their nation and to the Gentiles – a role foretold of the Servant in the Old Testament, but only now being fulfilled in succession to Jesus himself (13:47ff). That sense of privilege gave them such confidence in their preaching that it made Festus doubt the preacher's sanity (26:24) and made Felix tremble (24:25).

6. *Joy* was another powerful motive. There was no joy in the world like helping others to find the Saviour, and the first Christians knew it. There was joy on the radiant face of Stephen as he died, a martyr for his Lord. There was joy as the Ethiopian eunuch was led to faith (8:39). Tremendous joy filled Cornelius' house in Caesarea when the Spirit fell upon them (10:44ff). There was joy when the gospel spread out from Pisidian Antioch, despite the persecution it brought in its train (13:52). But to me one of the most amazing examples of the joy of evangelism is in the prison at Philippi. Inside are two men who have endured a Roman scourging for their street preaching. It is midnight. And what are they doing? Praising God for all they are worth (16:25). How could you express more graphically the tremendous joy that goes with telling others about Christ, however violent their reaction against you? The first Christians knew that there was no joy in the world like evangelism. That is one of the reasons why they kept at it.

7. I suppose that *vision* is another reason. Whenever we have a clear vision of anything, there is a strong motive to carry through and see that vision achieved. And this is very true in Christian service. Peter had a vision, a most unwelcome vision, of his call to proclaim Christ to those he considered beyond the pale (10:9ff). But he knew he was called to fulfil it. He did, and he defended his action vigorously to his detractors later. It was much the same with the way James got so gripped with a passage from Amos at the Jerusalem Council (15:15f). He had caught the prophet's vision of the rebuilt dwelling of David on the one hand, and of Gentiles called to the Lord on the other. He was determined to facilitate the achievement of that vision. Vision is a potent motivator.

8. But the greatest of all motivations to evangelism which we see on every page of the Acts is *the outward thrust of the Holy Spirit*. It is he who thrusts the infant church out on the streets, he who opens the way up to untouchables like the Samaritans and eunuchs, magicians and Roman soldiers. The Holy Spirit derives from a God who is always reaching out in love to the unlovely and the lost. And those who are filled with that same Spirit are inevitably driven in the same direction. 'I go, bound in the Spirit, not knowing what shall befall me,' said Paul (20:22). They could all have said something very similar. Ask Philip, ask Stephen, ask Timothy or Titus, ask the graduates of the school of Tyrannus. They would all have had to reply that they engaged in evangelism because the Holy Spirit was thrusting them out and would never allow them peace of mind if they sat back and rested on their laurels. Perhaps that is one of the reasons for their continual mobility. The Spirit called them to the regions beyond.

What about us? We have so little understanding of the awesomeness of Calvary, so little real conviction about the divinity of the one who suffered there, that our hearts are not warmed, and we do not move out in the power of that love. We frankly do not believe that men and women without Christ are in any serious need whatsoever: they are perfectly all right as they are. We must not invade their privacy by telling them about our faith. We have little compelling conviction that this is our responsibility, little sense of privilege that the Lord entrusts this thrilling commission to us. We have no clear vision of a waiting world and a risen Saviour longing to reach it through his church. As a result we in the West have a modern church which knows little of the joy of evangelism and little of the power of the Holy Spirit. For the Spirit of God, and indeed the joy of the Lord, are reserved for those who, in obedience to the Master's command, venture out with the gospel and *risk*!

Thankfully, our case is not hopeless. Christians in many parts of the world know precisely the zeal and the effectiveness of the first disciples. If we return to the paths which our forebears in Christ have so clearly mapped out for us in the pages of Acts, there is no reason why Europe and North America should not join the rest of the world in joyful, confident, effective outreach.

The priority of unity

Wherever there are human beings there is the danger of disunity. But one of the ways in which the church is intended to demonstrate its heavenly origin is by its unity. The church is a colony of heaven, and its relationships are meant to be a picture of God's ability to unite the seemingly irreconcilable in a single fellowship. If it fails to exhibit this, it compromises the very gospel that it preaches. Unity does not, of course, mean uniformity: God is no more interested in uniformity in the area of grace than he is in the area of nature. How dull and grey we would all be if we were clones of one another! But unity does entail a recognisable interdependence, and a recognition throughout the whole church of the membership and ministry of all. If we had that degree of unity in the church today it would silence many of our critics, and it would be very attractive to the many fragmented people out there who would love to be part of the church so long as they were welcome to bring their own individuality with them.

I am amazed at the ways in which the early Christians demonstrated their unity, and the lengths to which they were willing to go in order to preserve it.

1. They were *united in prayer* (1:14). Three disparate groups came together in united prayer before Pentecost: the disciples, the women, and the family of Jesus. It may well be that the other dimensions of their unity sprang from praying together. I have certainly noticed that happening in a city where all the ministers of the various churches meet together for regular prayer.

2. They were *united in testimony* (2:14). Though it was Peter who actually preached at Pentecost, the Eleven were right behind him, standing out there with him. It is an enormous encouragement to a

preacher to have a support group like that who can pray and encourage him into action.

3. There must have been some very *unitive administration*, too, if 3000 people from all over the known world could be organised in such a way that they continued in the apostles' doctrine and fellowship, the breaking of bread and the prayers (2:42). We are not told how it was done, but the organisation must have been remarkable, as it clearly was later with the daily administration of food to the widows.

4. They were *united also in the meeting of need*. Obviously some who joined the church at its inception were very poor, and this sparked a generous spirit of sharing not just in a small number of specially keen disciples, but in a widespread sharing of capital as well as income (2:44ff). Much disunity in church circles centres on money and property. The early Christians had a very original and effective way of avoiding such dissension.

5. They attended the Temple *together to worship* (3:1ff). There is a great power in united worship, transcending individuality and the tastes of the particular worshippers. It both encourages the congregation and builds them up: and it also has a significant impact on those who see and hear the worshippers. I am currently worshipping at a church which meets in an open-sided barn in the middle of a prestigious golf course, and the surrounding community loves it. Some of them are drawn in. Others comment favourably on the sound of hymns and the happy faces and helpfulness of the worshippers. As a result, the church has just been given land on which to build a school for the community. Attending worship together still has its double impact, internal and external.

6. Unity meant *mutual support* to these people. In 4:23 we see that the first thing the incarcerated apostles did after their release was to go back to 'their friends', to pray and praise God with them. It was in the context of this close support that they regained strength and vision for the next step of their advance. Some Christians only want to see their friends when they are feeling on good form: but the quality of this fellowship was such that the two apostles were not ashamed to return to it discouraged, afraid and dishevelled. That is the type of unity which is real and highly valuable.

7. They were *united in their leadership*. There was united leadership in Jerusalem among the Eleven; there was united leadership in those five men from such different backgrounds who shared the oversight of the church at Antioch (13:1). That is very remarkable. No less so is the way these leaders were open to the guidance of God. Somehow the Spirit prompted them to release Barnabas and Saul for pioneering missionary work. We do not know how the guidance was given. Since they were at prayer, it probably happened through the prophetic utterance of some member of the church. That by itself would not have sufficed. It might have been wrong. It might have been an ego trip by an hysterical individual. It was not until what was said was weighed by the congregation, and pondered in silence, that the conviction spread among them that this was indeed the Lord's purpose for their church. My own experience of the guidance of a congregation through prophetic utterance would confirm this. If the word really does come from God, there is no debate about it, no taking votes: everyone knows full well that God has spoken. All that remains is to obey.

8. The unity of these first Christians *in their decision-making* is just as impressive. As we saw in chapter 12, the Jerusalem Council debated a highly contentious issue. Yet they did not take a vote, and so leave an aggrieved minority. They did not set out to push their own conflicting positions: instead we find Peter adopting a 'Pauline' position in arguing for the free acceptance of Gentile believers (15:7ff). But together they sought the will of God, and they felt sure they had found it. James was able to sum up that 'it has seemed good to the Holy Spirit and to us . . .' Sensitive to the Spirit's guidance throughout the proceedings, they became united themselves. There was nothing dictatorial about this Apostolic Decree. Its regulations were minimal and the unity it guaranteed was priceless.

Christian unity is of the utmost importance, and the early Christians knew it. They contemplated division for only two causes. One was prominent and persistent public sin. The other was major doctrinal error. All else was secondary. They refused the temptation to split with brother Christians over money, ceremonial, differing interpretations of Scripture, different styles of church government, different modes of baptism, and all the things we find it so natural to divide over. These things did not justify dismembering the body of Christ. They refused to take the easy way out, to cut and run at the first sign of tension. They could so easily have spawned a conservative Jewish church, a liberal Jewish church, a Samaritan church, and a Gentile church, all within a decade of the start of the Christian movement. But it did not happen. Their unity stands like a beacon to us in our fragmentation. Christian unity is not a luxury. It is a top priority if the church is to stand firm and grow.

The priority of the Holy Spirit

The Spirit is the supreme reality in the Acts and he was the overwhelming priority in the lives of the disciples. They knew they were useless without him. At all costs they needed to be filled and to remain full of this marvellous Pentecost gift who equipped them for their mission. We have already considered the subject at some length. But now, at the end of the book, it may be worth reminding ourselves of some of the outstanding aspects of the Spirit in the church.

It was the Spirit who launched and sustained them in their evangelistic enterprise (2:38f). What courage it must have called for to stand and address those crowds! The Holy Spirit provided both the motivation and the courage.

It was the Spirit who made the Scriptures come alive (2:16ff). The disciples had known the Psalms and Joel since childhood, but now that the Spirit came upon them, the page sprang to life. The excitement of new discovery spills off the page as Peter proclaims, 'This is what was spoken by the prophet Joel . . . for David says concerning Jesus . . . being a prophet he foresaw and spoke of the resurrection of Christ . . .' The Spirit who inspired the Scriptures is given us to interpet them.

The Spirit was the secret of that transformation of life which was so remarkable in this new movement. It was all his work. Think of Saul, for example (9:17). He had only been a Christian for a few days, but once the Spirit was in control of his life, the impact was dramatic.

The Spirit was the key to refreshment and new power after exhaustion and prison (4:31). He was the one in whose strength they dared to take on naked evil (13:9). When the Spirit was in control, men and women could exhibit joy in the midst of persecution and privation (13:52). And in this twentieth century, when there has been more persecution of Christians than in all the previous nineteen centuries put together, we have been given many outstanding examples of Christian joy inspired by the Spirit in the midst of the most appalling circumstances.

The early Christians knew that they could not do effective pastoral work without the sensitive touch of the Holy Spirit (20:28). It was the Spirit who pointed out the ones who should exercise oversight, and it was he who enabled them to do it.

We have seen in the previous section how the Spirit was central to their guidance. It shows in their decision making, in contrast to so many church committees these days. It shows in their advance which was certainly not brought about by any apostolic planning. Nowhere is that more clear than in 16:6f where we can be sure that Paul and his company would have been most unlikely to cross the Aegean to the wild land of Macedonia – were it not for the Spirit's guidance. The consequences of that guidance and obedience have, of course, been world wide.

Indeed, the stability of the early church can be traced directly back to the supervision of the Holy Spirit: 'So the church throughout all Judaea and Galilee and Samaria had rest, and was built up: and walking in the fear of the Lord and the comfort of the Holy Spirit, it was multiplied' (9:31). What a lovely balance in that verse. The 'fear of the Lord' speaks of God's transcendence. The 'comfort of the Spirit' speaks of his immanence. That was the balance in which the earliest community was built up. That was the base from which it was multiplied.

The point is clear: the first Christians lived in total dependence on the Holy Spirit. This is one of the most conspicuous differences between them and us. We rely on our organisation, our education, our psychology, our finance, our plant and so forth. We show little sign of any overdependence on the Holy Spirit. We despise faith and call it pietism. We regard spiritual realities as somewhat unreal, and are embarrassed to talk about them. They fit untidily into this secular age in which we live. But although the culture of the first century was not a secular one, it was inimical to the Christian message, just as our own is. The broad-ranging concept of the Holy Spirit, who so inspired the lives of these men and women, was just as strange to first century society as to our own. Yet unlike us, they were not embarrassed. They rejoiced in his power and presence. They knew they were following in his wake. They knew that, above all, they needed to keep in the closest touch with him, their unseen guide. Nothing must be allowed to hinder the flow of the Holy Spirit in their lives.

If they were here today, I fancy they would want to reiterate some of the teaching about the Spirit which they left in the pages of the New Testament. They would want to tell us not to be afraid of the Holy Spirit. Nicodemus feared spiritual experience although he was a leader in Israel (John 3:7). Head knowledge was one thing, but actually to go and get baptised by John in the Jordan, actually to risk entrusting himself to the Spirit was very different. But we have nothing to fear from the Spirit of Jesus. It is tragic if we shrink from the Father's birthday gift to his church.

Equally, they would want to tell us not to resist the Holy Spirit (Acts 7:51). It is all too easy to do that, as at least one Jew to whom Stephen uttered the warning came to see, by hanging on to some attitude which is no longer helpful or appropriate but which blinds you to the new direction in which God is calling you now.

They would insist that we should not quench the Spirit (1 Thess. 5:19); and if we are to take seriously the context in which this injunction was uttered, it means that we should not write off the so-called charismatic gifts, such as prophecy.

They would be particularly anxious that we did not forget Ananias and Sapphira, and that we did not lie to the Holy Spirit, by allowing deceit in our hearts and lives, when integrity is sacrificed to appearances (Acts 5:3).

And mindful of the loving comfort of the Spirit, they would gently warn us not to grieve the Holy Spirit (Eph. 4:30). We grieve him when we knowingly sin either by commission or omission, and do not come back quickly in repentance and contrition.

Instead, they would have us do just two things. The first is to be filled with the Spirit (Eph. 5:18), and the second is to obey him (Acts 5:32). The filling needs constantly to be renewed. The obedience needs constantly to be maintained. In that obedience we shall gain greater insight into the mind of the Spirit as well as grow in likeness to our Master.

I remember feeling rebuked not long ago when an archbishop said reflectively to me, 'You know, I think the Evangelicals really see the heart of Christianity as understanding, and the Catholics as obedience.' There was more than a little truth in that gentle rebuke. Evangelical Christians are happy when debating some heresy, or arguing some abstruse point of doctrine – and maybe putting others down as they do so. Catholic Christians are often more willing to accept the unplumbed mysteries of the faith, and obey what they do understand.

The first Christians sought both to understand as much as they could of the divine revelation through the illumination of the Holy Spirit, and also to obey him, cost what it might. And it cost many of them their blood, the blood which has proved to be the seed of a worldwide harvest.

The priority of wholeheartedness

It would not be proper to conclude a book about first century disciples without drawing attention to their wholehearted obedience to Jesus Christ. We glanced at it earlier; it is one of the most striking features of the story in Acts. Christ is undeniably the head of his church, the unseen director of its operations. Luke tellingly hints at this in 1:1. 'In the first book, O Theophilus, I have dealt with all that Jesus began to do and to teach until the day when he was taken up.' The inference is plain. Jesus continued to 'do and teach' through his obedient disciples after he was taken up. And the rest of the book shows just how seriously they set about obeying their risen Lord.

We do not need to rehearse the evidence. It has been apparent throughout the Acts. These followers of Jesus were totally committed.

At the very outset the original disciples and the family of Jesus were wholehearted enough to sink their differences. They were whole-hearted enough to stand boldly for him in an unprecedented open air demonstration in the most public forum on the day of Pentecost. They were wholehearted enough quietly but firmly to withstand all the ecclesiastical pressure and political harassment to which they were subjected. Their obedience led them to face persecution, scourging, shipwreck, rejection and in many cases death. It enabled them to turn their backs on centuries of tradition and accept new converts without circumcising them. It gave them boldness on the streets and in the courts. It sent them to the ends of the earth with the good news of Jesus. At the end of the first half of Acts we see Peter, released from prison, disappearing to continue unchecked his spreading of the gospel: there was no thought of turning back, even though it led eventually to martyrdom in Rome. At the end of the second half of Acts we see Paul, in prison for his convictions and his dedication, but unfettered in the evangelism he was able to continue there, before he too was brought before a tyrannical Nero and executed. That same wholeheartedness marked the other main figure in the Acts, Stephen, whose steadfast faith in the face of his country's religious hierarchy led to a mob lynching. Paul's attitude could have stood for Peter, Stephen and the Hellenists, for Aquila and Priscilla and any of the others: 'I do not account my life of any value, nor as precious to myself, if only I may accomplish my course and the ministry which I received from the Lord Jesus, to testify to the gospel of the grace of God' (20:24).

There is no greater challenge to the contemporary church than this. Do we really believe that Jesus is God himself who has come to share our nature, rescue us from our alienation from God and accompany us not only alongside but inside our lives? If so there can be only one proper attitude for the disciple of such a Master: total and wholehearted obedience. I see it in many parts of Asia and Africa. I see it in Chinese who are prepared to tramp through trackless wastes of Mongolia to bring the gospel of Jesus to unreached areas. I see it in the fearless enthusiasm of Latin Americans who will stand shouting *'Gloria Dios!'* in a bus until almost all the passengers join in! I see it in the dedication of men like an African friend in Zaire who is prepared to go alone and without resources deep into the forest jungles to bring the gospel to the pygmy people. I see it in the skyscrapers and sophisticated business milieu of Singapore, where you are sure to get accosted by someone who is anxious to tell you about their Jesus. But I do not see it a great deal in the West.

Wholehearted obedience to Jesus Christ, the head of the church, may take many forms. But it is essential. He cannot work through disobedient disciples. If we wish to see any resurgency in our day of the vitality which marked the early church, we must look to our whole-heartedness. God gives his Holy Spirit to those who obey him.